WALKING AWAY
FROM NUREMBERG

Walking Away from Nuremberg

JUST WAR AND THE DOCTRINE OF
COMMAND RESPONSIBILITY

Lawrence P. Rockwood

UNIVERSITY OF MASSACHUSETTS PRESS
AMHERST

Copyright © 2007 by University of Massachusetts Press
All rights reserved
Printed in the United States of America

Cat   LC 2007011596
ISBN 978-1-55849-599-9 (paper); 598-2 (library cloth)

Designed by Jack Harrison
Set in Trump Medieval and Univers Light Condensed by dix!
Printed and bound by The Maple-Vail Book Manufacturing Group

Library of Congress Cataloging-in-Publication Data

Rockwood, Lawrence.
Walking away from Nuremberg : just war and the doctrine of command responsibility /
Lawrence P. Rockwood.
p. cm.
Includes bibliographical references and index.
ISBN 978-1-55849-598-2 (library cloth : alk. paper)—
ISBN 978-1-55849-599-9 (pbk. : alk. paper)
1. Military ethics—United States. 2. Command of troops. 3. Just war doctrine.
4. War crimes. I. Title.
U22.R67   2007
172'.42—dc22
2007011596

British Library Cataloguing in Publication data are available.

To the professionalism of the officers of July 20, 1944.

Ich hatt' einen Kameraden,

Einen bessern findst du nit.

Die Trommel schlug zum Streite,

Er ging an meiner Seite

In gleichem Schritt und Tritt.

Mein guter Kamerad!
Ludwig Uhland, 1809

CONTENTS

FOREWORD

Stephen Wrage, Professor of Political Science,
United States Naval Academy

THERE IS NO OTHER PERSON as qualified as Lawrence Rockwood to write this study of just war and command responsibility in the American military. His academic qualifications are absolutely first rate, but that is not the point. His study of both the long-standing traditions and the most recent applications of just war theory is thorough and insightful and is obviously the product of years of exhaustive reading and analysis, but that is not the point either. Rockwood is the single person most qualified to make this informed and impassioned argument about how the powerful must step forward and take full responsibility when they choose to use force, because Rockwood was there and he did just that.

He was the one to use force—he was a soldier—and when the time came, he alone stepped forward and took responsibility and fulfilled the obligations of the powerful toward the powerless. For doing so, Rockwood lost the military career that he loved and at which he had excelled, but he set an example of conscience-driven, principled behavior that has been discussed at the military academies and war colleges and is studied by every midshipman at the U.S. Naval Academy. In preparing a case study regarding his actions in Haiti in 1994, I interviewed Lawrence Rockwood, read the records of his court-martial and interviewed the Joint Task Force Commander, Lt. Gen. David C. Meade, among others. An account of Rockwood's experience in Haiti will show the strength of conviction and commitment that drove both his military career and his scholarship, and that underlies this outstanding and persuasive study.

In September of 1994, Capt. Lawrence Rockwood deployed to Haiti with the Tenth Mountain Division. His role as a counterintelligence officer was to seek out informants among the Haitian population and, through them, to uncover threats to American personnel. In preparing for this task, he had secured and studied reports from the CIA and other sources detailing the situation in Haiti. He had learned that the dictatorial regime of Raoul Cédras, which the American forces had been sent to remove, was holding hundreds of political prisoners and that in some prisons 90 percent or more of the prisoners were "guilty" of political crimes only. Cédras loyalists, he learned, were torturing and executing many of them, and the tempo of torture and murder was likely to increase as the guilty sought to silence voices and kill memories before they were forced to flee the country into exile.

Capt. Rockwood was very encouraged when he heard his commander in chief, President Bill Clinton, tell the nation on September 15 that the primary objective of Operation Uphold Democracy was "to stop the brutal atrocities that threaten tens of thousands of Haitians." He had been eager for months to see this operation get under way. He felt this was exactly the way the U.S. Army ought to be used, and he liked to quote Gen. Douglas MacArthur who said, "The protection of the weak and unarmed is the very essence and reason for [a soldier's] being."

It was clear to Rockwood from the first day of the invasion, however, that the operation wasn't going to be carried out the way he had hoped. Although he was pleased that Cédras yielded to diplomatic pressure and did not try to resist the American landings, he was shocked to see American troops stand by and watch while thugs from the Cédras regime beat pro-democracy demonstrators. In one instance, a demonstrator was beaten to death only a few feet from American troops who were allowed to do no more than set their jaws, angrily grip their weapons, and stare straight ahead.

Rockwood thought he had his marching orders from the president— "Stop the brutal atrocities"—but the Joint Task Force commander, Gen. Meade, clearly heard other orders from the commander in chief. On the eve of the troops' entry into Haiti, Clinton spoke in very different terms from the ones he had used four days before: "My first concern, and the most important one, is for the safety and security of our troops. . . . Protection of American lives is our first order of business." To Rockwood's dismay, "force protection" became the first, last, and only priority for Gen. Meade.

The rules of engagement forbade Americans from using force for any purpose but to save their own lives. Though they were 20,000 strong and heavily equipped, the word was: Don't go looking under rocks. Don't make any trouble with the remnants of the dictatorship. Stay inside the concertina wire. Stay behind the sand bags. Never be alone.

Never leave the compound except in convoy. Wear your helmets and body armor, even inside the compound. Get used to being mocked as "Ninja Turtles."

For Rockwood, in Haiti to save innocent people from brutal atrocities, the operation became a nightmare. What began as a noble mission spiraled down fast into a horrifying evasion of responsibility. The obsession with "force protection" was to his mind a formula for moral cowardice. The arguments he makes with such scholarly thoroughness in this volume are ones he first made to himself in Haiti as he struggled with his distress over his own army detachment's failure to protect the weak at a time when it seemed obligatory to do so.

Rockwood later said, "I sat night after night reading report after report of murder and torture and abduction" (including accounts of a beheaded body found in a swamp outside the city, and a mutilated torture victim being spirited out of the Belair jail at night). "It wasn't the Americans who were in danger. It was the Haitians! And we refused to do anything to help them, to protect them. Maybe we couldn't make every street in every slum safe, but we could go into the prisons. They were the worst places. They were where the torture and murder was going on, and we knew it."

Rockwood knew that the story was the same, or worse, in the countryside, but there Special Forces were not only allowed but had been directed to inspect the prisons. A Special Forces team entered a jail in the remote town of Les Cayes and the team commander, Lt. Col. Mike Jones, reported, "We found some pretty damning photographs. People being pulled apart by chains, people being beaten. We went into the jail that day. . . . Thirty-six people in one tiny cell, one guy lying on the ground with his spine exposed. . . . Lice infested. I've never seen anything like it in my life."

By night Rockwood pursued his counterintelligence role, seeking out informants and collating intelligence reports. By day, he pressed his superiors to live up to their obligations as the new occupying power. Then the two missions began to meld, because he found his informants were vanishing. He would talk to them one night, yet when he looked for the same people twenty-four hours later, they had disappeared. The first law of counterintelligence, he knew, is to protect your sources. If they were alive, they were probably in prisons, and the Americans, who had responsibility now for the prisons, weren't going to do anything to rescue them.

As the days passed, Rockwood grew anxious, almost frantic. He methodically worked his way up and down his chain of command and followed any other possible avenues, seeking authorization and assistance to inspect the prisons, particularly the National Penitentiary where he knew from a CIA report that almost all the prisoners were not criminals but simply political enemies of the Cédras dictatorship.

Rockwood went to the chaplain on the day he arrived in Haiti and was told to stay away from what the chaplain saw as essentially a political issue. He met with Judge Advocate General (JAG) officers and showed them the Civil-Military Operations Handbook for the Tenth Mountain Division, which contained a checklist of information to obtain about each site where prisoners were confined: "name, address, grid coordinate, telephone number, capacity of kitchens, name of warden, overall condition of facility and inmates." The JAG officers told him to stop worrying about Haitians and work on keeping Americans safe.

He brought his case to the military police, to his commanding officer, to the Inspector General, and to the chief of staff for Gen. Meade. Everyone told him that the prisons would be visited in time—probably in a matter of weeks—that there were no forces to spare at present, that no one wanted to become Haiti's new prison-keepers, and that nothing would be done that might provoke the old regime before their scheduled departure. Until the dictatorship left, the prisons would remain under domestic control.

"This is unbelievable," Rockwood wrote at the time. "This is moral cowardice on a massive scale. We came here on a great mission, like the American troops that liberated Czechoslovakia and Hungary and Poland. But now we pull up outside the Haitian equivalent of Auschwitz and declare that what is going on inside is none of our business."

This did not fit with the way Rockwood had been trained, or the way he had been brought up. He had risen fast in the army and had received outstanding evaluations. His officer fitness reports characterized his performance as "superb" or "excellent" and recommended he be promoted "ahead of his contemporaries." He had chosen his models carefully and had worked hard to mold himself in their pattern. In his cubicle back at Fort Drum in upstate New York, the Tenth Mountain Division's home base, he kept pictures of three men he admired: Gen. George Picard, a counterintelligence officer in the French army during the Dreyfus Affair who went to prison to protest Dreyfus' innocence; Col. Count von Stauffenberg of the German army who gave his life in an attempt to assassinate Adolf Hitler; and Chief Warrant Officer Hugh C. Thompson, the American helicopter pilot who saw the My Lai massacre in progress, lowered his helicopter into the middle of it, and ordered his door gunner to train his machine gun on American troops who were killing unarmed civilians.

Rockwood also remembered his father, also an officer, who fought in Europe in 1945 and later took his seven-year-old son to see the Nazi death camp at Dachau. "He told me that these camps are not the creation of a few evil, brutal men. They're really the creation of cynicism and blind obedience to authority. I knew that if I did nothing now, I would never be able to take my son and daughter to those places and tell them the things my father told me."

At around 5 p.m. on September 30 Capt. Lawrence Rockwood decided he had to act. He had been in the country for one week at that point, and the mission to Haiti was ten days old. "I knew that lives were in danger, and I knew that if I didn't do something, no one else would. My commanders weren't going to do anything to fulfill their humanitarian obligation under international law to help those helpless people."

Rockwood put on his battle dress utility outfit. He pulled on his flak jacket, donned his helmet, grabbed his rifle and full ammunition pouch, snapped on two canteens and a first-aid kit, and set out to inspect the National Penitentiary on his own. He knew he was putting at risk a spotless fifteen-year service record, a promising career, and an unbroken family tradition of service to their country that stretched back to the Civil War. "It was precisely those things that compelled me to do what I did."

He quietly made his way to the rim of the barracks compound, selecting a place where the barbed wire was penetrable. (If he had gone to the gate, he would have had to lie to the sentries. "An officer does not lie.") After he made sure he was not observed, he quickly scrambled over the wall of the barracks compound, dropped to the ground outside, and found himself in a Haitian slum.

With the help of a seven-year-old boy, he made a deal with a Haitian truck driver to take him to the penitentiary. He paid the driver forty dollars, plus ten dollars each to two other Haitians to serve as cover. They dropped him in front of the presidential palace, a few blocks from the prison.

He spent over an hour looking for the prison, attracting the attention of Haitian policemen and soldiers and being followed at times by num-

bers of curious persons. Finally he spied the gate with its sign, "Péniten-
cier National." Expecting a difficult confrontation, he approached
cautiously, but the gate stood ajar and he entered.

Once inside, he found himself outnumbered by armed Haitians eight
to one. He bluffed them, claiming to be the lead man of a larger team
that would soon arrive to carry out an inspection. (Officers don't lie, but
they sometimes confuse the enemy.) It was not clear whether they believed him, but at the outset no one put up resistance. At a later point
Rockwood blocked a door with his foot; at the end of his inspection
there was a round in his rifle.

The night warden, Haitian major Serge Justafor, happened to be a
graduate of the U.S. Army Infantry School at Fort Benning, Georgia,
and spoke good English. He let Rockwood into his office but claimed to
be unable to unlock the prison block. "I'm not responsible for what they
do to each other once I lock them in at night," he said darkly.

After being shown a few newly arrived inmates in good condition,
Rockwood made his own way down a hallway, across a courtyard, and
into the "infirmary." There he found twenty-six people, most of them
lying on the bare and filthy concrete floor. To Rockwood, who has a degree in nursing, they appeared to be suffering from various wasting
diseases: tuberculosis, AIDS, acute dysentery, and so on. Some were
amputees. Few had even a scrap of cardboard to lie on. Many were near
death. A trench along the wall was full of feces, urine, and flies.

Rockwood returned to the warden's office and demanded to see a list
of the prisoners. "My intent was to secure an inventory so that we could
return in two weeks and ask what had become of each individual." He
was told there was no such list. He again demanded entry to the main
cell block and was told that there could be no entry until morning.

Rockwood did not see the main cell block that night. The main cell
block, which actually was just a single chamber, contained over four
hundred prisoners with only one square meter per prisoner. The UN's
International Police Monitors group inspected the place a few days later
and called it "the worst prison we have ever seen." Five months later, in
February 1995, a delegation including U.S. Congressman Dan Burton
(R-IN) would visit the same prison. Burton would report that "prior to
my visit, there had been 500 people in a prison cell standing ankle deep
in excrement for up to 4 to 5 months and some of their feet rotted off.
They had gangrene and they had to have amputation."

Rockwood had seen enough. That night, faced with locked doors and hostile faces, he knew he had done what he could. In any case, he thought he had accomplished his mission. Now that he had opened the lid on this prison, he figured, the authorities couldn't ignore it. Now the Joint Task Force would have to take responsibility for the National Penitentiary, and what they found there would make them look in the rest of Haiti's prisons. Besides, he had a foolproof way to bring more American forces to the prison: call them to come and arrest him. He requested that the warden inform U.S. authorities of his presence there, then pulled up a chair in the courtyard and sat down to wait.

Rockwood had been in the prison for almost three hours when Maj. Spencer Lane, the U.S. military liaison in Port-au-Prince, arrived. Rockwood recalls that Lane upbraided him, telling him to toughen up and face facts. "The third world is full of hell holes like this one. What makes this one so special?" "This one, I told him, is different because it is being conducted in cooperation with the United States government and the United States Army."

Maj. Lane had arranged for a party of men to overpower Rockwood as he left the prison. This was far from necessary. In the event, Rockwood couldn't find it in himself to disobey a direct order. When told by a superior officer to accompany him to the barracks compound, he complied without resistance. Back in the barracks compound, Rockwood was given two psychiatric evaluations, found mentally sound, and told to wait in the hospital. He was also read his rights.

Rockwood was too pumped up to sit still. He left the hospital and sought out his commanding officer, Col. Frank Bragg, director of intelligence for Tenth Mountain. Bragg had been like a mentor to Rockwood, a stern but sympathetic voice. Now he was disappointed and upset. "How could you go off on your own like this? You had your orders."

Finally someone wanted to talk about orders, legal and illegal. "I don't just follow orders," Rockwood told him. "I am an American officer, not a Nazi officer." Bragg told him to lower his voice, but Rockwood pressed on, insisting that he alone was fulfilling the president's command intent. "My loyalty is to the Constitution, then to the commander in chief, not to the careers of my immediate superiors." "I looked around me," he recalled later, "and I didn't see anyone who outranked the president."

Rockwood went further and compared Gen. Meade to Gen. Yamashita, the commander of Japanese forces in the Philippines in 1945. Yamashita was hanged by a war crimes tribunal for his failure to protect American prisoners, even though he neither ordered nor knew of their execution by his soldiers. Gen. Meade, Rockwood charged, had direct and specific knowledge of human rights abuses in the Haitian penitentiaries—Rockwood himself had provided it to him—and was doing nothing to stop them.

Even after all this, court-martial was not inevitable. Rockwood could have resigned, or he could have accepted a reprimand from his commanding officer. There would have been a damaging letter added to his file, perhaps a fine deducted from his paycheck. The army offered him both alternatives. Rockwood insisted on a full court-martial and so opened himself to the distinct possibility of five or more years in prison.

The court-martial was convened in February 1995 at Tenth Mountain Division headquarters in Fort Drum, New York. It lasted two days, twelve hours each, and produced, with exhibits and expert witness statements, a fourteen-volume record of trial. The convening officer was Gen. David C. Meade, the same man Rockwood had compared unfavorably to a war criminal that the United States had hanged. The judge, the prosecutors, and all five jurors were appointed by Gen. Meade from among his command. He wrote their officer performance reports; their careers were in his hands. They also were people who had been implicitly indicted by Rockwood, since most had been in Haiti too and had failed in Rockwood's judgment to meet their obligations to the weak and to perform in accordance with international law and humanitarian duty.

The army chose to prosecute the case on the narrowest of grounds. Rockwood was charged with leaving his appointed place of duty (going off the compound) and disrespect to a superior officer (arguing with Col. Bragg), disobeying a superior officer (leaving the hospital contrary to an order from the psychiatrist who examined him), and conduct unbecoming an officer. To Rockwood those charges were beside the point, except the last one. Of course he had done those things, but under the pressure of necessity. Lives were at stake and were being lost. But conduct unbecoming an officer? He felt that he was the *only* officer who had conducted himself properly in Haiti.

Rockwood's defense was shaped on the largest possible claims: that he was obligated to fulfill the president's announced intent in Haiti to end human rights abuses, and that he was compelled under international humanitarian law to protect helpless people in danger for their lives. The defense was conducted for him by former attorney general Ramsey Clark, whose services had been procured for Rockwood by Amnesty International. There was plenty at stake for both sides. Gen. Meade was depicted as timid and indifferent to the real goals of the Haiti intervention. Rockwood was called a renegade who refused to follow orders. The army said it couldn't have rogue officers launching their own crusades. Rockwood told the army: "Be all that you can be."

The army asked Gen. Richard Potter, commander of Special Forces in Haiti, to testify against Rockwood. Potter declined. He had sent his teams into the prisons in his areas of operations. If Rockwood had been serving under Potter, he would have been doing his duty. Under Meade's command, he was a dangerous renegade, soon to become a convicted criminal.

Rockwood called another renegade, Hugh C. Thompson, in his defense. Thompson, it will be recalled, was the Vietnam-era helicopter pilot whose picture Rockwood kept in his carrel at Fort Drum.

Ramsey Clark summed up first: "You know what was going on in those prisons. Starvation. Neglect. Disease. You know people were dying in them. The hottest places in hell are preserved for those who, in times of moral crisis, do nothing." The army's prosecutor, Capt. Charles Pede, replied: "The Army looks uncaring, but it was not. There were just as many human rights being violated in the streets, and that's where our priority was. . . . Soldiers in the field must follow orders. . . . We must make an example of [Rockwood]."

The jury deliberated less than two hours and voted to convict on all charges. Rockwood faced dismissal from the army, possible large fines, and up to six years and three months in prison. He received dismissal, a $3,000 fine, and no prison. "I am not relieved," he told the press. "I am a soldier." Rockwood quotes the judge who sentenced Lt. Calley of My Lai to three years house arrest: "A soldier is a reasoning agent, obliged to respond, not as a machine, but as a person." His take on the Army as a whole: "The United States Army is the greatest human rights enforcer this world has ever known. The United States Army is the institution that brought the end of slavery in North America. The United States Army, with its allies, put the end to the concentration camp system. That is the true legacy of the United States Army."

Gen. Meade did not last long enough in that command to sign the conviction papers. He received an early and unscheduled retirement within days of the trial. Sources differ on the reason for his replacement, but all maintain that his clash with Rockwood contributed to his fall. As a consequence, Maj. Gen. Thomas Burnette, in his capacity as the court-martial convening authority upon assuming command of the division, threw out the conviction for conduct unbecoming an officer in his post-trial review of the case.

Meade's successor in Haiti, Twenty-Fifth Division deputy commander Gen. James Hill, took a different attitude. He made a practice of taking reporters on tours of the prisons and claimed that he personally had seen the inside of every prison in Haiti and had created exactly the kind of accounting system that Rockwood wanted. "We worked out a prisoner registration system, we worked out a tagging system, we've done some sanitation works, we fixed some showers. . . ." A reporter asked him whether giving an order to go into a prison should be a priority for the commander of the Joint Task Force. "Oh, absolutely. There is no doubt about that. There is no doubt about it, and we have made it a priority."

Rockwood pursued two appeals of his remaining convictions and hoped for years to be reinstated as an officer. The basis of his appeal was a challenge to the lack of jury instructions from the trial judge regarding the standard of command responsibility that Gen. Meade was subject to during the operation. This instruction as to what international humanitarian laws were applicable to the operation was central to Rockwood's defense and rationale for acting. "If I get back in," he joked, "I'll have my twenty years. I'll be right on track for general!" Through 1999 he was signing his e-mails "Captain Lawrence Rockwood, United States Army, on extended leave"; but in the end the Supreme Court refused to consider his final appeal. Even today, his email address remains soldier "But there are actions whose mere omission is a wrong; and they are called duties."

This book is a forceful, reasoned, informed, and convincing call to duty to the entire military. It comes from one who saw his duty and did it, and continues to do it to this day.

WALKING AWAY
FROM NUREMBERG

Nuremberg, Germany, November 20, 1945

IN HIS OPENING STATEMENT as the American chief counsel for the prosecution at the International Military Tribunal at Nuremberg, U.S. Supreme Court Justice Robert H. Jackson addressed the issue of whether the legacy of that tribunal would be simple "victor's justice" or the establishment of principles of international reciprocity in holding individuals accountable for war crimes: "We must never forget that the record on which we judge these defendants is the record on which history will judge us tomorrow. To pass these defendants a poisoned chalice is to put it to our lips as well."[1]

On loan from the U.S. Supreme Court for the purpose of negotiating the London Charter establishing the International Military Tribunal (IMT), and later serving as the tribunal's first lead prosecutor for the United States, Justice Jackson immediately understood that the trials he had arranged and the theory of his prosecution placed the American military profession in a historic ethical dilemma. In a 1946 article, published in what was then the professional journal of the U.S. Army, Jackson argued that the standards of liability that the IMT was holding as binding on the officers of the former Axis powers were, rather than novel initiatives, inherent in American military tradition and doctrine. Jackson, then, faced a formidable task in presenting his arguments, for many American military officers were concerned about firm precedents being established and the possibility that such precedents could be used against American commanders in the future.

Although the War Department had both initiated the tribunal process and crafted the charges, Jackson realized that it would be insufficient to portray the charter as simply a binding order initiated by a competent and recognized authority. Doctrine usually assumes a longevity that exceeds the tenure of an appointed or elected leadership.

Jackson had to present the charter to the American military profession as part of its own tradition. First, he had to balance the norms of military obedience to higher authority, especially civilian authority, with the concept that certain orders are by their nature manifestly illegal and should not be executed. Second, he had to address the reality that, although members of the military profession are by definition the managers of violence, they must abide by rules that recognized that the means that can be utilized in war are not unlimited and that military commanders are liable when the conduct of their subordinates exceeds those limitations.

The official position of the United States vis-à-vis Justice Jackson's ominous challenge has been one of steady retreat from a precise affirmative standard for holding individual commanders directly responsible for war crimes. Many of the principles of Nuremberg-era trials have their origin in the U.S. Civil War-era document *U.S. General Order No. 100*, also known as the Lieber Code (after its principal author, Francis Lieber), which incorporated all of the major principles of Augustinian just war doctrine. The U.S. Army, after administering the American war crimes program that included the IMT, incorporated a rigorous definition of command responsibility into its preeminent doctrinal manual on the law of war, Field Manual 27–10, the 1956 revision of which superseded earlier versions. During the course of the Vietnam war, however, the United States failed to hold its own military commanders responsible for dereliction in preventing grave breaches of international humanitarian law.[2] Subsequently, the United States consistently refused, and continues to refuse, to ratify international treaties and protocols that would replace the passive standard of command responsibility that the United States has enforced on its own military personnel with the affirmative standards inscribed in other recent international human rights statutes and war crime tribunal charters.

Rather than coming out of the tradition of legal positivism or political realism, many of the principles of the Nuremberg-era trials have their origin in the first modern codification of the laws of war during the U.S. Civil War, in *U.S. General Order No. 100*. Despite the continuities and discontinuities, the development of American military doctrine has been represented by the history of contested *weltanschauung* (worldviews) between those who championed functionally aristocratic models of military professionalism and those who championed democratic models. The basic assumptions of Augustinian just war doctrine and of *U.S. General Order No. 100* continued to retain their influence in the Nuremberg-era standard of command responsibility found in FM 27–10, but after that the situation changed. By his allusion to "drinking from a poisoned chalice" utilized in his opening statement as the American Chief Counsel for the prosecution at the International Military Tribunal (IMT) at Nuremberg, Justice Jackson addressed the issue of whether the ethical legacy of that tribunal would be more than a historical example of duplicity on the part of the victorious allies.

It must be kept in mind that, in a civil democracy, military leaders do not directly make decisions on national policy, including war crimes policy. They can, of course, influence such policy; and the degree of political deference to the military profession on issues of war and security by civilian political leaders continually fluctuates over time. Such changing political relationships, however, cannot provide a consistent basis on which to assess the American military profession's historical constancy to (or deviation from) the Nuremberg-era standards of command responsibility. On the other hand, the manner by which the military profession plans to implement national policy in the context of its own evolving institutional norms does provide a rather constant point of reference, one that can be used by the analyst to judge whether the military profession has kept faith with its own historical doctrinal values.

While current national policy obviously cannot be placed entirely on the shoulders of the military profession, the latter's systematic failure to hold its own soldiers to the standards of command responsibility that it has historically imposed on military personnel of its defeated adversaries must be viewed as an institutional failure. The United States failed to hold its own military commanders responsible for dereliction in preventing and suppressing breaches of international humanitarian law during the Vietnam War. The standards applied to American defendants involved in the perpetration and cover-up of the My Lai massacre, in particular, fell short of the standards that Jackson and his contemporaries held up to German and Japanese officers immediately after the cessation of hostilities in World War II. For example, in the My Lai case of Capt. Ernest Medina, the military judge instructed the jury that they must establish that Medina possessed actual knowledge that his subordinates were committing human rights violations in order for him to be held criminally liable as commander. That standard, referred to as the "must have known" standard, contrasts both with the "should have known" standards established in post-World War II war crimes tribunals and with contemporary standards on command responsibility found in a variety of recognized sources, such as the 1977Additional Protocol I to the Geneva Conventions, the statutes of the international tribunals for Rwanda and the former Yugoslavia, and the Rome Statute for the International Criminal Court.

In the direct aftermath of the U.S. failure to apply the Nuremberg-era standards of command responsibility in the trials following the disaster at My Lai, the United States took the lead in successfully negotiating the inclusion of an affirmative definition of command responsibility in Article 86 of Protocol I. Although the standard of command responsibility was not central to the Department of Defense's and the Reagan administration's subsequent overturning of the Army War College's recommendation for ratification of the protocol, the American reversal documented a conservative trend toward limiting the applicability of international humanitarian law for which a commander could be held liable.

In addition to initially supporting Protocol I, the United States supported the incorporation of Nuremberg-like standards of affirmative command responsibility into Article 6 of the statute of the International Criminal Tribunal for Rwanda (ICTR) and Article 7 of the statute of the International Criminal Tribunal for the Former Yugoslavia (ICTY). The nation's leadership, however, continues to oppose the ratification of treaties or the establishment of permanent and independent tribunals that could lead to the imposition of such standards on American citizens. Unlike U.S. decisions regarding Protocol I, the official U.S. position on the subsequent ad hoc tribunals and on the Rome treaty that created the International Criminal Court (ICC) was not established primarily on the basis of military-doctrinal analysis but rather on foreign policy and general political grounds. A formal examination of it therefore falls outside the scope of the present volume, even while occasional reference will be made to the attendant statutes and treaties.

Despite changing currents in both the internal, military sphere and the external, political sphere, the 1956 FM 27–10, with its affirmative, Nuremberg-era standard of command responsibility, remains the official keystone doctrine concerning the law of armed conflict. Minimalist standards of command responsibility, in line with those used in the case of My Lai and subsequently, have yet to be formally incorporated into American keystone doctrine. Rather, the rigorous definition of command responsibility remains doctrinally authoritative even as other doctrinal-guidance documents reveal a subtle trend toward the acceptance of a more relaxed standard.

Jackson's famous jeremiad was not directed merely at future governments of the United States or at the other wartime allies. It also pointed a righteous finger at the very institution he noted was responsible for planning, operating, and carrying out the judgments of the World War II–era American war crimes program, namely, the American military profession. Even when a doctrine, such as the command responsibility doctrine embodied in FM 27–10, is widely promulgated and has received clear political backing, it seldom reaches the point of being all-encompassing. It tends to stand on its own until challenged to extend or contract its reach. Nevertheless, doctrine, like law, possesses an institutional memory, a memory that can and does survive the ideological agendas of both political necessity and positive law. The simple and commonsense military principle mandating that *military commanders have an affirmative duty to protect the civilians and prisoners in the territory occupied or controlled by their forces, and that this duty extends to all military operations,* remains tenuously in effect as official U.S. policy. Disappointingly, however, it is only as military doctrine, rather than as legislated positive law or declared national policy that the principle continues to be validated.

This book examines the development of the concept of command responsibility as official military doctrine from the Civil War's General Order 100, or "Lieber Code," to contemporary U.S. military doctrine. JCS (Joint Chiefs of Staff) Pub 1, the definitive delineator of official U.S. military terminology, defines doctrine as "fundamental principles by which military forces or elements thereof guide their actions in support of national objectives."[3] Doctrine is distinct from law. It is authoritative, but a violation of doctrine does not necessarily involve a violation of law. Although doctrine often results in law and law often underpins doctrine, doctrine, perhaps more so than law, calls for judgment in its application (as against rote compliance). Unlike positive law based on legal jurisdiction, doctrine is based on professional consensus, even though the foundation of that consensus derives from on an internal institutional validation that is hierarchical and relatively narrow. Unlike law, doctrine is openly historicized in that it—specifically in the case of military doctrine—"captures the lessons of past wars, reflects the nature of war and conflict in its own time, and anticipates the intellectual and technological developments that will bring victory now and in the future," making it a test of professional rather than legal competence.[4]

Just as doctrine is distinct from law, doctrine is also distinct from drill. In a 1966 official doctrinal manual, Virgil Ney drew a distinction between drill manuals and modern military doctrine. He considered early manuals as "doctrine in infancy." One example of such proto-doctrine was the *Regulations,* or *Blue Book,* that Frederick William von Steuben developed to drill the Continental Army at Valley Forge in marching, weapons fire, and open-field battle maneuver. Doctrine proper involves strategic and operational concerns that are for more comprehensive than mere drill.[5] Additionally, doctrine is distinct from unofficial literature, no matter how influential, in that doctrine is usually officially published and may also carry an official imprimatur similar to that found in Catholic theological works signifying doctrinal correctness.

One benefit of an approach to command responsibility that looks at doctrine vis-à-vis law is that it avoids the perennial debate between natural law and positive law theorists. Following the views of Hugo Grotius (1583–1645) and the prominent late-medieval theologian, Saint Thomas Aquinas, natural law holds that there is an inescapable connection between law and morality. John Austin (1790–1859), legal positivism's leading historical proponent, countered such natural law theorists by drawing a sharp distinction between law and morality based on (1) the command doctrine, which stated that a law must constitute a threat of sanction; and (2) the doctrine of absolute sovereignty, which held that a law must be issued from a position of superiority.[6] Doctrine predates this debate. Specifically, an early just war concept, the doctrine of military necessity, which underpins command responsibility, predates the natural-versus-positive law argument and applies a normative criterion directly to the experience of war without requiring a philosophical discussion about the nature of law.

Like law, doctrine is hierarchal. In fact, no two sets of doctrinal publications can be equal in any given circumstance or contingency. This study is concerned only with doctrine that established a foundation for the general operation of an army and in changes in just war doctrine over time that necessitated modifications in subsidiary doctrines and even in the doctrines of other military services. Distinctions between doctrinal publications arose out of developments starting with the promulgation of (1) the *Field Service Regulations* early in the twentieth century, (2) the U.S. Army field manuals developed during World War II and utilized during the cold war, and (3) the current interservice or joint-service regulation systems now in the process of supplementing and replacing the separate doctrinal publication systems of the separate services. Current official policy places such doctrine into two major groups:

Capstone Doctrine: The highest category of doctrine publications in the "hierarchy of publications" that link doctrine to national strategy and the guidelines of other government agencies to include other members of international alliances and coalitions. .

Keystone Doctrine: Doctrinal publications that provides the foundation for a series of doctrine publications in the hierarchy of publication.[7]

The focus of the present study is army doctrine and publications, although it is recognized that the navy and the air force have developed similar doctrines based, in part, on what that the army laid out in executing its 'traditional role as the major source of both capstone and keystone doctrine. From the promulgation of U.S. Army *General Order No. 100* in the Civil War to the belated implementation of the Goldwater-Nichols Department of Defense Reorganization Act of 1986, a process not yet complete, first the War Department and, subsequently, the Department of the Army has been the principal agency for developing national war fighting doctrine in general and the laws of war in particular.

Doctrine is also comparable to law in that it posits a formal norm. Besides formal legal standards, regulations, and military orders, the 1990 edition of U.S. Army Field Manual 22–100, *Military Leadership*, includes traditional organizational values as formal norms. Informal norms include actual operating organizational values (such as careerism, peer pressure, and avoiding controversy), institutional pressures, and personal values. Unlike law, doctrinal norms do not necessarily imply uniformity or constancy. Despite its formal hierarchical structure, the human world of military leadership and subordination seldom provides for the uncontested development of formal norms. The process of the development of doctrine often is a complicated balancing act between current authoritative policy and past tradition. Norms can be arranged along a continuum from rigidly formal norms such as legal standards (laws, orders, and regulations), to semi-formal norms such as basic national values and traditional organizational values, to informal norms such as, again, actual operational values, institutional pressures,

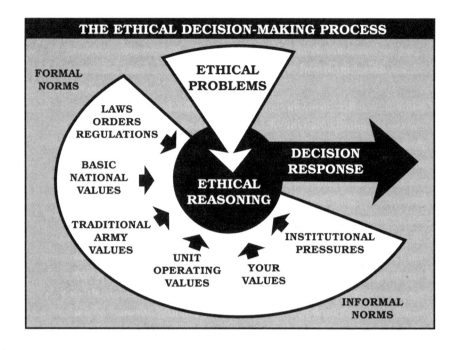

THE ETHICAL DECISION-MAKING PROCESS

ETHICAL
PROBLEMS

FORMAL
NORMS

LAWS
ORDERS
REGULATIONS

BASIC
NATIONAL
VALUES

DECISION
RESPONSE

ETHICAL
REASONING

TRADITIONAL
ARMY
VALUES

INSTITUTIONAL
PRESSURES

UNIT
OPERATING
VALUES

YOUR
VALUES

INFORMAL
NORMS

and personal values. Formal norms should always trump less formal norms. FM 22–100 defines a "true ethical dilemma" as that which occurs "when two or more deeply held values collide."[8]

Conflicts between formal norms and informal norms impact not only on the operational effectiveness of a command but also on the moral and ethical integrity of that command's actions. While intentionally avoiding old law journal debates about the nature of Justice Jackson's legal realism, this book does take as its subject the relationship between American military doctrine and the Nuremberg precedents.[9] Conservative, positivist commentators have pointed to the novelty of the Nuremberg process and criticized the "tendency to equate war crimes decisions, or Nuremberg precedents, with the law of war."[10] Rather than refute the legal positivist critique of Nuremberg, my purpose is to establish the Nuremberg precedents, their antecedents, and progeny as American military doctrine.

I argue that the ethics associated with traditional just war doctrine are not merely formal military norms but rather are, by now, international accepted norms of American parentage. Long a discipline left to staff officers and war colleges, military doctrine and its central role in defining institutional norms within the military profession have escaped the interest of both military historians and other scholars of civil-military affairs. Given the debate over the abuse of prisoners under American jurisdiction following the 9/11 terrorist attacks, however, the issue has moved to center stage. In 2005, Senator John McCain's amendment (no. 1557) to the National Defense Authorization Act for fiscal year 2006 mandated that the Department of Defense comply with army doctrine rather than with political and legal guidance provided by the Bush administration on the issue of interrogations and the handling of prisoners. On June 29, 2006, the Supreme Court struck down the military commissions President Bush had established to try enemy combatants. Ruling that the administration's overly expansive assertion of executive power was not in keeping with the requirements of the Geneva Convention, the court found that the president's action was neither required by military necessity nor authorized by federal law. This placed President Bush in the position of using his political capital in the 2006 election cycle for negotiating with Congress for legislation that would save major portions of his anti-Geneva detention and tribunal policies. As in the case of the 2005 McCain amendment, President Bush found opposition to policies developed by civilian White House lawyers with little to no military background being voiced by military defense lawyers, retired officers, and by senators from his own party serving on the Armed Serves Committee, the latter including John Warner (the committee chairman), Lindsey Graham, and, of course, former prisoner of war and torture victim John McCain.

The abuses and policies at issue, whether at Abu Ghraib Prison in Baghdad, at Guantánamo Bay in Cuba, or at incarceration centers in Afghanistan, did not result from a dearth of lawyering; in fact, the opposite is the case. And it will now take soldiers to fix the mess that lawyers have made. This conclusion, admittedly a somewhat extreme one, highlights and reinforces my thesis in this book regarding the ongoing relevance of military doctrine to issues of human rights, humanitarian law, and the historical development of professional military ethics.

According to John Austin, the preeminent theorist of positive law, every law is a command. The reverse, however, is not always the case: commands are not abstract laws. Laws never provide a sufficient basis for the legitimization of authority. John Adams may have been right to say "ours is a nation of laws and not men," but then so too were the southern Confederacy and the Third Reich based on law. It was the existence of the Nuremberg Laws of the 1930s, mandating the special treatment of Germany's Jewish population, that made Nuremberg such a compelling location for the trials of the very men who drafted and executed those laws. Indeed, it would be fair to say that legal positivism, as understood at the time, was the real defendant at Nuremberg. Six of those who sat in the dock at the International Military Tribunal were some of Germany's leading lawyers. One of the most senior, Hans Frank, the governor general of Poland, where the vast majority of extermination programs were carried out, never tired of praising the "majesty of law" over the course of his National Socialist career. Later, sixteen leading German judges were tried under Allied Control Law No. 10.[11] President Bush's policy of minimizing the possibility of humanitarian law being enforced on American nationals engaged in the so-called war on terror is merely the latest historical marker to an official worldview established as far back as the Reagan administration. This book is primarily neither a dispassionate legal analysis nor an interpretative study of national policy. Rather, it is an intellectual history of the development and practice of military professional ethics. This is a history unapologetically premised on direct professional experience and a historically informed intuition that a military commander who defers solely to lawyers on issues arising from the ethical reality of military conflict is simply not prepared for or fit to command. The chapters that follow expand on this proposition and more.

CHAPTER ONE

Just War Doctrine and
General Order No. 100

Men who take up arms against one another in public war do not cease on this
account to be moral beings, responsible to one another and to God.

General Order No. 100

DURING THE THIRD YEAR of the Civil War, the War Department issued
the *Instructions for the Government of the Armies of the United States
in the Field*—known officially as *General Order No. 100* and unofficially as the Lieber Code—to the deployed forces of the United States
Army. In a 1963 edition of the *International Review of the Red Cross*,
future World Court justice Richard R. Baxter called this military order
the "first modern codification of the Law of War."[1] Nine years later, retired U.S. Army Brigadier General Telford Taylor, former American
chief prosecutor at the Nuremberg war crimes trials conducted under
Allied Control Council Law No. 10, noted that *General Order No. 100*
"remained for half a century the official Army pronouncement on the
subject, furnished much of the material for the Hague Conventions of
1899 and 1907, and today still commands attention as the germinal document for the codification of the laws of land warfare."[2]

The theory of war found in *General Order No. 100* is distinct from
the three statist philosophies arising in the period following the end of
Europe's wars of religion: modern natural law theory; legal positivism;
and political realism. The Treaty of Westphalia in 1648 not only ended
the Wars of Reformation but also became the historical reference point
for a model of international relations centered on the early modern European shibboleths of anti-interventionism and noninterference based
on a theoretical equality of sovereignty between nation states. Unlike
the major schools of thought associated with this Westphalian system,
General Order No. 100 marked a return to traditional just war doctrine,

a premodern and less Eurocentric philosophy of warfare that (1) viewed war as an essentially moral undertaking; and (2) placed affirmative humanitarian obligations on a specialized group of individuals, namely, the military and the promulgators of military conduct.

Origins of *General Order No. 100*

Outside of Brussels at Waterloo in June 1815, the wars of the French Revolution came to an end. These wars marked the point of departure from the premodern to the modern in warfare. In the general vicinity of the battle, at Ligny, was a soldier in the service of the king of Prussia lying close to death from wounds he received during the final allied pursuit of Napoleon. This wounded soldier, a young Berliner named Francis Lieber, was the future drafter of U.S. Army *General Order No. 100*.[3]

After recovering from his near-mortal wounds, Lieber went on to unconventional warfare. His attempt to fight alongside Greek irregulars against the Ottoman Army was frustrated as a result of the treatment he received from his allies, a disillusioning experience that was shared by many other European volunteers who fought in the Greek war of independence.[4] Between his bouts of military service, Lieber received a doctor of philosophy degree from the University of Jena and spent time in jail for liberal agitation against the increasingly conservative Prussian state. Emigrating to the United States in 1827, he later became the chair of history and political economy at South Carolina College (1835–57). Subsequently he relocated to Columbia College in New York because of his antipathy to slavery. He was eventually appointed to a professorship of history, political science, and law. Lieber became one of the founding fathers of both American political science and, although he was never formally trained as a lawyer, American legal studies. His approach to law and politics were based upon the discipline of hermeneutics in the anti-idealistic and anti-rationalistic tradition of the German Protestant theologian Friedrich Schleiermacher and the German historian Wilhelm Dilthey. In fact, he was America's first leading exponent of classical hermeneutics.

For Lieber, laws and policies are subject to internal interpretation because they are composed in human languages whose component parts—words—have meanings that vary according to time, place, and the subjective worldview, or *weltanschauung,* of the original author(s). Lieber's political and legal hermeneutics resulted in a "practical" ethic that contrasts sharply with the extremes of both political realism, which posits an ethical aporia that holds actions of a state, either foreign or domestic, as existing independent of any ethical considerations, and legalism, which dismisses the political attributes and implications of law.[5] Lieber was a life-long critic of the conservative regime in Prussia and was a lifelong apologist for a revolutionary regime he adopted for his own, the United States. Lieber's political principles developed, to a large extent, in opposition to the Aristotelian principles of John C. Calhoun. Considered by many as the intellectual father of the Confederacy, Calhoun invested his writings with both proslavery and antiegalitarian sentiments. In reply to the Calhoun's conservative theory of "concurrent democracy," Lieber developed the theory of "institutional liberty" to explain the superiority of the American conception of nation to that of extreme revolutionary states such as France, which he had fought against, or reactionary nation-states such as Prussia, which he fought for but then rejected.[6] Reminiscent of Thomas Paine's role during the Revolutionary War, Lieber became the theoretic apologist of the Union cause during the Civil War, even initiating the discussion that would result in the revolutionary amendments to the Constitution adopted at the end of the war.[7]

By 1863, the Lincoln administration realized that the Rules and Articles of War, then in use, were not appropriate for a conflict with an enemy whose sovereignty it refused to recognize. As the eighteenth-century Westphalian system left the responsibility for the implementation of humanitarian concerns, such as the treatment of enemy prisoners, to be worked out between theoretically equal sovereign nation states, the threat that the Confederacy would exploit humanitarian practices under the custom and usages of war, such as granting prisoner-of-war status, was significant as a de facto recognition of sovereignty.

To resolve this conflict, Lincoln turned to Lieber to draft a "set of rules and definitions providing for most issues occurring under the Law and usages of War."[8] The result was *General Order No. 100*.[9] As its general provisions would later be incorporated into the Hague Conferences of 1899 and 1907, and it would also form the basis for similar codes in England, France, and even Prussia, the Lieber Code has usually been viewed primarily as a legal instrument. However, it would be a grave mistake to view *General Order No. 100* as having legal significance alone. Like the Emancipation Proclamation of the year before, the document was a military order from a civilian commander-in-chief to military commanders conducting ongoing military operations. The code remained in effect until it was superseded in 1917 by War Department Document No. 467, *Rules of Land Warfare*. Accordingly, *General Order No. 100* should be considered a foundational document for the general development of American military doctrine.[10]

As the first officially promulgated doctrine that addressed the overall conduct of tactical and strategic operations "rather than specialized functions such as simple drill," *General Order No. 100* constituted the U.S. military's first capstone doctrine.[11] Rather than being concerned with *how* to deploy tens of thousands of soldiers to march across open fields in increasingly costly battles, Lieber was concerned with *why* a state deploys soldiers in the first place. Next to Lieber, the most critical figure in the code's genesis was the general-in-chief of the Union armies, General Henry Wager Halleck, who was responsible both for selecting Lieber and for heading the military commission tasked with reviewing and approving the code. Hallack was the author not only of the most contemporary of the privately published tactical drill manuals utilized during the war but also of a major treatise on the laws of war, a work strongly influenced by Lieber's earlier writings.[12] Lieber's close collaboration with Gen. Halleck testifies to the relevance of *General Order No. 100* to the operational art of warfare, such as it existed during the Civil War.

On June 24, 1863, Confederate Secretary of War James A. Seddon wrote a letter to Washington rejecting *General Order No. 100*. Seddon correctly detected the revolutionary tone of Lieber's code, not only with respect to slavery but also in regard to the concepts of military necessity and the right of intervention in the affairs of another sovereign state—or (as in Seddon's case) states claiming sovereignty. Seddon attacked the code as an "assertion of dogmas" that were oppositional to the very foundation of Confederate authority.[13]

Contrary to sequentialist logic, the justification for major wars changes during their course, especially when their course is exceptionally longer and bloodier than expected. *General Order No. 100* represented the shift in Union war objectives from mere statist concern with the preservation of the Union to a revolutionary war of emancipation. To establish a precedent to allow humanitarian protocols without the statist criteria that could be used in support of Confederate foreign policy objectives, Lieber was indeed guilty of resorting to the non-state centered concepts that were considered by Seddon as premodern. However, just as "war antedates the state," as noted by the historian John Keegan,[14] efforts to establish normative codes for humanitarian concerns also antedate the state, at least the modern post-Westphalian state. The articles of *General Order No. 100* follow with remarkable consistency the central premodern principles of Augustinian just war doctrine.

Augustinian Just War Doctrine and Its Historical Significance

The principle that there is an *affirmative official duty to use force or coercion to assist others as predicated and conditioned by the principle of necessity* was laid down by the end of the fifth century as the concept of *justum bellum*, or just war.[15] The initial Western institutional base for just war doctrine was as a moral teaching of the leading theologians of the Roman Catholic Church. This sponsorship by a recognized supranational authority during the period of the doctrine's greatest influence gave just war doctrine a universal moral character. Later natural law theory, developing from just war tradition, would share this attribute of universality. Because, however, just war doctrine predates natural law theory and later legalist paradigms, including the Westphalian concept of the 'law of nations' and the 'laws of war,' it remains conceptually distinct from the perennial debate between positive law and natural law theorists over the continuity or discontinuity between law and morality.

Just war finds its classical foundation in the distinction between the usually interchangeable Latin words *lex* (law) and *jus* (justice). Marcus Tullius Cicero (106–43 BCE)—the great civic philosopher of republican Rome—in his infamous maxim, *silent enim leges inter arma*, stated that law is silenced in war, even though he continued to address wars in terms of their being either just or unjust.[16] Saint Augustine of Hippo (AD 354–430), the preeminent theologian of Western Christianity's first millennium, chose necessity rather than natural law as the moral foundation for any governmental use of force. The problem for Augustine in drafting the central principles of traditional just war doctrine at the end of the fifth century was defining an ethical role for Christian officials in an empire now ruled by Christian, specifically Catholic, emperors. As the political triumph of Christianity had not brought about a change in humankind's basic nature, this Christian empire, like its pagan predecessor, required the use of force, or the threat thereof, to maintain itself. Augustine's conundrum consisted of the fact that there was no practical alternative to the requirement for individual Christians to serve in positions of coercive authority. Although Augustine denied the self-defense argument for individuals, he argued for an affirmative obligation to defend others that superseded the pacifism associated with the early Church.[17]

One of the army's leading contemporary experts on just war doctrine has defined it as the mean between the two extremes of absolute pacifism and political realism.[18] The real demarcation between these categorical positions lies in a disagreement not over the nature of war but over the nature of peace.

While just war doctrine is effectively exemplified by the maxim of "no peace without justice," political realism favors the peace even at the expense of justice. Pacifism, on the other hand, denies any such opposition between peace and justice and posits instead that individuals, by avoiding the passive benefits of injustice, can work for justice as a means to gain peace.[19] Additionally, the pacifist sees war as the ultimate expression of injustice, while, for the political realist, all claims of justice must defer to the interests of a sovereign state, usually his or her own. Just war answers pacifism's categorical rejection of force by defending the use of force on the basis of the categorical value of human life, specifically the victim's.[20] Augustine separates just war doctrine from both political realism and pacifism by positing that the desire for peace does not in itself entail any virtue:

> Just as every single human being desires peace[,] in the same way they desire happiness. The love of peace, therefore, is not a virtue. When those who are leading their nations sing the praise of peace they are sincere. They seek war to achieve their peace. Even violent criminals demand peace, if only for themselves. They do not love war; they aspire to an unjust peace.[21]

Although not a systematic thinker in any modern sense, Augustine conceived the proper conduct of those holding state authority in terms directly related to the basic philosophical premises of his theology, namely, selfless love, encompassing the altruistic obligation to assist others for their own sake; and a human realism, based on what Hannah Arendt—one of his most famous twentieth-century interpreters—calls a "definite and obligatory equality among all people."[22] Just as the desire for peace entailed no positive value in itself, love according to

Augustine could be for either good or evil—and that is why actions responsibly undertaken for the welfare of others entailed a specific form of love, a selfless love, or *caritas*. The recourse to the utilization of force in war was not based on a passive acknowledgment of the action of a properly Christian state or a simple license for Christian participation in the official actions of such a state. Rather, it was an affirmative requirement of love necessitating an intervention in the affairs of humanity.

Following both the neo-Platonists and the Stoics, Augustine rejects the essentialism of Aristotle that legitimates war and even slavery on the basis of supposed inferior or superior natural attributes possessed by various human groups. The central premise of Aristotle's *Politics* was that humans are naturally destined from birth either to rule or be ruled, to be free or a slave, and that war is justified as a means of determining the essential differences in humanity manifested in higher and lower degrees of virtue.[23] Unlike Aristotle, Augustine argued for a unity of a shared human nature based on a sinful disposition to place one's selfish interests ahead of the interests of others. Augustine's teachings on just war, like his theology in general, is based on the foundation of human equality. Rather than an equality based on inherent human goodness, Augustine's human realism posited that humankind is inherently flawed and that this metaphysical truth accounts for both the existence of war and the recourse to it. Consequently, the most that can be hoped for are "momentary respites" from conflicts, not their complete end.[24] Despite his pessimistic assessment of human nature, however, Augustine considered the preservation and betterment of human society as our highest calling in the secular realm. He furthermore held that a peace founded on justice—at least a relative justice—is possible, and only after attaining such justice should a return to a state of peace be celebrated.[25]

Augustine was concerned with Christians serving the state in two basic functions: that of judge and that of a soldier. During the late Roman Empire, both were occupations intrinsically related, the role of soldier *(miles)* being more expansive than it is in contemporary societies, whose police and military function as largely separate entities. Unlike the later natural law theorists and political realists, Augustine spoke directly to the executors of state authority rather than to kings or statesmen. Living during the reign of the Roman Emperor Theodosius, who was championing Augustine's own version of Christianity, Augustine had the integrity to reject the views of many of his Catholic contemporaries, who held that wars conducted in defense of Christian states were inherently just while those conducted by pagan or heretical states were unjust. The commonly held belief attributing the holy war ideology of the Crusades to Augustine is not supported in the texts of his writings.[26]

The 1983 Pastoral Letter of the National Conference of Catholic Bishops, *The Challenge of Peace,* a document drafted under the guidance of the preeminent clerical just war authority, J. Bryan Hehir, affirmed the centrality of Saint Augustine to the establishment of just war doctrine that consists of "eight fundamental principles or criteria."[27]

1. Just Cause: The central tenet of traditional just war doctrine is Augustine's dictum that a war is "justified only by the injustice of an aggressor."[28]
2. Competent Authority: War is both a public and official act involving, to varying degrees, the act of judging the action of others or executing such a judgment under the orders of a superior official.
3. Comparative Justice: The claim of possessing a just cause in war is always relative and, consequently, parties to a conflict need to limit their objectives to the relative gravity of the offense being redressed.
4. Right Intention: While the justification of war is aggression or an unjust peace, the objective of a just war is a just peace.
5. Last Resort: Even when necessity demands it, war is a tragedy to be avoided at all costs, save justice.
6. Probability of Success: Nothing is more obstructive to the establishment of a just peace than indecisive or ineffective military action.
7. Proportionality: The unjust effects of warfare must be compensated for by the actual ends of justice attained by resorting to warfare.
8. Discrimination: There is a distinction between combatants and noncombatants and the intentional targeting of the latter is a criminal act, even in an otherwise just war.

Although not in a systematic form, all these major principles of just war doctrine can be found in Augustine. This is because the principles are not distinct, but inherently interconnected. For example, the principle of discrimination is already implied in the preceding criteria such as proportionality. The major just war theorist of the early cold war period, Paul Ramsey, argued "the justification of participation in conflict at the same time severely limits war's conduct. What justified, also limited."[29]

This traditional separation of just war principles into *jus ad bellum* (justice before war) principles and *jus in bello* (justice during war) principles also overlaps. For example, in their pastoral letter, the National

Conference of Catholic Bishops classified all just war principles except discrimination as *jus ad bellum*, with the central just war principle of proportionality as an overlapping theme between *jus ad bellum* and *jus in bello* principles.[30] To emphasize that *jus ad bellum* concerns are not set aside once a war is initiated, the leading secular theoretician on just war, Michael Walzer, makes the point that an unjust war can be fought justly, and a just war can be fought unjustly, thereby becoming unjust.[31]

This historical development of just war doctrine was characterized more by accommodation than by innovation. Augustine and early just war theory is often associated primarily with *jus ad bellum* concerns, and late just war theory with *jus in bello* concerns.[32] However, the innovations of *jus ad bellum* principles of just cause introduced by the Church in the eleventh century, such as indulgences for Crusaders and absolution for the fallen, find no basis in Augustinian just war doctrine. The significant authoritative events in the eleventh century on the conduct of war were the concept of the "Truce of God," put forward in 1041 by Abbot Odilo of the great Benedictine motherhouse of Cluny, which called for a cessation of hostilities on Holy Days; the "Peace of God," a call by the Council of Narbonne in 1054 to protect the Church and the poor from the effects of warfare; and, finally, the preaching of the First Crusade by Pope Urban II (also a Cluniac monk) at the Council of Clermont on November 27, 1095. While the former two can be seen as an extension of *jus in bello* prohibitions, the latter—with its arming of monks and priests, the indulgence giving total temporal pardon of all sin for participants (which would include war crimes committed over the course of the crusade), and a total absolution for those who died in battle—finds no foundation in Augustinian just war tenets, nor would they be authenticated by incorporation into the tenets of later just war theorists. The slaughter of noncombatants for belonging to another faith (although the de facto crusader principle of discrimination between Christians and non-Christians was not always honored anyway) also finds no basis in writings of Augustine. Crimes against civilians was something specifically of concern to later just war theorists writing in response to the sixteenth-century Amerindian genocide. In fact, Augustine discounted the entire *jus ad bellum* Cluniac rationale of Urban II, the protection of religious pilgrims. Augustine, like the early Greek Church, considered the act of pilgrimage to be of little importance.[33] Later just war theorists took great pains to avoid the appearance that they were adding anything to Augustine's conception of just war. Even Saint Thomas Aquinas (1227–1274), the official philosopher of the Roman Catholic Church during its second millennium, admitted to only expanding on principles already found in Augustine.[34]

Just as in the case of the initiatives following international community's lack of response to the genocides in 1994 in Rwanda and earlier in Nazi occupied Europe, most major humanitarian initiatives are responses to historic humanitarian disasters. Such was the case for the later just war theorists who responded to the failure of European empires to uphold Augustinian ethics in their conquest and subsequent genocidal actions against Amerindian populations. The Debate of Valladolid in 1550 between the Dominican bishop of Chiapas, Bartolomé de Las Cases, and the Aristotelian scholar Ginés de Sepúlveda marks the watershed between early and late just war theory. Based on his claim of the natural superiority of Christian Europeans over the pagan Amerindians, Sepúlveda argued that the European conquest was just. Las Cases countered with his famous "Aristotle, farewell" response: "The natural laws and rules and rights of men are common to all nations, Christian and gentile, and whatever their sect, law, state, color and condition, without any difference."[35]

Continuing Las Cases's defense of Amerindian populations, a fellow Dominican, Francisco de Vitoria (1480–1520), and a Jesuit, Francisco Suárez (1548–1617), placed the *jus in bello* criteria of proportionality and discrimination at the center of their writings.[36] Vitoria, in his *On the Law of War*, associated the attribution of innocence to noncombatants for the first time. Even so, he does not provide them an absolute dispensation against the effects of warfare, going so far as to allow innocents to be enslaved as long as it does not go "beyond the limits which the necessities of warfare demands."[37]

The major differences between early and later just war theory is one of emphasis. Just as nothing of Augustine is left out of Vitoria, nothing in Vitoria directly contradicts Augustine. As stated by Father Hehir, "the logic of the argument from Augustine through Vitoria, Michael Walzer and Paul Ramsey has been the same."[38] This is primarily owing to the fact that each of the just war doctrine's component parts suggests the rest of the doctrine.

With rise of the Spanish School of international law that included Vitoria, Suárez, and the Dutchman Hugo Grotius, the concept of natural law was reintroduced into just war doctrine. Natural law was added to just war principles without replacing them. The major innovation of natural law theory was that it placed its emphasis of the statist conception of law above the more ethical conception of justice. Although Aquinas is principally known as the father of modern natural law theory, and for introducing the ideas of Aristotle in scholastic philosophy, he did not apply either to the concept of just war. Natural law was incorporated into just war theory by his disciple Francisco de Vitoria.[39] Aquinas divided all law into four categories: divine, or eternal, law—*lex divina;* natural law, or *jus naturae;* the law of nations, or *jus gentium;* and positive law, or *lex humana.* According to Aquinas, natural law is a rational appreciation of eternal law by human beings.[40]

Natural law was an opportune instrument for theorists responding to the failure of Christian Europeans to apply humanitarian norms in warfare especially with those who did not share their creed, as was clearly demonstrated in both the conquest of the Americas and the wars of religion between Catholic and Protestant states that culminated in the bloody Thirty Years War (1618–1648). This lack of reciprocity by Europeans in applying humanitarian norms to their enemies of alien cultures and religions finds no basis in Augustine's actual teachings on war. Rather, it was established as precedent during the Crusades and found continued expression in the conduct of the Christian conquest of the Iberian Peninsula, the Protestant English conquest of Catholic Ireland, the destruction of the indigenous populations of the Americas, and, finally, the military and civil violence of the Reformation and Counter-Reformation.[41]

In the seventeenth century, Hugo Grotius (1583–1645), a Protestant who advocated religious toleration, in his *On the Law of War and Peace* attempted to secularize just war doctrine by utilizing natural law theory. In addition to accepting the claims of Vitoria that the jurisdiction of natural law was universal, Grotius added three major innovations: the relations of states can be judged as if they were individuals; crimes by nations can be addressed in the same way as individual crimes; and, the reciprocity of malice among nations must be replaced by a reciprocity of trust.[42]

Grotius's optimistic view of the human condition contrasts with both Augustinian human realism and the political realism of Grotius's contemporary, Thomas Hobbes (1588–1679). Hobbes's infamous work, *Leviathan,* represented a counter to optimistic premises of Grotian natural law that continues to be cited by contemporary legal positivists and political realists.[43] As a result of viewing war—rather than God's or man's reason—as the true basis of natural law, a view that sees human life as "solitary, poor, nasty, brutish, and short," Hobbes preached an absolute preference for peace based an absolute deference to the will of a sovereign ruler of a nation-state. [44] According to Hobbes, human law is simply an authoritative enactment based on the "coercive power, to compel equally to the performance" of obligations by individuals to a sovereign who does not in turn answer to other sovereigns, their subjects, or any universal law(s) ascribed to a higher power.[45]

For all their differences, Grotius and Hobbes each influenced, and were influenced by, the Westphalian state-centered virtues of nonintervention in interstate affairs and general noninterference. Writing primarily for statesmen rather than for soldiers, Grotius and Hobbes took up different aspects of Augustinian just war theory: justice, in case of the former; and a realistic view of human nature, in the later. Successor theorists in the Westphalian tradition, such as Cornelius van Bynkershoek (1673–1743), Emmerich de Vattel (1714–1767), and Georg Friedrich von Martins (1756–1821), in various combinations, blended the natural law concepts of Grotius with the legal positivism and political realism of Hobbes while maintaining the statism of both.[46]

Grotius is distinct from Hobbes in that he posited a universal maxim for humanitarian norms that would be binding on states regardless of their religious or ideological leaning. It is ironic that the modern concept of natural law, originating partly as a device to deal with the failure of Europeans to act on the basis on humanitarian reciprocity in dealing with populations that they considered alien, is used contemporaneously to justify lack of action by Western powers in dealing with humanitarian conflicts, including genocides, in non-Western nations. This was exemplified in the 1990s when the Western statist emphasis on noninterference was cited most often in connection with humanitarian interventions in nations whose societal norms could be portrayed as not sharing in Western legalist traditions. Anticipating the contemporary debate on whether the norms of universal human rights are based on a culturally specific Western individualist discourse or whether they emphasize social obligations of the kind associated with many non-Western cultures, the universality of the Grotian stress on passive legalisms is certainly debatable. Given the distrust of religious sanctions as evidenced in the bloody conflicts of his time, Grotius sought a secular universal norm that would transcend the religious disputes of his time.

Grotius utilized the passive injunction of the pagan Roman Emperor Septimius Severus (146–211)—"Do not do to another what you do not wish to be done to you"—rather than the affirmative injunction of the Golden Rule found in Matthew 7:12-"Always treat others as you would like them to treat you."[47] In contrast to religiously derived affirmative obligations placed upon combatants in Augustinian just war doctrine, Grotius's categorical maxim is a passive proscription of actions that cause harm to others, a passivity that would become idiosyncratic to the Western-legalistic approach to human rights.

In 1758, the Swiss scholar Emerich de Vattel published his encyclopedic *Droit des gens* (Eng. trans., *Law of Nations*, 1760). Vattel emphasized concepts that were directly opposite those posited by Augustinian just war doctrine, namely, the concepts of neutrality and voluntary state action. Neutrality, says Vattel, is the belief that a state or institution can maintain an unprejudiced relationship to all parties to the conflict. His second concept, that of the "voluntary law of nations," left the final decision on whether to apply humanitarian norms to the discretion of states, whose sovereignty Vattel considered absolute.[48]

This Grotian natural law tradition of passive obligations reaches it apex in the "categorical imperative" of the eighteenth-century German idealist philosopher Immanuel Kant (1724–1804). "Act always in such a manner," wrote Kant, "that the immediate motive or maxim of thy will may become a universal rule in a obligatory legislation for all intelligent beings."[49] Rather than comprising a universal norm shared across time and space, the passivity of ethical imperatives in both Kant and Grotius have been characterized as unique to modern European philosophical and religious thought.[50] In contrast, just war doctrine is based on an affirmative obligation for the care and protection of others acknowledged in various forms by most of the major world religions. Additionally, specific humanitarian norms placed upon combatants as individuals, similar to those articulated by Augustine, are also found in the scriptural and classical ethical codes of almost every major world culture. While the respective weights placed on *jus ad bellum* versus *jus in bello* vary from society to society, these two basic components of early just war doctrine are not unique to Augustine, to Christianity, or to the West. However, the Western emphasis on the *jus ad bellum* is certainly owing in part to the greater interest among post-Westphalian theorists, whether natural law or positivist, in the actions of rulers and statesmen who initiate conflicts, as compared to the actions of soldiers who conduct them. By contrast, Islamic law, for instance, stresses the conduct of war and the mitigation of its "harmful consequences" rather than the just or unjust causes of wars. Additionally, many Asian and African religious and ethical codes emphasize *jus in bello* ethics in the conduct of war. [51]

In the West, war is a political action by the state. From Aristotle to Lieber, the intellectual analysis of warfare is usually related to the conception of the state held by the analyst. Georg Friedrich Hegel, the eminent statist philosopher of the nineteenth century, considered the state as a godlike manifestation of the ethical force of history.[52] Lieber, in his *Political Ethics*, returned to a view of the state as a living or organic institution, in the sense that it is composed of living human beings—a view that was shared by Augustine. For both Lieber and Augustine, the existence of a state always involves a certain level of societal consensus on moral and ideological principles, principles that influence the means by which a given state achieves it ends, including war. It is not surprising, considering their shared instrumentalist understanding of the nature of the state and their mutual antipathy to anti-Aristotelian views on ethics—especially as regards slavery—that Lieber and Augustine, although writing a millennium apart, would display a theoretical congruence on the normative principles of warfare.[53]

The perennial debate between proponents of natural law and legal positivism has not only polarized the discussion of humanitarian norms in war over the last three centuries; it underpins the current debate over the universality of human rights in general. The Westphalian emphasis on law over justice plays into the hands of the advocates of Western exceptionalism, who emphasize, in contradistinction to Eastern traditions, (1) individual rights over communitarian obligations; and (2) political and civil rights over social, cultural, and economic rights.[54] Critics of the concept of universal norms, such as the political scientist Samuel P. Huntington, have claimed that the concept of natural law, as one of the unique components of "the rule of law," is one of the "distinguishing characteristics of Western society" and that to apply it to other civilizations is a "universalist pretension." [55] Yet such an East-West dichotomy regarding human rights norms does not apply to Augustinian just war doctrine. Because it is free of both natural and positivist forms of Western legalism, and because it emphasizes obligations rather than rights, traditional just war theory is far more universal than the political legacy of Europe's Westphalian system.

One does not have to look to other cultures and times to find alternatives to Westphalian legalism that follow the basic assumptions of Augustinian just war doctrine. The Protestant theologian Reinhold Niebuhr (1892–1971) argued in favor of Augustinian realism over natural law. Associating the Aristotelian need to find a historical order that conforms to nature, a need that always is compromised by the forces of self-interest, Niebuhr maintained that the "supposed sanctities of the law" are always tainted by ideology. Although he was considered the spiritual father of cold war–era political realism, he also differentiated his realism from the vulgar form of political realism maintained by those who "see only their own interest and failing thereby to do justice to their interest where they are involved in the with the interest of others."[56] Although usually associated with the views of Catholic theologians, just war doctrine finds other non-Catholic parallels in the teachings on ethics of violence and war—as found, for example, in the teaching of such non-Catholic forums as the National Council of Churches.[57]

Just War Criteria and *General Order No. 100*

Richard R. Baxter, the author of the successor document to *General Order No. 100*, the Department of the Army's still-current Field Manual 27-10, *The Law of Armed Conflict*,[58] stated that the Lieber Code was "little more than an amplification of the ideas" that Lieber had expressed twenty-five years before.[59] In his 1838–1839 *Manual of Political Ethics*, Lieber succinctly summarized traditional just war doctrine:

> A war, to be justified, must be undertaken on just grounds—that is, to repel or avert wrongful force, or to establish a right; must be the last resort—that is, after all other means of reparation are unavailable or have miscarried; it must be necessary—that is, the evil to be addressed should be a great one; and it must be wise—that is, there must be reasonable prospect of obtaining reparation, or the averting of the evil, and the acquiescence in the evil must be greater than the evils of the contest.[60]

Even though Lieber, as a lay leader of the Anglican Church in America, would certainly have been aware of Augustine's writings, he probably did not draw directly on Augustine in either his *Manual of Political Ethics* or his preparation of *General Order No. 100*. His choices regarding the international law sources he drew upon, however, indicate the aspects of the laws of war that he accepted and those that he did not. He was most critical, for example, of Vattel; he ignored Hobbes, and he acknowledged Kant.[61] Although the term "just war" does not appear in Lieber's code, the substance of its 147 articles falls substantially within the eight traditional just war principles. Because it avoids the natural law tenets of late just war theorists and the post-Westphalian legalists, the articles of *General Order No. 100* are more in accord with the affirmative obligations and the human realism of early, or Augustinian, just war doctrine.

Just Cause

The Augustinian requirement that a war must be a response to an injustice or an aggression is not modified by the existence of the modern territorial state. While *General Order No. 100* posits that the object of war lies beyond war in the realm of the political, the political end must be just:

> Article 30: Ever since the formation and coexistence of modern nations, and ever since wars have become great national wars, war has come to be acknowledged not for its own end, but the means to attain great ends of state, or to consist in defense against wrong; and no conventional restriction of the modes adopted to injure the enemy is any longer admitted; but the law of war imposes many limitations and restrictions on principles of justice, faith, and honor.
>
> Article 68: Modern wars are not internecine wars, in which the killing of the enemy is the object. The destruction of the enemy in modern, and, indeed, modern war itself, are means to obtain that object of the belligerent which lies beyond the war.

Like Grotius, Lieber goes beyond Augustine's requirement that a just peace is war's object in claiming that peace is the normal condition of mankind and "war is the exception."[62] There are some, however, injustices that cannot be tolerated, either for *raison d'état* or in the name of peace. One such injustice, for Lieber, was slavery. Lieber must have known that his code's claim that "The law of nature and nations has never acknowledged it (slavery)" contradicted natural law theorists of the Spanish School , such as Vitoria, and the notion of natural law posited by Aristotle.[63] As a resident of antebellum South Carolina for two decades, his code's declaratory statement on the institution of slavery bypassed the contemporary debate about the character of slavery. Lieber was well acquainted with the arguments made by his contemporary intellectual rival, John C. Calhoun, in defense of the institution on the basis of Aristotelian natural law. Although—as evidenced by his earlier works and lectures—no one was better qualified than Lieber to discuss precedents, legal or otherwise, regarding slavery, *General Order No. 100* stipulated, as self-evident, the "just cause" of the Union aim to end the slave system in the South.

In Lieber's *Political Ethics* the author wrote, "the state is an institution for a distinct moral end."[64] In the context of both his life's work and his code's reference to the American Civil War, the "great ends of state" are never morally neutral.

Competent Authority

Grotius, like Hobbes, spoke of authority in absolute terms, of a sovereign power whose independent actions are not subject to any other power.[65] Lieber's writings on war, however, are dominated by a pre-Westphalian emphasis on those who execute authority rather than on the rights and prerogatives of rulers (who were likely to be the monarchs that Lieber so despised). Lieber, like Augustine, realized that soldiers often err in determining who has competent authority over them, the result being one of the major proximate cause of war in their times. Much of Augustine's views on the military profession are derived from his correspondence with Boniface, a renegade Roman general, in which the theologian counseled a return by the military man to a proper allegiance with Rome.[66] Lieber, similarly, watched as thousands of soldiers followed key American military leaders in taking up arms against the United States by granting their allegiance to an authority—the Confederacy—whose competence Lieber (and others) challenged. Tragically for Lieber, one of the soldiers who made this mistake in judgment was his own son, who died in the battle of Williamsburg in 1862. One of the major acts of the wartime U.S. Congress was to ensure that such a bloody referendum would never be repeated. During the course of the war, legislation was passed that clearly defined and prioritized the criteria that soldiers must utilize in determining proper competent authority. The oath of office that soldiers take upon entering military service—pledging allegiance to the Constitution, the president, and their appointed military leadership, in that precise order—remains in use to this day.[67]

For Augustine, soldiers were related to the civil judges of his day insofar as they acted not as individuals but as agents of a higher authority. As flawed human individuals, moreover, a judge or a soldier can at most be an imperfect instrument of justice. Although it is never a personal act, the unavoidable exercise of the coercive prerogatives of government is always contaminated by personal hypocrisy. Therefore, according to Augustine, all officials are faced with the incongruity of exercising competent, but not credible, authority.[68] Although their official status made soldiers and judges distinct from other human beings, Augustine admonished his fellow civilians that they "must not think that no one who serves as a soldier, using arms for warfare, can be acceptable to God."[69]

For both Lieber and Augustine, soldiers who killed the enemy differed from murderers not simply because their acts were official. Official acts also had to be competent; specifically, they had to integrate moral and ethical concerns regarding justice into a professional field of expertise. Lieber went further than Augustine in approving a special sanction for those held under arms for having committed acts that would be criminal or sinful if based on personal motivation; he held that soldiers—owing to the trust bestowed upon them—must adhere to even higher ethical and moral standards than civilians. In Article 4, discussing martial law, Lieber posited that it was incumbent on those who exercised martial law to recognize the "principles of justice, honor, and humanity—virtues adorning a soldier even more than other men, for the very reason that he possesses the power of his arms against the unarmed." For both Lieber and Augustine, soldiers were not passive beings blindly following someone else's orders; rather, a soldier's competence should always be the result of an active and properly understood obligation.

Lieber and Augustine, by giving military duties an affirmative character that compels action rather than inaction, make the soldier—as a tool of the state—subject to being guilty of a "double injustice" if inaction on his or her part leads to the harm of those that he or she is bound to defend. When soldiers commit crimes in the direct performance of their military duties, therefore, they are always crimes of omission rather than commission. Such crimes of omission are more grievous than crimes of commission, because such crimes of commission are additionally crimes of omission resulting from a soldier's failure to maintain the ethical basis of his or her profession.[70]

Comparative Justice

The most problematic aspect of the legalistic approach to the establishment of enforceable humanitarian norms in warfare is that of the application of guilt to collective entities. Augustinian just war doctrine does not, as some have claimed, posit that only one combatant can lay total claim to virtuous intent or conduct. [71] Virtue and guilt, as determined by imperfect human judges, are imperfectly determined. Unlike Vattel, who argued that "war cannot be just on both sides," and that opposing combatants are to "be considered as two individuals disputing on the truth of a proposition; and it is impossible that two contrary sentiments should be true at the same time"; neither Augustine nor Lieber held to such a simplistic or absolutist understanding of justice in situations involving oppositional conflict.[72]

On June 1, 498, the pagan citizens of the North African town of Calama engaged in an anti-Christian riot that led to the loss of life. Nectarius, a distinguished pagan Roman official wrote to Augustine asking him to intercede on behalf of his fellow townsmen, who, he claimed, were not responsible for the act. Augustine counseled his petitioner that he was doing his fellow citizens a disservice by not acknowledging that there are many levels in which individuals are guilty for collective acts, and that it might not be possible to "distinguish the innocent from the guilty out of the whole city, but only the less guilty from the more guilty." Augustine provided three levels of individual complicity in collective acts. Those who, out of fear, "lacked the offer to help" a victim or victims "were guilty of only a minor sin." Those who "actually committed" harmful acts were "implicated more deeply." And, finally, "those who instigated" the acts were implicated "most deeply of all."[73]

Like Augustine, Lieber did not hold that a just cause should manifest itself as a *crusade against evildoers,* or a campaign against collective entities composed of individuals who were considered equally guilty for the injustices perpetrated by the collective and, therefore, liable to uniform treatment by the opposing forces. In his code, no loyal citizen of the Confederacy was an innocent entitled to be totally spared from the consequences of the war.[74] *General Order No. 100* places all enemy citizens into two major categories: unarmed and armed. The former subdivided further into seven subdivisions, each with separate protections accorded to their life and property:

1. Private Citizens. Noncombatants serving in no official capacity are protected from being "murdered, enslaved, or carried off to distant parts." (Article 22)
2. Magistrates and Civil Officers. Commanding generals are allowed to

force oaths of temporary allegiance or to expel those who refuse. (Article 23)

3. Slaves. Those formally held in bondage are "immediately entitled to the rights and privileges of a freeman." (Article 43)

4. Noncombatants Accompanying an Army. Commanders are permitted to confine and process as prisoners of war. (Article 50)

5. Heads of State and Diplomatic Agents. Unless previously granted safe passage, they are to be treated as prisoners of war. (Article 50)

6. Spies. All espionage is punishable by death. (Article 88)

7. Guides. Their treatment varies from no punishment for those forced into service to death for those intentionally misleading a force. (Articles 94–97)

General Order No. 100 subdivides enemy combatants into nineteen distinct categories, each entailing specific treatment upon capture:

1. Prisoners of War. Soldiers taken prisoner, who have committed no otherwise unlawful acts, are not subject to "punishment for being a public enemy, nor is any revenge (to be) wrecked upon him by the intentional infliction of any suffering, or disgrace, by cruel imprisonment, want of food, by mutilations, death, or any other barbarity." (Article 56)

2. Deserters. Former soldiers of the U.S. Army, taken in the service of the Confederacy, are to be put to death. (Article 48)

3. Chaplains and Medical Staff. May be treated as prisoners of war either by a commander's determination of necessity or their own voluntary request. (Article 53)

4. Hostages. Although rarely used in modern war, they are to be treated as prisoners of war. (Article 55)

5. Criminals. Enemy soldiers who have committed crimes against their own forces or people, before being captured, can be punished by their own authorities. (Article 59)

6. Deniers of Quarter. Those have failed to give others quarter are to be denied quarter in turn. (Articles 61–62)

7. Soldiers Captured in the Uniform of Their Enemy. Like spies, such soldiers are also given no quarter. (Articles 63 and 83)

8. Outposts, sentinels, and pickets. Unless it is determined of military necessity, opportunistic firing upon their position is prohibited. (Article 69)

9. Users of Poison. Offenders are to be put to death. (Article 70)

10. Assaulters of the Injured: Offenders are to be put to death. (Article 70)

11. Escapees. While firing upon prisoners in the process of escape is permitted, the attempt is not a crime unless it is part of a general conspiracy. (Article 77)

12. Partisans. Defined as "soldiers armed and wearing the uniform of their

army" but detached from the main body of the enemy, they are to be treated as prisoners of war. (Article 81)

13. Brigands and Pirates. Soldiers committing acts of private violence are subject to death. (Article 82)
14. Irregulars not wearing uniforms. Armed civilians or insurrectionists who kill, steal, or destroy infrastructure or materials of the occupying are not entitles to be treated as prisoners of war. (Articles 84–85)
15. War Traitor. Non-enemy personal who provide information to the enemy become an enemy who may be punished by death. (Articles 89–91).
16. Messengers. If in uniform, they are to be treated as prisoners of war. (Article 99)
17. Bearers of flags of truce. They are to be cautiously admitted. If admitted under false pretenses, they are to be treated as spies. (Articles 104–109)
18. Breakers of Parole. Released prisoners of war, who have violated their voluntary pledge not to engage in future acts of warfare, can be put to death upon recapture. (Article 124)
19. Officers / noncommissioned officers. They are allowed special honors and treatment. (Articles 73 and 127)

General Order No. 100, as it applied humanitarian considerations to an enemy whose legitimacy was not recognized by the United States, was an exercise of comparative justice in its entirety. Even though the final article (Article 157) defined the "armed or unarmed resistance by citizens of the United States against the lawful movements of their troops" as treason, the document stated that all enemy citizens—whether combatants or noncombatants—were entitled to certain norms of humanitarian treatment. This, despite their being expected to bear a higher burden in the war than "manifestly loyal citizens." (Article 156).

As with Augustinian just war doctrine, the natural law association of non-combatancy with legal innocence is absent from *General Order No. 100*. Additionally, the sloppy attribution of collective guilt, defined as holding individuals responsible for the collective actions of organizations or institutions by mere membership without any evidence of an individual act, is also absent.

Right Intention

While the justification for war is aggression or an unjust peace, for Augustine the objective of war is a just peace. "Peace ought to be what you want, war only what necessity demands."[75] The hackneyed phrase "the end justifies the means" has never been an accurate description of just war doctrine. Rather, just ends justify proportional means. Just war doctrine predates the legalist debate between naturalism and positivism; it also predates the philosophical debate between ethical normativism and ethical consequentialism. Normative, or deontological ethics, is the theory that the efficacy of moral action stands in reference to formal rules or norms of conduct. Consequentialist, or teleological, ethical theories stress that it is consequences rather than intentions that determine the correctness of any given action. Both Augustine and Lieber were seminal ethical theorists who argued that actions are only moral when both intention and result are integrated.[76]

Echoing Augustine, Lieber argued, "wars are not internecine wars, in which the destruction of the enemy is the object"; rather, war is a "means to obtain that object of the belligerent which lies beyond the war" (Article 68). A just war entered into by competent authority for a just cause can still be fought with unjust intent by either the leadership or the actual participants of a conflict. Soldiers cannot see into the hearts of their leaders. Sometimes, that may be fortunate. However, soldiers can never categorically abandon their consciences to higher authority. Except for criminal behavior, a soldiers acts on his (or her) intentions when he is "armed by a sovereign government and takes a soldier's oath of fidelity, he (then) is a belligerent, his killing, wounding, or other warlike acts are not individual crimes or offenses" (Article 57). Although the decision for the soldier to enlist is often coerced, soldiers are partially responsible for justice or injustice of the cause for which they fight at the time that they first don their uniforms. Just as the electorate is accountable for the future actions of politicians they support when they dropped their ballots, soldiers are responsible, as far as their understanding and knowledge allows, for historical justice or injustice as executed by the military institution they are joining. Only when soldiers (or the electorate) obtain new information indicating criminality on the part of those whose authority they have previously validated, can they claim to be faced with a new ethical decision.[77] Consequently, soldiers must proceed not with blind faith, but with a common sense and an informed faith regarding the actions of their superiors in the context of the stated political and ethical ends of a war. Unfortunately, history is replete with examples of wars lost because national and military leaders who have betrayed this trust have employed military means incongruent with the political and moral ends sought.

Last Resort

Even when necessity demands it, war is a tragedy to be avoided at all costs, save the realization of justice. Augustine still demanded that no matter how just the cause, those in positions of authority must begin by "bewailing the necessity he is under of waging wars, even just wars."[78] Augustine naturally argued that it is better to achieve justice without recourse to war. "However, greater glory is still merited by not killing men with swords, but war with words, and acquiring or achieving peace not through war but through peace itself."[79] Augustine reflected the position found in Sun Tzu's Chinese classic, written down nine hundred years before: "To subdue the enemy without fighting is the acme of skill."[80] If a resort to war becomes justified, however, the war must be successful. Just as all nations do not exist in a state of Westphalian equality, neither are all wars equal. If the preferred level of war is no war at all, it follows that larger wars require greater justification than more limited wars.

It is clear that the Confederacy, with less material and human resources, would have benefited if both sides had resorted to a more "limited" war. The Civil War was fought under the conflicting legacy of two previous wars: the American War of Independence and the wars of the French Revolution. At the outbreak of the Civil War, the Confederacy styled itself as fighting the second phase of the American War of Independence; the United States initially styled itself as fighting a limited statist, post-Westphalian war for the preservation of the Union. Unlike the American Revolution, the French Revolution introduced warfare that was revolutionary not only in its ends but in its level of warfare. *General Order No. 100* was a testament to the new level of war to which the United States government in 1863 was going to resort, that is, a revolutionary level of war. For that reason, Lieber's code was categorically rejected by the Confederacy. In limited wars, such as in the campaigns of Frederick the Great of Prussia, the genius of a general utilizing maneuver could win out over an enemy possessing greater resources, or, in the case of wars for independence, belligerent forces could press the war past the threshold of cost that an enemy was willing to bear. Unfortunately for the South, no amount of battlefield genius, or even the greater human losses suffered by the other side, would overcome the political and moral determination of the side having greater material and human resources to resort to a less restricted war.[81]

In his June 24, 1863, letter to Washington rejecting *General Order No. 100*, Confederate secretary of war James Seddon claimed that Lieber's Code was an opportunistic justification by the United States for its resorting to a level of war that he found unacceptable. Seddon could not have failed to appreciate the timing of the release of *General Order No. 100* (starting in May 1863), just as Lincoln was issuing a plan for the southern reconstruction based on the end of slavery and as Gen. Ulysses S. Grant was deploying his forces for his victory at Vicksburg (May 19-July 4), leading to the ascendancy of a commanding general who was willing to expend a revolutionary level of casualties to achieve a revolutionary end. Simultaneously, Gen. Robert E. Lee was engaged in his final attempt to win the war by maneuver, resulting in his defeat at Gettysburg (July 1-4) and the demise of the Confederate effort to win a limited war of maneuver in a conflict that was rapidly becoming a revolutionary war of attrition.[82]

Probability of Success

The central concept of *General Order No. 100* is the doctrine of affirmative military responsibility based upon, rather than in contradiction with, military necessity. Like Lieber, Augustine understood that a just war could not bring about justice in defeat and that only "when victory goes to the side that had a juster cause (is it) surely a matter of human rejoicing, and the peace is one to be welcomed."[83] Augustine also wrote, "Therefore it ought to be necessity, and not your will, that destroys the enemy who is fighting you."[84] Nothing is more obstructive to the establishment of a just peace than indecisive or ineffective military action. The most unjust outcome in war—of which there are numerous contemporary examples—is one in which neither combatant attains, or is allowed to attain, success.

The doctrine of military necessity is the major conceptual link between Lieber's code and Augustinian just war doctrine. For Lieber, military necessity consisted of two major components. First, "no conventional restriction of the modes adopted to injure the enemy is any longer admitted," he wrote. Yet, second, "the law of war imposes many limitations and restrictions on principles of justice, faith, and honor" (Article 30). Articles 14–16 are the most cited articles of the code and consist of Lieber's attempt to clarify these two seemingly contradictory themes:

Military necessity, as understood by modern civilized nations, consists in the necessity of those measures which are indispensable for securing the ends of war, and which are lawful according to the modern law and usages of war. (Article 14)

Military necessity admits of all destruction of life or limb of armed enemies, and of other persons whose destruction is incidentally unavoidable in the armed contests of the war; it allows of the capturing of every armed enemy, and every enemy of importance to the hostile government, or of particular danger to the captor; it allows of all destruction of property, and obstruction of the ways and channels of traffic, travel, or communication, and of all withholding of sustenance or means of life from the enemy; of the appropriation of whatever an enemy's country affords necessary for the subsistence and safety of the army, and of such deception as does not involve the breaking of good faith either positively pledged, regarding agreements entered into during the war, or supposed by the modern law of war to exist. Men who take up arms against one another in public war do not cease on this account to be moral beings, responsible to one another and to God. (Article 15)

Military necessity does not admit of cruelty—that is, the infliction of suffering for the sake of suffering or for revenge, nor of maiming or wounding except in fight, nor for torture to extort confessions. It does not admit of the use of poison in any way, nor wanton devastation of a district. It admits of deception, but disclaims acts of perfidy; and in general, military necessity does not include any act of hostility which makes the return to peace unnecessarily difficult. (Article 16).

Proportionality

Even success in a just war does not result in nirvana, but only a more just peace. The justness of the peace sought must compensate for the suffering created by the decision to resort to warfare. Augustine wrote that faith must be kept not only with the "friend, for whose sake one is fighting," but "even with an enemy against whom one is waging war."[85] That faith is violated when the means to attain an end are not commensurate with the end that is sought. Proportionality is impossible in the absence of a recognition of reciprocity in the value of life and the dignity of the human populations (on each side) affected by the conflict. Proportionality is based on an understanding that the humanity of the enemy is equal to the humanity of one's own side or kind.

Advances in technology always challenge proportionality. The longevity of *General Order No. 100* as official doctrine was likely the result of Lieber's avoidance of issues related to technology.[86] For Lieber,

what is proportional is simply what is necessary. "Unnecessary or revengeful destruction of life is not lawful" (Article 68). During the cold
war, discussions as to whether the use of nuclear weapons could ever be
considered proportional dominated discussions among modern just war
theorists.[87] Authoritative decisions regarding proportionality and the
utilization of new technologies, at least in nominally democratic states,
are made by civilians. No matter how much weight civilian leaders give
to the opinion of military advisors, the decision of the Allies to fire-
bomb cities and resort to nuclear warfare during World War II was legally and constitutionally the responsibility of civilians.

Discrimination

Out of all the criteria associated with just war doctrine, the function
that is most particularly the soldier's is that of discriminating between
the combatant and the noncombatant. The term "noncombatant" refers
not only to civilians but also to disarmed combatants and other cap-
tives. Writing to a soldier, Augustine wrote, "And just as you use force
against the rebel or opponent, so you ought to use mercy towards the
defeated or the captive."[88] However, just as there is nothing in Augustine or Lieber to attribute innocence to noncombatants and guilt to combatants, so there is also no categorical prohibition against actions
involving "unintentional" noncombatant casualties. As in the case of
military necessity, discrimination—for Lieber—consists of two distinct
components.

> The citizen or native of a hostile country is thus an enemy, as one of the
> constituents of the hostile state or nation, and as such is subjected to the
> hardships of the war. (Article 21).

> Nevertheless, as civilization has advanced during the last centuries, so
> has likewise steadily advanced, especially in war on land, the distinction
> between the private individual belonging to a hostile country and the
> hostile country itself, with its men in arms. The principle has been more
> and more acknowledged that the unarmed citizen is to be spared in per-
> son, property, and honor as much as the exigencies of war will admit.
> (Article 22)

For Lieber, the combatant/noncombatant distinction is a relative one
based on the degree of participation by an individual in a war effort. Although the determination of relativity is accomplished by referring to
other traditional just war criteria—specifically comparative justice and
proportionality—the intentional, nonincidental murder of a noncom-

batant is always a crime. The one exception to this rule for Lieber was a limited form of retaliation to be used against a "reckless enemy" who leaves to "his opponent no other means of securing himself against the repetition of barbarous outrage." (Article 27)

> Retaliation will, therefore, never be resorted to as a measure of mere revenge, but only as a means of protective retribution, and cautiously and unavoidably; that is to say, retaliation shall on5ly be resorted to after careful inquiry into the real occurrence, and the character of the misdeed that may demand retribution. Unjust or inconsiderate retaliation removes the belligerents further and further from the mitigating rules of regular war, and by rapid steps leads them nearer to the internecine war of savages. (Article 28)

The Legacy of *General Order No. 100*

The most controversial aspects of Lieber's code include the author's liberal use of the death penalty for offenses proscribed by the code and his failure to categorically reject the right of retaliation and to deny quarter in cases where quarter is not reciprocated.[89] While the right to quarter was unequivocally standardized in the Hague Conventions, retaliation was not completely outlawed from the law and usages of war until the Geneva Conventions of 1949. Until that time, retaliation was allowed in order to ensure that humanitarian norms would be followed by each side of a conflict on the basis of reciprocity. Despite Lieber's failure to categorically prohibit retaliation, as he did in the use of torture, the United States Army carried out no retaliatory executions of Confederate noncombatants during the war.

While modern human rights activists may take pause at Lieber's tentative endorsement of reprisal, his categorical prohibition of the use of torture (Article 16) is far in advance of some prominent contemporary civil rights activists and legal scholars, as well as the behavior tolerated by the contemporary international community.[90]

Only a year after Lieber's code was promulgated, the Swiss humanitarian Jean-Henri Dunant drew upon the work of his fellow countryman, Emmeric de Vattel, to found a code based upon the concepts of neutrality and voluntary state action. *The Geneva Convention of 1964 for the Amelioration of the Conditions of the Wounded and Sick in the Armies in the Field*, based on a draft by Dunant, provided for the protection of military hospitals and offered a protocol for the medical treatment of wounded soldiers based on a premise of reciprocity

between opposing armies.[91] Just as Lieber's code is accepted as foundational in the development of the modern "laws of war," or "laws of
armed conflict,' so was Dunant's work and his establishment of the
International Committee of the Red Cross in 1863 pivotal to development of the modern conception known as international humanitarian
law (IHL). The contemporary use of these terms is more reflective of
the institutional affiliation—military in the case of the "laws of war"
and nongovernment in that of IHL—than one indicating a distinct area
of expertise. However, it is possible to discern conceptual distinctions
in the development of what would eventually become shared areas of
specialization.

Unlike Lieber, who wrote for soldiers, Dunant was concerned with
organizing civilians to work cooperatively with military forces to mitigate unnecessary suffering. As a witness to the Battle of Solferino involving French and Austrian forces on June 24, 1859, Dunant noted that
neither side benefited from the suffering of wounded soldiers who were
left unattended to die on the field. If a neutral entity could provide relief
under such circumstances, why would either side not voluntarily allow
the provision of such neutral humanitarian aid? Upon this logic of neutrality and voluntarism, he established the International Committee of
the Red Cross. The ICRC's cherished ideal of neutrality has lost much
of its luster following the Rwandan genocide of 1994, in which the international community voluntarily chose to emphasize neutrality over
humanitarianism as 800,000 noncombatants were slaughtered in plain
view.[92]

Passive obligations easily become supplemental or secondary to obligations considered primary or affirmative. In other words, passive obligations lead to passive execution. Whether one looks at the international
response to the 1994 Rwandan genocide or to the infamous—but proce-
durally correct—ICRC visit to the model Theresienstadt concentration
camp during the Holocaust, the twentieth century provides ample material for those who question the effectiveness of passive virtues of voluntarism and neutrality in establishing humanitarian norms.[93] Dunant,
at least, unlike the leadership cadre of such modern nongovernmental
human rights organizations as Amnesty International and Human
Rights Watch, did not look upon the profession of the military as an ad-
versary incapable of humanitarian concerns. Both Lieber and Dunant
appealed to soldiers' sense of military honor. For Lieber, however, humanitarian norms could not be associated with passive obligations that

busy military commanders could consider merely supplemental or secondary to other objectives.

Just as it is clear that contemporary commentators like Howard Zinn are outside of Augustinian just war tradition when they attribute *absolute* noncombatant immunity to traditional just war teaching, so too it would not be fair to hold Dunant responsible for the absurdities that have been associated with his conceptual framework in the late twentieth century by those claiming to be his heirs.[94] He would have likely found the modern notion that an armed force can claim neutrality even while holding ground on foreign territory as incomprehensible. Despite their disparate approaches to military affairs, both Lieber and Dunant recognized the benefit of engagement with the military profession in the effort to mitigate humanitarian suffering in war along with the efficacy of appealing to soldiers' sense of honor. The antimilitary essentialist bias found among the leadership of such modern nongovernmental organizations (NGOs) as Amnesty International and Human Rights Watch finds its historical base in the Vietnam War-era antiwar movement rather than in the influence of Dunant and his ICRC.

The difference in content and emphasis for Lieber and Dunant underlie contrasting, although not necessarily antagonistic, approaches to the end of removing unnecessary suffering in war. The 1863 *General Order No. 100* and the 1864 First Geneva Convention serve as foundational texts for the two major schools of modern international humanitarian law or the law of armed conflict, namely, the Law of the Hague and the Law of Geneva. As the inspiration for The Hague Convention of 1899 and 1907, *General Order No. 100* provides a historical foundation for the affirmative limits placed on conduct of war itself associated with the Law of The Hague. Conversely, Dunant's convention is the foundation for the more passive and voluntary protections for specific classes of individuals such as the protections afforded wounded soldiers, prisoners of war, and medical personnel traditionally associated with the Law of Geneva.[95]

The Andersonville Trial

The obligatory discrimination between combatants and noncombatants is the one responsibility that a combatant cannot transfer to a noncombatant. Rather than harming those they are bound by definition to inflict harm upon, soldiers commit war crimes by failing to render protection to those they are legally required to protect. While the murder of a noncombatant may be a very active and voluntary act, it is—in terms of a soldier's affirmative obligations—an act of omission rather than an act of commission. A soldier has not only an affirmative responsibility not to violate this most soldierly of all the just war criteria, he has an affirmative obligation to prevent other soldiers from violating it as well. *General Order No. 100* in addressing cases of "wonton violence" against noncombatants—which includes robbery, pillage, sacking, rape, wounding, maiming, and murder—posits that "A soldier, officer or private, in the act of committing such violence, and disobeying a superior ordering him to abstain from it, may be lawfully killed on the spot by such superior" (Article 44). This requirement to enforce the just war principle of discrimination is nothing less than the historical foundation of the doctrine of command responsibility.

> Whoever intentionally inflicts additional wounds upon an enemy already wholly disabled, or kills such an enemy, *or who orders or encourages soldiers to do so* [italics mine], shall suffer death, if duly convicted, whether he belongs to the Army of the United States, or is an enemy captured after having committed his misdeed. (Article 71)

Telford Taylor argued that *General Order No. 100* was problematic in that it had "little to say about enforcement of the laws of war, or about the bounds of 'superior orders' and 'command responsibility.' "[96] Whether or not one accepts these principles as inherent or implied in *General Order No. 100*, they certainly were central in the immediate postwar court-martial of Major Henry Wirz, the former Confederate commandant of the prisoner-of-war camp at Andersonville, Georgia, for conspiracy to "injure the health and destroy the lives of soldiers in the military service of the United States."[97]

During the course of the American Civil War, Henry Wirz was the only soldier tried as a war criminal for failing to adhere to the humanitarian standards contained in *General Order No. 100*. The simple answer of "victor's justice" does not sufficiently address the complexity of the decision to try Wirz and not others. Union occupation policies and scorched-earth tactics against Southern property and infrastructure have often and inaccurately been compared to modern war crimes. While such practices were novel at the time and condemned by the Confederacy, they were authorized by *General Order No. 100* and pale in comparison to permissible actions against enemy infrastructure found in modern warfare. Despite the ludicrous claims of some apologists of the "lost cause," there were no My Lai's perpetrated on the population of the Confederacy during Sherman's March or anywhere else.[98] Even the American historian Charles Royster's recent brutal depiction of Sherman stresses that, "The actions of Sherman's men bore little resemblance to the killing of civilians in twentieth-century war. Few if any writers have contended that Sherman made those mass killings possible or necessary, that twentieth-century war would have taken a different course without Sherman's example."[99]

While the lack of war crimes prosecutions against United States soldiers can be explained in terms of either a lack of evidence of criminal activity or an unwillingness of a sovereign power to hold its own forces accountable for violations of the laws of war, the question why the decision was made to try Wirz for war crimes and not other senior Confederate leaders is more difficult to answer. On May 30, 1863, the Confederate Congress issued a policy allowing the execution of U.S. Army officers commanding black units. Subsequently, on August 12, 1863, War Secretary Seddon sent a letter to Lt. Gen. Kirby Smith (CSA) initiating the Trans-Mississippi command policy to kill all blacks captured in uniform. Actual executions of African-American U.S. soldiers by Confederate forces occurred on June 7, 1863, at the Battle of Milliken's Bend (Louisiana), under Gen. Richard Tylor (CSA); on April 12, 1864, at the Fort Pillow Massacre (Tennessee), under Gen. Nathan Bedford Forrest (CSA); on April 18, 1864, at the Poison Springs Massacre (Arkansas), under Gen. Samuel Bell Maxey (CSA); on April 17–20, 1864, during the Confederate recapture of Plymouth, N.C., under Gen. R. F. Hoke (CSA); on June 25, 1864, at the Battle of the Crater (Petersburg, Va.), under General William Mahone (CSA); and on October 2, 1864, at the Battle of Saltville, Va., under Gen. Felix Huston Robertson (CSA).

When the United States Army discovered that its own soldiers, those of African decent, were being systemically murdered or enslaved upon capture, it chose not to retaliate in kind. Rather, it prudently chose the option of discontinuing the practice of prisoner exchange that had served the interests of the manpower—and labor-starved Confederacy. It could have implemented its privilege of retaliation under Article 28 of *General Order No. 100* but did not.

This breakdown of the prisoner exchange led to the development of one of the least chivalrous realities of the Civil War: the horrendous prison conditions that took the lives of 60,194 prisoners of war, 30,218 in Confederate prison camps and 29,976 in camps run by U.S. military authorities.[100] The claim of victor's justice in the case of Wirz's conviction and subsequent execution was posited by none other than former Confederate president Jefferson Davis—originally named as a co-conspirator with Wirz in the draft indictment but later dropped from it—who in a series on articles in 1890 claimed that the United States Government was exclusively responsible for the conditions at Andersonville owing to its failure to continue the prisoner exchanges, and moreover that conditions in Confederate camps were no more inhuman than those in the North.[101] The historian James McPherson, in his seminal *Battle Cry of Freedom*, dismisses the oft-made claim of equivalency between northern and southern prisons (a claim made after the war in defense of Wirz and the South) by pointing to the fact that all northern prisons had at least provided shelter from the elements and that the twenty-nine percent mortality rate (13,000 out of 45,000) at Andersonville dwarfed the mortality rates for northern prison camps.[102]

While Wirz's defense attempted to dispute the secondary charge of murder, evidence that Andersonville was a de facto death camp was presented by fellow Confederate officers and even by Wirz's own defense witness, Father (later Bishop) Peter Whelen.[103] Wirz addressed the primary charge of conspiracy "to impair and injure and to destroy the lives" of U.S. Army prisoners by making recourse to the defense of superior orders (the first such defense in the modern era), claiming that as a "subaltern officer [he] merely obeyed the legal orders of [his] superiors in the discharge of [his] duties" and that he could not "be held responsible for the motives that dictated such orders."[104] Wirz's defense mirrored sentiments he expressed in a letter written upon his arrest at Andersonville on May 7, 1865, in which he stated that he was "only the medium, or may I better say, the tool, in the hands of my superiors."[105]

In response, Col. N. P. Chipman, Wirz's prosecutor, argued a theory of command responsibility that anticipated by eighty years the position found in the 1945 London Charter for the establishment of the International Military Tribunal at Nuremberg:[106]

> A superior officer cannot order a subordinate to do an illegal act, and if a subordinate obey such an order and disastrous consequences result, the superior and the subordinate must answer for it. General Winder (Wirz's direct superior) could no more command the prisoner to violate the laws of war than could the prisoner do so without orders. The conclusion is plain, that where such orders exist both are guilty.[107]

Forty-six years later, Chipman admitted that he was directly ordered by the War Department to remove the names of President Jefferson Davis, Secretary James A. Seddon, and other high Confederate officials as co-conspirators on the indictment.[108] Besides the obvious political expediency of this order, the case against Wirz's superiors was complicated by the death of his immediate superior, Gen. John H. Winder.[109]

Almost all the major issues associated with the American War Crime Program of the Nuremberg era surfaced during the Andersonville trial, including claims of victor's justice and ex post facto justice.[110] The dual concepts of command responsibility and superior orders were central in the prosecution and defense of Maj. Wirz. Just as in the case of subsequent prosecutions that held forth a strict level of command accountability for war crimes, the Andersonville trial continues to be questioned by some in terms of "law."[111] It is not the purpose of the present work to present a legal treatise in defense of a stricter level of command responsibility in the case of war crimes, as implied in traditional just war doctrine, in *General Order No 100*, and explicitly posited by the prosecution during the Andersonville trial. Regardless of the validity of the legalistic criticisms of the Andersonville trial, *the doctrinal significance of such cases for the American military profession is not diminished.* Seven out of eight of the military panel that convicted and sentenced Wirz to be hanged were general officers. The secretary of war and the president as commander-in-chief upheld both the conviction and the sentence. The report of the trial was officially published and distributed by the U.S. government. Whether are not the definition of command responsibility utilized during the trial was based upon a proceeding comprised of "good law," it was and is doctrine.

The principle that there is an affirmative official duty to use force or coercion to assist others, as predicated on and conditioned by the principle of necessity, is found formally in the foundational document of the modern laws of war, U.S. Army *General Order 100*. Dr. Francis Lieber utilized the principle of necessity to reintroduce the basic principals of Augustinian just war doctrine into *General Order 100*. The code's affirmative obligations to minimize human suffering was enforced by the U.S. Army military tribunal that convicted and sentenced to death Henry Wirz, the commandant of Andersonville Prison, for his failure in addressing the inhuman conditions of Union prisoners during the Civil War.

General Order No. 100 was also a pivotal milestone in the development of formal military doctrine in the American military profession. As a representation of a major change in national strategy affecting the conduct of Union forces, it provides the first example of a national operational capstone doctrine. As the initial authoritative basis for a series of doctrinal publications on the laws of war that was binding on all branches of the service, it was also the first major historical example of keystone doctrine.

As doctrine, it remains outside of the major traditions arising out of post-Westphalian legalism, that is, political realism, legal positivism, and the neutral voluntarism associated with 1864 Geneva Convention along with the humanitarian law tradition of Dunant and his ICRC. Finally, it was the product of those who possessed direct experience of the reality of armed conflict; it consisted of an executive order by the commander in chief of the armed forces to his commanding officers in the field; and it was intended to be utilized primarily by operational military commanders rather than by lawyers.

CHAPTER TWO

The Doctrinal Development of the American Military Profession

I see many soldiers: would that I saw many warriors! "Uniform" one calls what they
wear: would that what it conceals were not uniform!

FRIEDRICH NIETZSCHE

THE FUTURE AUTHOR of a book that would serve as scripture for the
conservative political realists of late twentieth-century American military and diplomatic officialdom, Carl von Clausewitz, was serving as a
staff officer in the rear guard of the Prussian forces seeking to cut off
the French forces trying to reinforce Napoleon at Waterloo. A few miles
away, the future author of *General Order No. 100*, Francis Lieber, a
Prussian enlisted soldier, lay wounded and near death. Many of the
philosophic inclinations of Clausewitz were the reverse of Lieber's. In
fact, the two men's contrasting views of the nature of war would mark a
key point of divergence between informal and formal norms in the
American military profession. It is ironic that the two key individuals
associated with such disparate martial legacies at one point shared the
same uniform and participated in the same campaign.

Clausewitz is only known to history because the French Revolutionary army followed the common customs and usages of war at the time
in granting him quarter and providing him medical care after he fell
wounded in an earlier battle in 1806.[1] Following his recovery and parole, Clausewitz joined Field Marshals August Wilhelm Gneisenau and
Gelhard Johann von Scharnhorst in modernizing and reforming the defeated and antiquated Prussian army. Being the most politically conservative and antirevolutionary of the Prussian military reformers,
Clausewitz discarded his uniform and donned a Russian one in 1812
rather than fight for Napoleon, not returning to Prussian service until
his sovereign had discovered the error of his ways by turning on the
French Emperor after his defeat in Russia. After his retirement, Clause-

witz put down his military insights and observations in a book that
would end up being one of the most selectively read texts in history.
The significance of its belated adoption by conservative American military theorists can only be compared to the reception in the English-
speaking world of the King James Bible in the sixteenth century.

In 1832, Clausewitz died in the midst of a major revision of his seminal *On War*, completing only its first chapter.[2] Although the author died
in relative obscurity, the sponsorship of Clausewitz's ideas by Field
Marshals Helmuth von Moltke and Colmar von der Goltz in the late
nineteenth century, as they undertook to prepare the new nation of
Germany for total war, turned Clausewitz into a military icon. Clausewitz's influence in Europe rose steadily until this ideal of total war was
experienced first-hand by Europeans during the First World War.[3]

Aside from the many questionable historical processes for which he
has been either blamed or credited, it is fairly incontrovertible that
Clausewitz understood the nature of war as intrinsically violent, political, unpredictable, and resistant to positivistic scientific systematiza-
tion. For someone with no formal university training, the philosophical
influences on Clausewitz were considerable. His posited dichotomy between absolute war and actual war places him in the idealist tradition
of Immanuel Kant, and his reification of the nation-state reflects the
influence of Georg Friedrich Hegel.[4] Insofar as he considered some societies more naturally virtuous than others, Clausewitz was completely
Aristotelian in his views on ethical or humanitarian conduct in warfare. For Clausewitz, normative patterns of humanitarian conduct in
war were societal rather than professional. In *On War*, Clausewitz
wrote that "if wars between civilized nations are far less cruel and destructive than wars between savages, the reason lies in the social conditions of the states themselves and in their relationship to one another";
and that "to introduce the principle of moderation into the theory of
war itself would always lead to logical absurdity."[5] Unlike Lieber and
Augustine, Clausewitz separates justice and morality from warfare. Like
Thomas Hobbes, and Niccolò Machiavelli before him, his writings are
addressed to those working on behalf of a self-interested nation-state in
a zero-sum competition, where adjustments in the balance of power at
the expense of other nation-states occur with no other justification than
that of *raison d'état*.[6]

Clausewitz contra Lieber

Clausewitz, however, who was not translated into English until 1873, did not became a formal influence over American military thinking until the advent of the cold war, and specifically the so-called Clausewitzian renaissance after the American military defeat in Vietnam. It is historically problematic, therefore, to apply this "neo-Clausewitzian" *weltanschauung*, identified with so many contemporary military analysts and political pundits, to the development of American military professionalism in the late nineteenth century. Theorists who belong to this neo-Clausewitzian consensus include Samuel P. Huntington, Henry A. Kissinger, and Harry G. Summers Jr.[7] Since Clausewitz was one of the major reformers of the Prussian military, a short examination of his actual writings is warranted in connection with the general influence that Prussian military reform exerted on the development of American military doctrine.[8]

Unlike Lieber, Clausewitz wrote a code for statesmen or heads of states, not only for soldiers, using his direct experience of war to integrate his personal life experiences with selected historical references. Also unlike Lieber, Clausewitz and his Napoleonic contemporaries were fixated on conventional warfare between large regular military formations. On the other hand, the genesis of Lieber's code, like most doctrinal developments, was an effort to address contemporary doctrinal deficiencies. Lieber was specifically tasked with addressing those aspects of war—such as constabulary functions and the handling of irregular forces—that historically have constituted the U.S. Army's most prevalent activity, even while such activities are traditionally minimized or avoided by American military professionals.

The strongest similarity between Lieber's and Clausewitz's view on war is the *supremacy of political over purely military ends.* In his most famous dictum, Clausewitz wrote that "war is not merely an act of policy, but a true political instrument, a continuation of political intercourse, carried on by other means."[9]

In *General Order No. 100,* Lieber appears to have paraphrased Clausewitz: "war has come to be acknowledged not to be its own end, but the means to obtain the great ends of state."[10] Recognition of this congruity between Lieber and Clausewitz does not, however, extend to the self-proclaimed American heirs of Clausewitz. In fact, the particular form of neo-Clausewitzianism that eventually took hold in America ended up turning Clausewitz on his head, by advocating a de facto political deference to military ends above policy goals. The American version of Clausewitz contradicts not only Clausewitz but also the tradition of both *General Order No. 100* and the political allegiance mandated in the soldiers' and officers' commissioning oaths as derived form the Civil War. This reversal of the Prussian's position is, for the purposes of this study, one of the primary points of departure between true, classical Clausewitzianism and neo-Clausewitzianism.

Constitutional Allegiance and the U.S. Military Profession

Between the Civil War and World War II, the process of the development of military doctrine was formalized with the introduction of a standard publication system. The period was characterized by contested visions of military professionalism. Those favoring a domestic, democratic conception of military professionalism gradually supplanted those that drew on a functionally aristocratic model of an officer corps associated with Prussia and Germany.

Most discussions of the development of the military profession have centered on a presumed "civil-military gap" in values, attitudes, and worldviews that have developed between the military and civil society, and particularly on the political and societal consequences resulting from such a gap. The point of departure for any new military doctrine is the precedent that it replaces or modifies. The subject of the present analysis is the changes and consistencies in the development of American military doctrine in the context of preexisting doctrine, specifically the evolution of formal doctrine from the promulgation of *General Order No. 100* during the American Civil War to the present.

The development of doctrine provides a historical record of the intellectual foundation of the military profession in the United States. Although certainly affected by external forces and political expediency, military doctrine is an internal system of normative values.

The doctrinal significance of *General Order No. 100* and the just war precepts contained within it cannot be separated from the constitutional conflict that was contemporaneous with its publication. The American Civil War was a referendum for and by the American military profession on the meaning of allegiance. From 1790 to 1861, the oaths that officers took upon accepting military commissions did not consistently mention the Constitution. This changed as the result of the American Civil War, ending with a decision in favor of those holding primary loyalty to the federal government and its Constitution as opposed to those holding primary loyalty to state governments and their constitutions. This was subsequently formalized by legislation. In 1862, the Radical Republicans controlling the U.S. Congress mandated that an officer's political allegiance to the Constitution was to be unqualified and specified by law. From 1862 onward, the words of the presidential oath of office as found in the U.S. Constitution, to "support and defend the Constitution of the United States," was incorporated into all official oaths of office, including both the enlisted and commissioning oath still used to this day:[11]

> Officer's Commissioning: I, _____, do solemnly swear (or affirm) that I will support and defend the Constitution of the United States against all enemies, foreign and domestic; that I will bear true faith and allegiance to the same; that I take this obligation freely, without any mental reservation or purpose of evasion; and that I will and faithfully discharge the duties of the office on which I am about to enter. So help me God.[12]

> Enlisted: I, _____, do solemnly swear (or affirm) that I will support and defend the Constitution of the United States against all enemies, foreign and domestic; that I will bear true faith and allegiance to the same; and that I will obey the orders of the President of the United States and the orders of the officers appointed over me, according to regulations and the Uniform Code of Military Justice. So help me God.[13]

Evocative of the fifth-century just war maxims of Saint Augustine exhorting Roman soldiers to examine the moral foundation of their service and conduct, these oaths forced individuals entering military service to personally acknowledge the basis of the authority under which they entered into military service and the source of the legitimacy of their actions while in military service. As the oath requires allegiance to a particular constitution, the political and ideological premises of this constitution are distinct from other contemporary armies who pledged their allegiance to other arrangements of political authority. The formal basis of military allegiance in the United States, in contrast to the major European powers of the day, was also institutional rather merely national in an organic sense. However, the end of the Civil War did not result in a consensus regarding military professionalism and the nature of its historical development. Different interpretations and views on the institutional lessons of the Civil War and the efficacy of using foreign models of military professionalism, specifically that of Prussia, as a model for institutional reform divided those who would have the most influence over the establishment of future military doctrine in America.

The centrality of an individual affirmation of duty in the oaths of political allegiance resonates well with both Francis Lieber's *General Order No. 100* and the traditional just war doctrines contained within it. This, however, conflicted with the general assumptions associated with that other notable Prussian, Carl von Clausewitz. American scholars and members of the American military profession have utilized Clausewitz and the Prussian military tradition to ground theories of military professionalism that contrast strikingly with the democratic and just war doctrine put forward by Lieber.

Emory Upton's Love Affair with Prussia

Although the popularity of Clausewitz among American military professionals is understandable, the thinker's historical reach is limited. Clausewitz did not have a direct individual impact on the development of the American profession during its most important period of development, that lying between the Civil War and World War II. Basing the impetus of military professionalism in America on Clausewitz, as distinct from the Prussian military reformers in general, is just bad history. It was not through Clausewitz but rather through the French writer Antoine Henri, Baron de Jomini, that Napoleonic strategy was conveyed to America. The reason for this was that Jomini's writings were clearer and more understandable than Clausewitz's classic.[14] Clausewitz's influence on the American military between the Civil War and the Second World War must be understood in conjunction with the nineteenth-century Prussian military in general; Clausewitz can at most be considered an usually uncited source for a view of military professionalism that has came to play an informal role in the development of American military professionalism until the time that the United States was defeated in Vietnam.

Such a view is at odds with the premier theoretical work on American military professionalism, Samuel P. Huntington's *The Soldier and the State*. Huntington argues that modern military professionalism was spawned in post-Napoleonic War Prussia and was epitomized by the theories of Clausewitz. Prior to this, according to Huntington,

America could claim to possess only a proto-military professionalism, and this was to be found mainly in the slave-holding South and embodied in the policies of Secretary of War John C. Calhoun. The greatest weakness of Huntington's historical thesis is the absence of documentation concerning how the culture of professionalism migrated from Prussia to the United States.[15]

As Clausewitz could not be directly credited for the transplantation of military professionalism from Prussia to the United States, the mantle usually falls on the shoulders of Maj. Gen. Emory Upton. After serving as commandant of the U.S. Military Academy from 1870 to 1875, Upton was sent by the war secretary on a tour of Europe in search of military organizational models worthy of imitation. Four years after the conclusion of the Franco-Prussian War and the creation of a new German empire, the task of locating the belle of the ball was hardly difficult. Upton's admiration for the Prussian/German military reinforced his preference for smaller, more professional armies as against larger, ad hoc ones, a preference developed during his service in the American Civil War. Consequent to Lincoln's recharacterization of the war as a national war of emancipation (rather than a limited war to preserve the Union), Upton became highly critical of what he considered the deficiencies in the Union Army resulting from the political interference of civilian leadership and the appointment of noncareer officers to major commands. The preeminent military historian Russell F. Weigley credits Upton with the dubious distinction of having first asserted the requirement for national policy to conform to military imperatives, rather than the other way around. Upton argued, says Weigley, "that all the defects of the American military system rested upon a fundamental, underlying flaw, excessive civilian control of the military." Consequently, Weigley credits Upton with causing lasting damage to the army by establishing a model of civil-military relations that emphasized antagonism over accommodation to civilian society.[16]

Upton's choice of Prussia as a model for military professionalism was not without precedents, for the American military already possessed a genuine Prussian heritage beginning with the Revolutionary War. The legacy of Prussia precedes the advent of the Prussian military reformers of the Napoleonic period. In 1778, Friedrich Wilhelm (Frederick William) von Steuben arrived at the Valley Forge encampment of the American Continental Army with the assignment, arranged by Benjamin Franklin in Paris, to provide a system of drill and discipline based

on a model other than that of the British enemy. Drawing on his service
in the army of Frederick the Great, Steuben drafted his *Regulations,* or
Blue Book, that established a uniquely American manual of arms, one
that is nominally utilized to this day. Steuben's legacy, however, was
confined to drill and not to general or "keystone" doctrine, and his military experience predated the Napoleonic-era Prussian military reforms
that were later exalted by Upton.

Upton's admiration for the Prussian institutions of the reform period
was generalized; his writings contain no systematic analysis of the
writings of the Napoleonic War-era military reformers. Upton's position on the connection between political ends and military action was
the opposite of Lieber's and Clausewitz's, whose works are not cited in
Upton's own. It was, rather, the ideas of Lieber's archrival, John C. Calhoun, that Upton drew on as a base for his proposal regarding an expandable army.[17] In a time of war, such an army would be comprised of
personnel from the regular army, national volunteers, and the militias,
all of whom would be "regulars in drill, discipline, and courage" and be
placed under the command of professional soldiers.[18] Taking his own
life in 1881, Upton despaired of ever seeing an expandable regular army
free of civilian interference or seeing his ideas officially endorsed or
published by the army. He did, however, leave an unfinished manu-
script, which was posthumously published as *The Military Policy of the
United States* and unofficially disseminated among the officer corps. It
generated enough discussion (in support and opposition) to facilitate the
creation of the first official keystone doctrine since the promulgation of
General Order No. 100.[19]

One doctrinal specialist who wrote in opposition to Upton was Maj.
Arthur L. Wagner, U.S. Army, an instructor in the "Art of War" at the
U.S. Infantry and Cavalry School at Fort Leavenworth, Kansas. In 1866,
Wagner wrote a study that strongly criticized the Prussian military for
ignoring the lessons concerning mass armies during the American
Civil War. He argued that foreign doctrine, especially Prussian doctrines, must cede precedents to the Republican forms of a distinctly
American civil-military relationship.[20] Wagner's major work, *Organization and Tactics,* divided the art of war into two major divisions:
(1) strategy, or the movement and disposition of an army in a "theater of
operations"; and (2) tactics, the movements of soldiers on a battlefield.
Calling Upton's focus on drill and discipline to mind, Wagner felt that
"it was not sufficient that an army be composed of intelligent, well-

instructed, brave, and obedient soldiers, well armed and equipped;" he also considered drill as "merely one of the means, not the end" of military discipline. [21]In believing that there are too many diverse elements in war to keeps the art of it from becoming a science based on universal laws, Wagner was probably more familiar with the actual writing of Clausewitz than was Upton, who believed in the existence of laws that have been in operation throughout American military history. For Wagner, the art of war was a human science rather than an exact science.[22]

Wagner's greatest difference with Upton had to do with the relative effectiveness and discipline of the republicanized United States Army during the Civil War, as compared to that of contemporary professionalized European armies. Wagner favored the former, and Upton the latter.[23] Wagner, unlike Upton, received official endorsement for his doctrinal positions. In 1897, the second edition of Wagner's *Organization and Tactics* contained an official imprimatur from the adjutant-general's office and was officially recommended by the Headquarters of the Army for officers undergoing examination for promotion. It contained a preface written by the commander of the U.S. Infantry and Cavalry School, the direct precursor to the Command and General Staff School. It was not until twenty-three years after his death that Upton's *Military Policy of the United States* was officially published by the Army, and even then its contents received only a tentative endorsement.

While the works of Upton and Wagner made only modest headway toward providing a doctrinal foundation for the military profession on land, Capt. Alfred Thayer Mahan supplied an intellectual rationale for American naval and foreign policy that would be utilized through the twentieth century. Unlike the army, the navy already possessed a functional War College by 1890, the year that Mahan, a faculty member, had his lectures published as *The Influence of Sea Power on History, 1660–1783*. Mahan founded his naval worldview on the strategy of Henri de Jomini rather than on Clausewitz or other Prussian military reformers, and he recommended Great Britain rather than despotic Prussia as a historical model for policy. It was a time when America was assuming its role as an imperial world power.[24] The difference in the level of professionalism between America's naval forces and its ground forces was clearly demonstrated in America's first major overseas military intervention.

Elihu Root and the Birth of Military Professionalism

A year after America's tangled victory in the Spanish-American War (1898), President William McKinley appointed the Wall Street lawyer Elihu Root to be his secretary of war. Root was charged with cleaning up the military mess in the newly acquired Philippine Islands, then occupied by U.S. Marine and U.S. Army ground forces. From 1899 to 1904, Root conducted the most extensive military reform in American history (at least until that occurring four decades later under Gen. George C. Marshall). He reorganized the administrative system of the War Department and modernized promotions. He carried out many policies envisioned by Upton, including the founding of a War College, the creation of a general staff, and the strengthening of federal control over the National Guard. Root also was forced to address the fact that army's performance in the Spanish-American War and the subsequent Philippine Insurrection (1899–1906) exposed an army in doctrinal crises.

The major activity of the army between Root's time and the Civil War had been the carrying out of constabulary functions in the South during Reconstruction and on the western frontier. Morris Janowitz, an early critic of Huntington's theory of civil-military relations, argued that, although such functions have always been a persistent activity for regular military forces, they have always been a source of doctrinal neglect.[25] With its first regular military action in thirty-four years, the U.S. Army's performance, while leading to victory, was disappointing. Despite the army's wealth of historical experience with such operations, American forces were unable to conduct disciplined constabulary functions during the American occupation of the Philippines following the war. The worst incident followed a massacre of 59 Americans at Balangiga, on the island of Samar. Marines under the command of U.S. Army Gen. Jacob F. Smith, an officer who had participated in the Wounded Knee Massacre of 1890, engaged in a genocidal riot that left 165 villages burned and thousands of Philippines murdered, the majority of whom were clearly noncombatants.[26]

On February 21, 1903, seven months after the court-martial of Gen. Smith for his force's conduct on Samar, Root laid the cornerstone of the Army War College in Washington, D.C. Root used this occasion to deliver a eulogy for Upton and his quest for greater professionalism in the American military.[27] A year later, Root agreed to the publication of an official, edited version of Upton's *Military Policy of the United States.*

In his preface to the document, however, Root offered only a partial endorsement of Upton's ideas. After pointing out that many of the author's concerns had already been addressed, Root pointed out that Upton failed "to appreciate difficulties arising from our form of government and the habits and opinions of our people"; and moreover that Upton's views were "colored by the strong feelings natural to a man who had been a participant in the great conflict of the civil war."[28]

Root was well aware of great divisions among officers during the Civil War, specifically between regular West Point-trained officers like Upton and citizen-soldiers elected to their commissions by their men or politically appointed. At the center of this controversy was Gen. George McClellan, who was first relieved as general-in-chief after the failure of the Peninsula Campaign in 1862, later reinstated commander of the Army of the Potomac, and relieved for the final time a few months later after failing to follow up the Union victory at Antietam. The traditional depiction of McClellan's action and his removal as a controversy over civilian control of the military is misleadingly one-dimensional. While McClellan strongly resented interference in military affairs by the Congress and by President Lincoln—a resentment shared by Upton—he held his military superiors in the same contempt as his civilian superiors did. He never hesitated to go over their heads to appeal to civilians, as in the case of Gen. Winfield Scott and Gen. Henry W. Halleck, his predecessor and his successor, respectively, in the role of general-in-chief.

It was not the military or civilian character of his superiors that McClellan objected to; rather, it was the change in war aims from a smaller, more traditionally statist one of preserving the Union to a larger, ideological goal centered on emancipation. To paraphrase Clausewitz, McClellan would have no part in a war that was the continuation of policies with which he did not agree. These policies would soon be definitely expressed in the Emancipation Proclamation and in *General Order No. 100*, the latter at the initiative of Halleck.[29] While it would be unfair to call Upton a simple McClellanite, he clearly shared McClellan's opposition to the influence of the Lincoln administration and the Republican Congress on the conduct of the war. In chapter 25 of his *Military Policy*, Upton offers sympathetic criticism of McClellan's civil-military decisions.[30] Additionally, Upton, like McClellan, opposed the change in war aims when the Civil War became a larger war of emancipation.[31]

Root, conversely, was acutely aware of *General Order No. 100* during his tenure as secretary of war. In 1901, an American general publicly announced that the insurgents in the Philippines had violated twenty-six articles of the "Lieber Code" and claimed that the United States was justified in not according such belligerents the protections accorded lawful combatants according to the most controversial doctrine contained in *General Order No. 100*, that of reprisal. Root did not agree. Although he accepted Lieber's principle that soldiers fighting an enemy that engages in unlawful conduct may respond in a manner that would not otherwise be sanctioned, Root claimed that the extreme form of retaliation being carried out by American forces in the Philippines was beyond any justification. Both Gen. Jacob Smith and his direct subordinate, Maj. Littleton Waller, unsuccessfully tried during their court-martials to use the Lieber Code's doctrine of retaliation to justify the Samar outrages. Although he was later widely criticized for being both too soft and too hard in what he admitted was the superficial war crime trials of American officers in Manila, Root, upon hearing reports of the excessive reprisals carried out under Gen. Smith, cabled that "nothing can justify or will be held to justify, the use of torture or inhuman conduct on the part of the American Army." In a personal letter to Senator Henry Cabot Lodge, Root criticized the tactic of utilizing *General Order No. 100* to justify the disproportionate reprisals occurring in the Philippines. [32]

On July 21, 1902, Root responded to criticism by Gen. Granville Dodge, who considered Root's decision to court-martial American personnel as an error in judgment based on a naïve understanding of the reality of war: "I think if you could read the testimony in the Waller case [who was tried prior to General Smith and established the evidentiary record subsequently used against Smith] you would change your views. I had very much the same views of the case as you express, but careful examination of the entire record and evidence extremely distressing to me." [33]

The suspect use of the Lieber Code in war crimes cases to defend American atrocities in the Philippines did not dampen Root's enthusiasm for *General Order No. 100* and its author, Francis Lieber. Five years after the Manila court-martials, Root, as secretary of state, directed the American delegation to the second Hague Conference to radically expand the reach of laws of war. Root considered the Lieber Code as the source that "made possible the success of the Hague Conferences.[34] During the second Hague Conference, Root's ambition to expand international law at the expense of traditional prerogatives of the nation-state was frustrated by his bête noire, Germany. It was probably Root's anti-German antagonism that accounts for his partiality for the anti-Prussian Lieber over the pro-Prussian Upton. Root took the occasion of the presidential address at the seventh annual meeting of the American Society of International Law in 1913 to celebrate the fiftieth anniversary of adoption of the Lieber Code. In his eulogy of Lieber, Root described the man as a German whose love of country urged him "to the support of a government which the love of liberty urged them to condemn" in that the "people of Prussia were held in the strictest subjection to an autocratic government of inveterate and uncompromising traditions."[35] In Root's speech, there was nothing of the qualified endorsement so obvious in the secretary's eulogy for Upton ten years earlier. Although, as secretary of war, Root is credited with implementing many of Upton's recommendations regarding the professionalization of the American Military, he kept his distance from the Uptonian celebration of Prussian efficiency and professionalism at the expense of democratic principles. Root closed his presidential address with the following:

> It stirs the imagination that the boy who lay wounded on the battlefield at Namur for his country's sake and who languished in prison for liberty's sake and who left his native land that he might be free, should bind his life into the structure of American self-government and leave a name honored by scholars and patriots the world over. If our Society, at once national and international, were about to choose a patron saint, and the roll were to be called, my voice for one would answer "Francis Lieber."[36]

It is significant that the period of the greatest advances in military professionalism took place under the direct tutelage of celebrated personages of another entirely distinct profession, the legal profession. Between 1897 and the Second World War, eleven of the fourteen serving secretaries of war were lawyers' the most notable of whom were Elihu Root (1899–1904), William Howard Taft (1904–1908), and Henry Lewis Stimson (1940–1945). For the historian Robert H. Wiebe, who argued that late nineteenth century witnessed the beginning of the transformation of American society from the individualized values of small towns and communities to the values of the urban middle-class and professional bureaucrats, as epitomized by the legal profession, nowhere was this transformation better embodied than in the career of Root. Administering the most important period of the professionalization of the American military, Root considered professional bureaucracy a necessary instrument to counter the contemporary challenges to a premod-

ern system of government.[37] Given that Stimson, who served twice as
secretary of war, started his legal career in firm of Root & Clark, it could
even be claimed that the most critical periods of military professionalization took place under the tutelage of one law firm.

The Formalization and Specialization of American Military Doctrine

Except for *General Order No. 100,* the creation of military doctrine in
the United States prior to the twentieth century was decentralized and
informal. Except for the edited writings of Emory Upton and those of
Arthur L. Wagner, doctrinal texts utilized by the American military
during the nineteenth century were commercially published, sometimes with and sometimes without an imprimatur. As the American
military profession underwent formalization and specialization in the
early twentieth century, so too did American military doctrine.

With the publication of *Field Service Regulations* in 1910, the army
under Root's successor as war secretary, William H. Taft, introduced
what was to be the first formal series of doctrinal publications. This
document served simultaneously as a "capstone" publication, officially
articulating national war fighting doctrine, and a "keystone" publication, providing a base for all other supplemental doctrinal publications.[38] The *Field Service Regulations* were not the product of a single
author holding an official endorsement; rather, the manual was the
responsibility of a Field Service Regulations Board charged with drafting a centralized and current war fighting doctrine. It was the first
time since the promulgation of *General Order No. 100* that a single volume could be described as the official military doctrine of the United
States. Seven new editions of the series would be issued between
1908 and 1941, when Field Manual 100–5, *Operations,* would super-
sede the older series. The FM 100–5 series would remain the primary
keystone doctrinal series after the creation of the Department of
the Army by the National Security Act of 1947 until the end of the
twentieth century, when the Army's traditional role as the major de-
veloper of keystone doctrine was superseded by the Department of
Defense (DoD).[39]

Lt. Col. Walter Kretchik of the U.S. Army Command and General
Staff College, a leading expert on the historical development of army
doctrine, considered the first edition of *Field Service Regulations* to
contain the ideas of both of the major post-Napoleonic military theo-

rists, Jomini and Clausewitz, but "transmitted though the writings of Henry W. Halleck, Emory Upton, and Arthur L. Wagner."[40] The legacy of Francis Lieber also figured prominently in the manual. The entirety of Article XII in the first edition of the manual consisted of a reprint of *General Order No. 100*. The position of *General Order No. 100* in subsequent editions, however, became increasing peripheral. By the 1914 edition of *Field Service Regulations*, only a summary of the Lieber's provisions was included in an appendix titled "Extracts from International Conventions and Conferences."[41]

In two editions promulgated before and after the experience of the American expeditionary force in the First World War, the *Field Service Regulations* emphasized decisive offensive operations over passive defensive tactics. The contemporaneous reaction to the recent experience of static trench warfare in Europe reinforced the traditional American doctrinal emphasis on affirmative, decisive action going back to the pre-Civil War writings of Henry Halleck. The same emphasis is also found in the traditional just war requirement for a high probability of success and the principle of military necessity found in *General Order No. 100*, of which Halleck was the major sponsor. Maj. Gen. J. L. Hines, acting chief of staff, in his preface to the 1923 edition of the *Field Service Regulations*, wrote, "War is positive and requires positive action. All training should, therefore, aim to develop positive qualities of character rather than to encourage negative traits. The basis of training will be the attack."[42]

In this same edition, however, the humanitarian significance of the need for decisive action is not openly acknowledged, in contrast to *General Order No. 100* and earlier versions of the regulations that contained summarized versions of *General Order No. 100*. This change was in keeping with the concept of the passive humanitarian obligations in war, associated with the influence of the International Committee of the Red Cross, that was gaining in influence at the expense of the affirmative obligations associated with traditional just war doctrine. By 1923, the appendix to *Field Service Regulations* summarizing *General Order No. 100* was finally dropped from the manual. As the false dichotomy between operational decisiveness and humanitarian concerns in war became more accepted, officers would now have to consult more specialized manuals for guidance on the humanitarian norms of war.

What the precepts contained in *General Order No. 100* may have lost in terms of their capstone significance by their removal from *Field Ser-*

vice Regulations, however, they gained in specialized keystone significance by means of other publications. In 1913, Col. Edwin F. Glenn at
the Army War College was tasked with drawing up an authoritative and
updated doctrinal manual to succeed *General Order No. 100.*[43] Titled
Rules of Land Warfare, Glenn's manual was to be the first of an authoritative doctrinal series that would apply across separate military services.
It has yet to be superseded. In its preface, the integration of Lieber's doctrinal legacy with contemporaneous material is categorically affirmed.
"It will be found that everything vital contained in G. O. 100 of A. G. O.
of April 24, 1863, 'Instructions for the Government of Armies of the
United States in the Field,' has been incorporated into this manual,"
Glenn wrote. "Wherever practicable the original text has been used
herein, because it is believed that the long familiarity with this text and
its interpretation by our officers should not be interfered with if possible
to avoid doing so."[44]

The Department of War issued new editions of *Rules for Land Warfare* in 1934 and, as Field Manual 27–10, in 1940. The Department of the
Army promulgated the current edition of FM 27–10, titled *Laws of Land
Warfare,* in 1956. Although the manual was far more specialized than
either *General Order No. 100* or the summation of the Lieber Code in
the early editions of the *Field Service Regulations,* the new manual was
intended as a reference for all professional officers rather than as a handbook for lawyers. As the title of the manual from the 1914 to the 1940
edition indicates, the emphasis is on normative "rules" rather than legalistic "laws," placing the manual clearly within the purview of military doctrine rather than positive law.

Over time, however, more and more conventions from international
law were incorporated into the manual. Although the 1914 edition did
not list the Geneva Conventions of 1868, the Hague Conventions of
1899, or the majority of the Hague Conventions of 1907 as instruments
binding on the American military, it fully incorporated an expansive interpretation of the modern theory of customary international law: "In
addition to the written rules there exist certain other well-recognized
usages and customs that have become recognized as rules of warfare.
These usages are still in the process of development."[45]

The 1940 edition added the Red Cross conventions of 1864, the Hague
Conventions of 1899, and the additional Geneva Conventions of 1929 to
the list of instruments "in force."[46] Despite the expanding applicability
of international humanitarian law, the most consistent feature of the

succeeding editions of the *Rules of Land Warfare* between 1914 and 1940 remained the verbatim reaffirmations of the major just war doctrines of *General Order No. 100*, including the doctrine of military necessity, reprisals, and protections of prisoners of war.[47] In other areas, the *Rules of Land Warfare* expanded the protections found in *General Order No. 100*, such as expanded prohibitions on denying quarter, collateral damage, care of prisoners, and care for sick and wounded.[48] The only major area of retreat in the maintenance and extension of the humanitarian norms of *General Order No. 100* was in the area of command responsibility and superior orders. This is not surprising for an era in which Secretary of State Robert Lansing, embraced at the Paris Peace Conference in 1919 the pre-war German position regarding the exclusion of humanitarian law, as actions of state, in criminal prosecutions. Lansing's conservative, positivistic position flies in the face of the idealistic international tone associated with the Wilson administration's foreign policy. Lansing's minimalist position would, unfortunately, hold sway until the height of the Second World War.[49]

The Re-Democratization of the American Military

Not all initiatives regarding the professionalization of the armed forces can be attributed to the tutelage of members of the legal profession. The most eminent reformer of the Progressive period, following Root, was Maj. Gen. Leonard Wood, whose professional training was that of a medical doctor. Serving as chief of staff of the army from 1912 to 1914, mostly under Root's protégé, Henry Stimson, Wood embodied Stimson's vision of an army representing a democratic society rather than a "career of a chosen class."[50] Between the years immediately prior to the First World War and the American involvement in the Second World War, a battle was waged between the adherents of Emory Upton and Leonard Wood. In the words of John K. Mahon, America's preeminent historian of the citizen-soldier: "Emory Upton, although long dead, gave the definitive expression to the professional position, and he supplied the ideas to which Elihu Root, as far as it was politically possible, embraced. The most influential spokesman on the other side was Major General Leonard Wood. Wood's insistence that citizens could be trained in a few months was unacceptable to hard-core professionals."[51]

Following Leonard Wood in the non-Uptonian citizen-army tradition would be Brig. Gen. John McAuley Palmer and General of the Army

George Catlett Marshall. The professional models for all three would be characterized by the democratic ideal of universal military service (UMT) in which citizenship, like in the classical examples of the Greek and Roman republics, would be synonymous with military service.

Leonard Wood's program for democratization was wedded to his plan for the professionalization of the military based on the insights of the managerial revolution associated with the Progressive era.[52] However, Wood's ideas were at odds with the conception of the citizen-soldier championed by the supporters of the National Guard in which individual state prerogatives and unit cohesion would be given greater weight than centralized managerial efficiency. For Wood, all standardizations of training, especially that of officers, had to be controlled by the War Department. In his first year as chief of staff, Wood oversaw the establishment of military training camps for college students. By 1916, this initiative would overhaul the ineffective training of students attending land-grant colleges, as required by the Morrill Act of 1862, and make it into the modern Reserve Officers Training Corps (ROTC). When the pool of manpower for recruitment of officers was unable to meet the requirements of the national army called for in the wake of the First World War, Wood supported the so-called Plattsburg idea, which entailed opening up training camps to older men with professional, nonmilitary credentials. This program would provide the foundation of the formal Officer Training Schools (OTSs) established during World War I. As civilian candidates would receive training over several months and then be commissioned, they earned the lasting nickname "ninety-day wonders."

By the year after the end of the First World War, the U.S. Army was radically democratized by the commissioning of 80,568 line officers. This democratization was not one of quantity alone, but also of demographic representation. For the first time, African Americans recruits were incorporated into the officer training system, some attending segregated and others integrated OTS facilities.[53] Leading this democratized army was General of the Armies, John J. Pershing. Partly as a result of their experience as aides to Pershing during the war, Generals Palmer and Marshall would move further, even, than Wood in their criticism of Uptonion professionalism.

It was John Palmer who provided the concept of the citizen-soldier with a firm theoretical foundation. Being both a graduate of West Point and the son of an illustrious Civil War citizen-soldier, Maj. Gen. John

McAuley Palmer, Palmer viewed the expandable professional army concept associated with John C. Calhoun and Emory Upton as outdated in the age of national mass armies. As a mere captain, Palmer assisted Secretary of War Stimson before the war in the latter's attempt to gain support in the military profession for a deployable professionalized citizen army. The result of this effort was the War Department report "The Organization of the Land Forces of the United States." As a colonel in 1919, Palmer testified before and worked with Congress on legislation that would be influential in the creation of the National Defense Act of 1920. Like Leonard Wood before him and George C. Marshall after him, Palmer failed to establish a complete national system of universal military training (UMT) to feed recruits into his democratized citizen army. These ideas were not exclusive to Palmer. During the war these ideas were also championed by the National Association of Universal Military Training, whose advisory board included former Secretaries of War Root and Stimson. What made Palmer unique was his belief that the Uptonian model of professionalism was not only impractical; it was also inconsistent with the "genius of American institutions." General Palmer wrote: "The forms of military institutions must be determined on political grounds, with due regard to national genius and tradition. The military pedant may fail by proposing adequate and economical forces under forms that are intolerable to the national genius."[54]

In 1939, the new chief of staff of the army, Gen. George C. Marshall, approved a new version of the army capstone doctrinal manual, *Field Service Regulations.* Rechristened Field Manual (FM) 100–5, *Operations,* the manual was a watershed in establishing the ideal of the citizen-soldier as a formal norm. The manual called for instilling "symbolic ideals emplaced by tradition and national culture" into American soldiers as basis of their military service.[55] Marshall was a great critic of the neo-Clausewitzian "principles of war" enshrined in the 1923 and later versions of Army capstone doctrine. In 1939 he issued an infantry handbook prepared under his direction that stated "the art of war has no traffic with rules, for the infinitely varied circumstances and conditions of combat never produce exactly the same situation twice."[56] For Marshall, like Palmer, military operations and organization had to be both pragmatic and aligned with democratic institutions.

In response to the new non-isolationist foreign policy objectives contained in Roosevelt's "Four Freedom's" address to Congress, Marshall took it as his primary task upon being appointed chief of staff to create a nation in arms to meet both the contingencies of an armed peace or eventual war. Like Leonard Wood, Marshall understood that a mass citizen army had to be led primarily by professionalized citizen-officers. In 1940, on the twenty-fifth anniversary of Leonard Wood's original Plattsburg camp in upstate New York, Elihu Root, Henry Stimson, and retired Brigadier General John Palmer met to draw up a plan for a national military conscription that would follow as close as possible to their cherished vision of universal military service. Palmer took the plan to the new army chief of staff, Gen. Marshall. In the face of congressional opposition, President Roosevelt passed the Selective Service Training Act of September 16, 1940. Requiring all men between the ages of twenty-one and thirty-five to register for one year of military service, it was the closest approximation to the concept of universal military training that would ever be achieved in the United States. In order to implement it, Roosevelt called Stimson back to serve a second term as secretary of war to work with Marshall.[57]

Marshall was willing to move much further than Leonard Wood or even Secretary Stimson from the Uptonian conception of a professional officer class. For Marshall, it was common sense that an experienced noncommissioned officer (NCO) in the infantry was far more of a professional than was, say, a civilian manager of a bank. The Selective Service Act would provide a constant pool of recruits for officer candidacy, a great improvement over the training camps for businessmen during the World War I-Plattsburg era. Marshall, however, was confronted with more determined resistance to his ideas on democratizing officer candidacy than he had faced with his doctrinal reforms. When Stimson was on the verge of instituting OTS-style "training camps for the sons of the rich without going thru the draft," Marshall informed Stimson that he considered it "a colossal mistake" that would have to be done without him: "I went to Mr. Stimson and told him I had done my best and said the entire staff with me on this. 'I will tell you now I am going to resign the day you do it.'"[58]

In 1941, two months before the Japanese attack on Pearl Harbor, Gen. Omar Bradley, the commandant of the newly established Officer Candidate School (OCS), read a letter by Marshall for the commissioning ceremony of the school's first graduates, which included the author's father. The letter encapsulated the ideal of a non-Uptonian professionalized citizen army. In this army, although there might not be a Napoleonic marshal's baton found in every trooper's rucksack, there would be a possible gold lieutenant's bar nesting under every gold sergeant's strip. The words read out to the new lieutenants clearly followed the model first conceptualized by Gen. Palmer, and it was this philosophy of a democratized military profession that Marshall had put his career on the line to implement.

> Our Army differs from all other armies. The very characteristics which make our men potentially the best soldiers in the world can be in some respects a source of weakness. Racially we are not a homogeneous people, like the British for example, who can glorify a defeat by their stubborn and dogged discipline. We have no common racial group, and we deliberately cultivated individual initiative and independence of thought and action. Our men are intelligent and resourceful to an unusual degree. These characteristics, those qualities may be, in effect explosive or potentially destructive in a military organization, especially under adverse conditions, unless leadership is wise and determined and unless the leader commands the complete respect of his men . . . Your class is the first of what I believe will be the finest group of troop leaders in the world.[59]

A truly democratized Army not only had to be lifted out of class-consciousness; it had to be more representative of American society at large. While the Army would remain racially segregated under Marshall during the Second World War, the positions of leadership available to African Americans would be greatly expanded, especially in aviation. The integration of the American military after the war under President Truman, who was greatly under Marshall's influence, was the logical next step. Marshall also expanded the role of women in the Armed forces, both commissioned and enlisted, by his support of the Women's Army Auxiliary Corps, granting the organization military status in 1943. Also during Marshall's tenure as chief of staff, the first Catholic priest served as chief of the Chaplain's Corps.

When Marshall was sworn in as chief of staff on the day Hitler invaded Poland, the army consisted of less than 200,000 men. By the time Marshall left that office in 1945, the army numbered over 8,000,000. Marshall knew that the army organization he experienced for most of his career, an expandable professional army, would not return after the war. Although the Uptonian dream of a functional elite officer corps was far from dead, Marshall's concept of the professionalized citizen-soldier provided the doctrinal and intellectual foundation for the modern American army.

In the fifth century, Saint Augustine appealed to Christians that military service was not forbidden and that they should conduct themselves under arms in an individual affirmation of shared Christian ethics. Generals Palmer and Marshall held that American military professionals should conduct themselves under arms as individuals affirming shared democratic ethics. As in Augustinian just war doctrine, the focal point of professionalism resided in the individual soldier or commander. The enforcement mechanism to ensure that this individual affirmation would be consummated in actual military policies was the expansion of the principle of individual and command responsibility during the course of World War II.

CHAPTER THREE

Command Responsibility and the Meaning of Nuremberg

The commander is responsible for everything his unit does or fails to do.
Army Field Manual 71–100, *Division Operations* (1996)

Duty requires each of us to accept responsibility not only for our own actions, but also of those entrusted to our care.
Army Field Manual 100–1, *The Army* (1986)

THE WORLD WAR II–ERA American war crimes program established a standard of command responsibility as part of a wider American war crimes policy. The central tenets of command responsibility and superior orders were first initiated as a change in military doctrine and were later imposed by U.S. military tribunals on defendants of the defeated Axis powers. After receiving international validation, these standards were then reincorporated into U.S. military doctrine. This entire process was planned and administered by members of the American military profession in the U.S. War Department.

In the U.S. military, the word "command" has two separate definitions that are simultaneously both distinct and overlapping. First, command is simply the authority that a military commander "lawfully exercises over subordinates by virtue of rank or assignment." Second, it is a "unit or units, an organization, or an area under the command of one individual."[1] The individuals assigned to a command are collectively and reflexively associated with the person of the commander. The word "responsibility" also shares two major distinct, yet reflexive, definitions. Responsibility is both the "quality or state" of being a responsible moral agent and "something for which one is responsible."[2] Additionally, command responsibility includes both a superior's liability for the commission of a war crime by a subordinate and a defense by a subordinate that such as crime was the result of his or her complying with "superior orders."[3]

Both senses of "command responsibility" were brought to bear in the court-martial of Maj. Gen. Jacob Smith during the Philippine Insurrection (1899–1906). In 1901, Smith was court-martialed and then forced to retire for the conduct of his operations against noncombatants on the island of Samar that year.[4] The general unsuccessfully argued that the actions of his command represented permissible forms of retaliation under *General Order No. 100,* still in effect at the time. Later his subordinates similarly argued, unsuccessfully, that their actions were permissible under the concept of superior orders.

The future Nobel Peace Prize recipient George C. Marshall, while serving as a lieutenant in the Philippines, noted that gratuitous reprisals against the civilian population of the country were widespread and that, in his opinion, more soldiers than Smith and his subordinates should have been arrested and court-martialed.[5] Forty-three years later, as chief of staff of the army, Marshall would be in position to extend and formalize the concept of command responsibility to allow prosecution of military personnel regardless of claims of superior orders. On November 14, 1944, the War Department, under Marshall's signature, issued Change 1 to its Field Manual 27–10, *The Rules of Land Warfare* (1940):

> Liability of offending individuals and organizations who violate the accepted laws and customs of war may be punished therefore. However, the fact that the acts complained of were done pursuant to an order of a superior or government sanction may be taken into consideration in determining culpability, either by way of defense or in mitigation of punishment. The person giving such orders may also be punished.[6]

The Origins of Nuremberg

The 1944 change in military doctrine supplanted the previously existing American policy positions concerning responsibility for war crimes as established at the end of World War I. Drawn up by the American delegation under the leadership of Secretary of State Robert Lansing, the American reservations regarding proposed war crimes trials at the Paris Peace Conference in 1919 articulated an unqualified defense of the principle of sovereign immunity. Lansing and his team also rejected the Allied attempt to hold the German Kaiser accountable for provocation of the First World War and violations of the laws and customs of war by

German forces during the course of the conflict. Embodying concerns over the politicized utilization of legal innovations by the Allied powers at the expense of the defeated powers, the general tone of the American dissent was couched in the conventional language of conservative legal positivism that included a general distrust of any movement toward establishing an international regime of war crimes prosecution based on the enforcement of consistent reciprocal standards and jurisprudence between nations.[7]

For example, the American Memorandum of Reservations noted that there were "two classes of responsibilities, those of a legal nature and those of a moral nature." Accordingly, legal offenses were subject to trial proceedings by legitimate tribunals," while moral offenses, "however iniquitous and infamous and however terrible in their results," were outside the jurisdiction of judicial action and "subject only to moral sanctions." In direct contrast to the natural law-just war perspective of Francis Lieber and *General Order No. 100,* Lansing held that the "laws and principles of humanity vary with the individual, which, if for no other reason, should exclude them from the consideration in a court of justice" and that "there is no fixed and universal standard of humanity." Specifically, the American delegation opposed the "doctrine of negative criminality," which held individuals liable who "abstained form preventing, putting an end to, or repressing, violations of the laws and customs of war." Finally, the proposition that an international tribunal might have jurisdiction for the prosecution of war crimes was categorically rejected: "The American representatives know of no international statute or convention making a violation of the laws and customs of war—not to speak the laws or principles of humanity—an international crime, affixing a punishment to it, and declaring the court that has jurisdiction over the defense."[8]

The American war crimes program, initiated in the final year of the Second World War, represented not only a transformation in American policy but also a mechanism to link that policy to international norms. The 1907 Hague Conventions restricted the application of the "laws, rights, and duties of war" only to formations "commanded by a person responsible for his subordinates."[9] According to the view of legal positivists, however, military commanders could only be held responsible under the domestic laws of their own country. The 1928 Kellogg-Briand Pact criminalized the resort to aggressive war. As ratified by the U.S. Senate, it certainly created a challenge to Secretary Lansing's conservative legal positivism at the Paris Peace Conference. However, it still contained no enforcement mechanism that could be applied to citizens of other nations. Notions of command and individual responsibility, without a credible threat of punitive sanctions imposed by entities other than those benefiting from criminal behavior, provide little solace to the victims or potential victims of war crimes or aggression. Because legal positivism cannot address the possibility that a nation-state can be a criminal enterprise, it cannot provide credible redress for criminal acts of state.

The first systematic and operationally binding international standard that placed the individual perpetrators of state actions under the jurisdiction of tribunals, other than those administered by the authorities of the very state for whose benefit the criminal acts were perpetrated, was initiated by a directed change to standing American military doctrine. Penalties placed on individuals for noncompliance with international standards would be imposed on the citizens of the defeated powers by the multilateral action of the victorious states by overturning one of the central tenets of legal positivism. Most important, the victorious powers would claim that they would be bound, henceforth, by same universalistic standards they were imposing on the citizens of other nations.

This revolutionary change in American policy was generated in the midst of the greatest interdepartmental power struggle in the U.S. government during the course of the Second World War. This conflict, which would come to be known as "The Great German War on the Potomac,"[10] did not result from a policy fight between Lansing's successors at the State Department and the War Department. Rather, it was the result of Secretary of War Henry L. Stimson's and Assistant Secretary of War John J. McCloy's opposition to Treasury Secretary Henry Morgenthau's plans for a Carthaginian peace, which was intended to economically "castrate the German people," as well as to Winston Churchill's initial position in favor of the summary executions of some German leaders.[11] With the State Department taking a passive position in the dispute between Stimson and Morgenthau, the Department of War was at first isolated in pushing for a reconstruction of Germany rather than its dismemberment.

To set an example for the re-legitimization of the rule of law in Germany, Stimson's policy was to cultivate Germany as a future strategic ally by utilizing the very trials established to deal with German war criminals. It is hardly surprising that Germany's future role as a bulwark of democratic constitutionalism against both Nazism and Communism, which would play a pivotal role in the West's victory in the cold war, was not obvious to the many critics of Stimson's position. While the coming cold war may have been foreseeable to some American officials, the role of a divided Germany whose border would serve as the military and ideological pivot of Europe was hardly a certainty in 1944.[12] Even those who would eventually champion a central role for Germany in the cold war, either as a unified neutral or a divided state with its western portion integrated into the Western alliance, voiced concerns that the American war crimes program was an impediment, rather than an asset, to that process. Reinhold Niebuhr, one of the fathers of cold war realism, warned that moving beyond the holding of individuals responsible for "crimes against commonly accepted standards of humanity" would lead to the dismissal of the program as vindictive "victor's justice," as in the case of the discredited Morgenthau Plan to deindustrialize Germany. Niebuhr's concerns over the more controversial aspects of the Nuremberg process would be addressed by the inclusion of protections (Articles 10–12) against guilt by association in the 1949 Universal Declaration of Human Rights.[13] Another of the realist theorists of the early cold war, George F. Kennan, was more categorically dismissive of the American war crimes program, holding that "the Allied Commanders had standing instructions that if any of these men [the Nazi leaders] fell into the hand of Allied Forces they should, once their identity is established beyond doubt, be executed forthwith." Kennan argued that it was impossible for trials to undo crimes of such magnitude and that the inclusion of Soviet judges who carried out Stalin's purges would "make a mockery" of the trials.[14]

While Stimson's policies toward Germany may have been proven sound with the benefit of post-cold war hindsight, the American war crimes program constituted one of the most controversial and criticized policies of the immediate post war period. Stimson was initially assisted by Army Chief of Staff George Marshall and Judge Advocate Maj. Gen. Myron C. Cramer in his efforts to fight back Morgenthau's plan for a draconian peace and Churchill's preference for summary executions. In his diary, Stimson wrote that it was "very interesting to find that Army officers have a better respect for the law in those matters than civilians who talk about them and are anxious to go chop everybody's head off without a trial or hearing."[15] The first product of the effort was the November 11, 1944, draft "Memorandum for the President from the Secretaries of State, War, and Navy" prepared by the army lawyer Lt. Col. Murry C. Bernays under the direction of John McCloy. The memorandum preceded by only four days the publication of Change 1 of November 15, 1944, to War Department Field Manual 27–10, *The Rules of Land Warfare*, issued under Marshall's signature.[16] The November 11 memorandum included what critics and defenders would claim to be the most legally innovative part of the initiatives that were put forward by the Department of War in establishing the foundations of the Nuremberg trials. These "Bernays' additions" included the concepts of (1) criminal conspiracy to wage aggressive war; and (2) criminal-organizations, a novel and controversial initiative to collectively try the SS and other entities of the Third Reich legally responsible for war crimes.

Unlike the November 11 "Bernays' additions," which would be long delayed by the indifference of other departments and a lack of clear guidance from the president, Marshall's change to FM 27–10 was effective immediately and did not attract interdepartmental and inter-Allied opposition. The repudiation of the defense of superior orders and the standard of command responsibility found in the change to FM 27–10 constituted the third major element, along with "the Bernays additions," in what would become the "Nuremberg Ideas" associated with the War Department war crimes initiatives sponsored under the leadership of Secretary Stimson.[17]

The initiatives of this "Stimson Group," with the addition of the concept of crimes against humanity, had been discussed without much official notice in the deliberations of the United Nations War Crimes Commission (UNWCC), which had started meeting in London on October 20, 1943. Even after the November 1, 1943, Moscow Conference Declaration by Roosevelt, Churchill, and Stalin of Allied intentions to prosecute individual Germans responsible for war atrocities, the UNWCC provided not much more than a platform to pacify the concerns of occupied governments in exile regarding Axis outrages on their respective populations and territories. By the end of 1944, both the British and American representatives to the UNWCC had left the process. Sir Cecil Hurst resigned over the British Foreign Office's opposition to a war crimes tribunal established by treaty. Herbert C. Pell, the American representative, was forced out when his position became unfunded owing to his disagreement with the State Department over his support for including prewar crimes against German Jews under the jurisdiction of any proposed Allied war crimes tribunal.[18]

Aided by the public outcry following the revelation of the December 17, 1944, massacre of seventy American POWs at Malmedy, Belgium, during the Battle of the Bulge by members of the First SS Panzer Regiment, the Stimson group in the War Department succeeded in obtaining an interdepartmental consensus on central points of war crimes policy, resulting in the three secretaries' (War, State, and Justice) agreement of January 22, 1945. The War Department still failed in both obtaining the formal approval of President Roosevelt and in overcoming opposition to formal trials by the British Foreign Office. With the U.S War Department arguing for an extension of current international law and the British foreign office objecting to war crimes trials on traditional positive legalistic grounds, the resulting American and British positions were 180 degrees opposite those taken in the aftermath of World War I. Even though British opposition was slightly counter-balanced by the support of Gen. Charles de Gaulle, president of the interim government of France, the impasse over war crimes policies was not broken until after Roosevelt's death on April 12, 1945. Eight days later, President Truman ordered that the American war crimes program, as articulated in the three secretaries' agreement, be acted upon as the stated policy of the United States. Truman then succeeded in convincing one of the most influential officials of the New Deal, Supreme Court justice Robert H. Jackson, to serve as his representative and chief counsel for war crimes in the final negotiations for the trials and also to serve as the tribunal's first U.S. chief prosecutor.[19]

With the appointment of Jackson, the discussion of war crimes trials reverted to the international arena, with the War Department personnel supporting Jackson's leadership of the American effort. An important addition to the Stimson group with Col. Bernays was Maj. Gen. William J. Donovan, head and founder of the Office of Strategic Services (OSS). General Donovan brought the resources of the American military intelligence to relieve Jackson's acute shortage of evidentiary documentation. On June 26, 1945, Truman, Stalin, and Churchill (later to be replaced by Clement Attlee) met at the Potsdam Conference outside Berlin. Concurrently, American, British, French, and Soviet delegations met at Church House in London to finalize the London Charter on the International Conference on Military Trials, which later came to be generally known as the Nuremberg Charter. The pressure to have a general agreement in place prior to the adjournment of the Potsdam conference pushed the representatives toward a consensus.

While detailed description of the London conference is beyond the
scope of the present work, a few relevant factors regarding the resulting document should be noted. The electoral defeat of Churchill and
the Conservatives in Britain broke the American-British impasse on
holding war crimes trials. Now the greatest challenge to the American policy came from the Soviet delegation. The London Conference
called for the creation of an International Military Tribunal (IMT),
with judges serving from each of the major European Allied powers
appointed to try the "major war criminals of the European Axis." Jackson was well aware of the problems relating to having Soviet participation on a tribunal in the aftermath of the Stalinist purges and the
Nazi-Soviet Pact. Jackson's assistant and successor, Brig. Gen. Telford
Taylor, called the presence of Soviet judges the "biggest wart" of the
IMT.[20] The main point of contention between Jackson and the Soviets
was over the wording of principles. Jackson called for the text to emphasize universal reciprocity rather than victors' justice. When the Soviets
insisted that only the crimes of the "European Axis" were of concern to
the trials, Jackson wrote to the president in Berlin on June 6 arguing that
having no agreement would be better than sacrificing principle on this
issue:

> If certain acts of violations of treaties are crimes, they are crimes whether
> the United States does them or whether Germany does them, and we are
> not prepared to lay down a rule of criminal conduct against others which
> we would not be willing to have invoked against us. Therefore, we think
> the clause "carried out by the European Axis" so qualifies the statement
> that it deprives it of all standing and fairness as a juridical principle.[21]

Despite his lack of success in convincing the Soviets on this point,
Jackson was successful in gaining eventual Soviet agreement on many
other issues. The charges that would be brought against twenty-one defendants in the first trial of the Nuremberg process were condensed into
four major counts: (1) planning crimes against peace; (2) initiating or
waging crimes against peace; (3) war crimes; and (4) crimes against
humanity. The initiatives of the Stimson group fared well in the outcome of the London Conference. Although the Bernays Additions would
be restricted to crimes against peace for individual defendants, repudiation of the defense of superior orders as found in Marshall's change
to FM 27–10 were clearly articulated in Articles 7–8 of the London
Charter:

Article 7. The official position of defendants, whether as Heads of State or responsible officials in Government Departments, shall not be considered as freeing them from responsibility or mitigating punishment.

Article 8. The fact that the Defendant acted pursuant to order of his Government or of a superior shall not free him from responsibility, but may be considered in mitigation of the punishment if the Tribunal determines that justice so requires.[22]

On October 10, 1945, the representatives of the United States, France, Britain, and the Soviet Union signed the "Charter of the International Military Tribunal" in Berlin. The signers were, respectively, Robert H. Jackson, Francois de Menthon, Hartley Shawcross, and R. Rudenko. Twenty-four individuals were named in the indictment signed in Berlin.

The International Military Tribunal (IMT) and the Nuremberg Principles

Although the major precedents of command responsibility are usually associated with later Nuremberg trials under Allied Control Council Law No. 10, which followed the trial of the major leaders of the Third Reich, the issue of the defense of superior orders was also central in the International Military Tribunal (IMT) held in Nuremberg between November 20, 1945, and September 30, 1946. The major military defendants at the IMT included Field Marshal Wilhelm Keitel, Hitler's ranking officer in the Wehrmacht; Gen. Alfred Jodl, Hitler's chief of staff; and Admirals Erich Raeder and Karl Doenitz, the successive commanders of the German navy. [23]

All four of these defendants unsuccessfully articulated the principle of absolute obedience to superior orders in their statements before the tribunal. In his statement, given before his sentence was read on August 31, 1946, Adm. Raeder argued that a refusal to follow orders was a political act that infringed upon the political neutrality he associated with military professionalism: "If I have incurred guilt in any way, then this was chiefly in the sense that in spite of my purely military position I should perhaps have been not only a soldier, but also up to a certain point a politician, which, however, was in contradiction to the entire tradition of the German Armed Forces."[24]

The defendants rejected the most relevant historical example of officers resisting Hitler's authority. Under cross-examination, Gen. Jodl

condemned the July 20, 1944, conspiracy by German general staff officers led by Col. Claus von Stauffenberg to assassinate Hitler. Jodl stated
that the plot was the "blackest day which German history has seen as
yet and will probably remain so for all times." He went on to explain the
military code of ethics that governed his conclusion:

> Judge Owen J. Roberts: Why was it such a black day for Germany?
> Because someone tried to assassinate a man whom you now admit was a
> murderer?
>   General Jodl: Should I—at a moment when I am to be blown up in a cow-
> ardly, insidious manner by one of my own comrades, together with many
> opponents of the regime—should I perhaps approve of it all? That was to
> me the worst thing that happened. If the man with a pistol in his hand had
> shot the Fuehrer and had then given himself up, it would have been en-
> tirely different. But these tactics I considered most repulsive to any officer.
> I spoke under the impression of those events, which are actually among
> the worst I know, and I maintain today what I said then.
>   Judge Roberts: I do not want to argue with you, but do you think it is any
> more dastardly than shooting those 50 American soldiers who landed in
> the north of Italy to destroy a military target, shooting them like dogs?
>   General Jodl: That also was murder, undoubtedly. But it is not the task
> of a soldier to be the judge of his commander-in-chief. May history or the
> Almighty do that.[25]

Jodl then articulated his view of the ethical code of a soldier:

> And as for the ethical code of my action, I must say that it was obedience—
> for obedience is really the ethical basis of the military profession. That I
> was far from extending this code of obedience to the blind code of obedi-
> ence imposed on the slave has, I consider, been proved beyond all manner
> of doubt by my previous testimony. Nevertheless, you cannot get around
> the fact that, especially in operational matters of this particular kind,
> there can be no other course for the soldier but obedience.[26]

Field Marshall Keitel, in turn, appeared to have some regret over
his decision to serve according to the principle of absolute obedience to
orders in his pre-sentencing statement. When asked how he would
respond if he were placed in the "same position again," he answered
that he "would rather choose death than to let [himself] be drawn into
the net of such pernicious methods." In one of the most credible statements of remorse given by a defendant before the IMT, Keitel admitted
that German military honor had been compromised under the Third
Reich:

I believed, but I erred, and I was not in a position to prevent what ought to have been prevented. That is my guilt. It is tragic to have to realize that the best I had to give as a soldier, obedience and loyalty, was exploited for purposes which could not be recognized at the time, and that I did not see that there is a limit set even for a soldier's performance of his duty. That is my fate.[27]

Military professionals were especially interested in the case of Adm. Doenitz. Although a fanatical Nazi who was appointed by Hitler as head of state prior to his suicide, Doenitz's role in the war was seen as the most operationally military of any of the major defendants before the IMT. An argument for considering as war crimes the Allied aerial bombings and the use of the atom bomb, which disproportionately resulted in civilian casualties, has been made by some, the suggestion being that the American war crimes program was no more than victor's justice.[28] The defendants of the defeated powers were charged with no crimes that were identical to actions allowed under Allied policies, except in the case of Adm. Doenitz, who was charged with waging submarine warfare in a manner exactly like that of the Allies. While this was technically allowed by the London Charter, which forbade the use of *tu quoque* ("hypocrisy of the prosecution") in the tribunal, Doenitz's lawyer, Otto Kranzbuhler, a former German naval officer and lawyer, succeeded in obtaining the cooperation of American admiral Chester Nimitz and the British Admiralty to respond to interrogatories regarding the submarine tactics in question, specifically that of refusing to rescue survivors, which was also an Allied practice. The success of Kranzbuhler and Nimitz in avoiding a conviction of Doenitz on this specific charge was the high-water mark for the ethical integrity of the tribunal.[29]

The tribunal found all four military defendants guilty of following and disseminating a particular illegal order, "The Commando Order," which mandated the execution of enemy commandos. Following Article 23 of the Hague Convention, the tribunal held that commando operations were a legitimate military tactic, thus giving commando members protection as POWs if captured. Keitel and Jodl were convicted on all counts and were hanged by American soldiers. Raeder was convicted on all counts except crimes against humanity and was given a life sentence. Doenitz was convicted of planning, preparing, initiating, and conducting a war of aggression but not of participating in a conspiracy to carry out such a war. Doenitz was also convicted of war crimes, but he was found not guilty on the charge of crimes against humanity. Although three of the four were found guilty of counts stemming from the Bernays Additions, only those major military defendants found guilty of "crimes against humanity" under the principle of command/individual responsibility were executed.[30]

On December 11, 1946, seventy-one days after the IMT handed down its sentences, the newly born UN General Assembly affirmed the Principles of International Law recognized by the Charter of the Nuremberg Tribunal that included the U.S. War Department's thesis on superior orders and command responsibility:

Principle I: Any person who commits an act which constitutes a crime under international law is responsible therefore and liable to punishment.

Principle II: The fact that internal law does not impose a penalty for an act which constitutes a crime under international law does not relieve the person who committed the act from responsibility under international law.

Principle III: The fact that a person who committed an act which constitutes a crime under international law acted as Head of State or responsible Government official does not relieve him from responsibility under international law.

Principle IV: The fact that a person acted pursuant to order of his Government or of a superior does not relieve him from responsibility under international law, provided a moral choice was in fact possible to him.

Principle V: Any person charged with a crime under international law has the right to a fair trial on the facts and law.

Principle VI: The crimes hereinafter set out are punishable as crimes under international law:
   Crimes against peace: (i) Planning, preparation, initiation or waging of a war of aggression or a war in violation of international treaties, agreements or assurances; (ii) Participation in a common plan or conspiracy for the accomplishment of any of the acts mentioned under (i).
   War crimes: Violations of the laws or customs of war which include, but are not limited to, murder, ill-treatment or deportation to slave-labor or for any other purpose of civilian population of or in occupied territory, murder or ill-treatment of prisoners of war, of persons on the seas, killing of hostages, plunder of public or private property, wanton destruction of cities, towns, or villages, or devastation not justified by military necessity.
   Crimes against humanity: Murder, extermination, enslavement, depor-

tation and other inhuman acts done against any civilian population, or persecutions on political, racial or religious grounds, when such acts are done or such persecutions are carried on in execution of or in connection with any crime against peace or any war crime.

Principle VII: Complicity in the commission of a crime against peace, a war crime, or a crime against humanity as set forth in Principles VI is a crime under international law.[31]

The Yamashita Precedent

The most noted of the Nuremberg-era trials, insofar as the standards of command responsibility are concerned, was undertaken outside of the formal structure of the London Charter. The trial of Japanese General Tomoyuki Yamashita was contemporaneous with the IMT and was referenced in the subsequent trials in Europe authorized under the Allied Control Council's Control Law No. 10. It is still the most cited standard of command responsibility to this day. On October 8, 1945, two days before the London Charter was signed in Berlin, Gen. Yamashita was arraigned by a military tribunal consisting of veteran American general rank officers under the direct authority of Gen. Douglas MacArthur, Supreme Commander Asia and Pacific (SCAP). Yamashita was put on trial for his "command responsibility" in failing to prevent or punish the killing of civilians and prisoners of war during the Japanese defense against the American reconquest of the Philippines in 1945. Yamashita's forces were responsible for killing 8,000 civilians, committing 500 rapes, and carrying out other atrocities in and around Manila. Although these forces were under Yamashita's formal command, the general's defense team argued that Yamashita did not have effective control of the forces in question as a result of his inability to communicate orders or receive reports from them, a consequence of American forces having disrupted his command infrastructure. The tribunal charged that Yamashita "unlawfully disregarded and failed to discharge his duty as commander to control the operations of members of his command, permitting them to commit brutal atrocities against people of the United States and of its allies and dependencies."[32]

The American military commission trying the Yamashita case addressed the defense's claim regarding Yamashita's innocence by putting forth a broadly defined standard of command responsibility, one that entailed an affirmative, positive obligation on the part of the leader:

Clearly, assignment to command military troops is accompanied by broad authority and heavy responsibility. This has been true of all armies throughout history. It is absurd, however, to consider a commander a murderer or rapist because one of his soldiers commits a murder or a vicious rape. Nevertheless, where murder and rape and vicious, revengeful actions are widespread offenses, and *there is no effective attempt by a commander to discover and control the criminal acts, such a commander may be held responsible* [italics mine], even criminally liable, for the lawless acts of his troops, depending upon their nature and the circumstances surrounding them.[33]

This most rigorous of all standards of command responsibility, known as the "Yamashita precedent," was a complete, formal repudiation of the pre-World War II American legal position that "neither knowledge of commission, nor ability to prevent is alone sufficient" to convict a leader or commander for the crimes of his subordinates.[34] Following the defense's appeal to the Supreme Court, the standard was explicitly affirmed and the sentence of execution was upheld, reinforcing the notion of an active, rather than a passive, command obligation:

It is evident that the conduct of military operations by troops whose excesses are unrestrained by the orders or efforts of their commander would almost certainly result in violation which it is the purpose of the law of war to prevent. Its purpose to protect civilian populations and prisoners of war from brutality would largely be defeated if the commander of an invading army could with impunity neglect to take reasonable measures for their protection. Hence the law of war presupposes that its violation is to be avoided through the control of operations by commanders who are to some extent responsible for their subordinates.

This is recognized by the Annex to the Fourth Hague Convention of 1907. Article I lays down as a condition which an armed force must fulfill in order to be accorded the rights of lawful belligerents, that it must be "commanded by a person responsible for his subordinates.[35]

In the minority dissent, Supreme Court justice Loren E. Murphy accepted the defense's claim that "nowhere was it alleged that the petitioner personally committed any of the atrocities, or that he ordered their commission, or that he had any knowledge of the commission thereof by member of his command"; and that the positive obligation of "failing to take action" was without prior legal precedent.[36] Justice Wiley Rutledge, in his supporting dissent, argued that there are no precedents for imputing "mass guilt" to individuals in cases "where the person is not charged or shown actively to have participated in or knowingly to have failed in taking action to prevent wrongs done by others.[37]

Gen. MacArthur confirmed Yamashita's sentence of hanging and issued a statement that articulated the ethical professional obligation of command responsibility, in keeping with the general antipositivist tone of the American war crimes program. It is worth repeating MacArthur's words, which should be familiar to any American soldier:

> The soldier, be he friend or foe, is charged with the protection of the weak and unarmed. It is his very essence and reason for his being. When he violates this trust, he not only profanes his entire cult but threatens the very fabric of international society. The traditions of fighting men are long and honorable. They are based upon the noblest of human traits— sacrifice.[38]

Trials under Control Council Law No. 10

On December 20, 1945, thirteen days after Gen. Yamashita's sentencing, Allied Control Council Law No. 10 established the basis for "the prosecution of war criminals and similar offenders," following the charges as previously outlined in the London Charter establishing the IMT. Justice Jackson's deputy, Gen. Taylor took over as chief U.S. prosecutor during this next phase of the trials. During the war, Taylor served as a military intelligence officer and was one of the leading experts of the organization of the German armed forces during the war. Taylor had the support of the military governor, Gen. Lucius Clay, and the Allied high commissioner John McCloy, who agreed with Stimson's view of the trials as integral to the construction of a new democratic Germany. These military trials, unlike those to be established in the Far East following the Yamashita trial, focused on trying military leaders for straightforward war crimes and avoided the more novel aspects of the IMT associated with the Bernays Additions, such as conspiracy to wage aggressive war and membership in criminal organizations. Between 1945 and 1949, the United States prosecuted twelve major trials under Control Council Law No. 10. Two trials, the High Command case and the Hostage case, left important legal and historical precedents regarding the concept of command responsibility.

The German High Command Case
(United States v. Wilhelm von Leeb et al.)

Between December 30, 1947, and October 28, 1948, Field Marshal Wilhelm von Leeb and thirteen other general officers were tried on four counts: crimes against peace; war crimes; crimes against humanity;

and conspiracy to commit crimes charged on other counts. Von Leeb, the senior defendant, served as the commander in chief of Army Group North on the Russian Front until he resigned on January 16, 1942, to protest Hitler's interference with the conduct of his command. The charges against von Leeb included participating in a plan or conspiracy to implement the Commissars Order, an illegal order for German forces to execute Soviet commissars and other Soviet Communist officials, and the Command Order, an illegal order for German forces to execute enemy personnel captured in areas to the rear of conventional combat operations. Von Leeb was acquitted of this charge because he was able to demonstrate that he not only did not disseminate the order but he openly opposed it. Like Yamashita, von Leeb's defense argued that he was unaware of the criminal actions carried out by his subordinates. Accordingly, the tribunal ruled that criminal responsibility did not attach to a commander "merely on the theory of subordination and overall command."[39]

Although the tribunal in this case qualified and somewhat narrowed the range of indirect command responsibility stemming from the Yamashita precedent, in that it held that "the responsibility is not unlimited," it also provided a more nuanced and detailed description of the affirmative duties placed on a commander. The tribunal ruled that a commander "cannot set aside or ignore by reasons of the activities of his own state within his area [of responsibility]" because he is "the instrument by which the occupancy exists." The tribunal also held that the care required for the civilian population in the area under the commander's control is "analogous" to the protections that a commander must provide for combatant prisoners of war. In sum, a commander either "must have knowledge" or be held criminally negligent in failing to prevent crimes committed by his subordinates. Although von Leeb was not found guilty under the principle of command responsibility for the execution of the Commando Order, he was found guilty of knowingly disseminating a similar order, the Barbarossa Jurisdiction Order that ordered German forces to summarily execute civilians.[40]

The Hostage Case (United States v. Wilhelm List et al.)

If the High Command case can be viewed as moving away from the standard of command responsibility laid down by the Yamashita precedent, the Hostage case, undertaken between July 15, 1947, and February 19, 1948, should be viewed as moving back in the direction of

Yamashita. Field Marshal Wilhelm List and eleven other defendants were charged with both direct and indirect responsibility for the executions of thousands of civilians in Greece, Yugoslavia, Norway, and Albania from September 1939 to May 1945, executions that were held to be "unjustified by military necessity."[41] Unlike the decision in the High Command case, the tribunal's ruling in the Hostage case was written in response to the prosecution's successful effort to deny credibility to the defendants' claim of ignorance regarding crimes committed by subordinates in their area of responsibility. Field Marshall List was shown to have been aware of the killing of civilians by his forces and to have failed to take any disciplinary actions or preventive measures. List also claimed that many of the crimes were committed by forces not under his direct command. The tribunal's ruling clearly upheld the concept of indirect subordination:

> [List] contends further that many of these executions were carried out by units of the SS, the SD [Sicherheitsdienst], and local police units which were not tactically subordinated to him. The evidence sustains this contention but it must be borne in mind that in his capacity as commanding general of an occupied area, he is charged with the duty and responsibility of maintaining order and safety, the protection of the lives and property of the population, and the punishment of crime. This not only implies a control of the inhabitants in the accomplishment of these purposes, but the control of other lawless persons or groups. He cannot escape responsibility by a claim of a want if authority. The authority is inherent in his position as commanding general of occupied territory.[42]

The defense claimed that List was not responsible for illegal reprisal orders that were neither issued by his superiors nor signed by him. The tribunal responded by ruling that an officer is bound only by lawful orders and "one who distributes, issues, or carries out a criminal order becomes criminal *if he knew or should have known* [my italics] of its criminal character."[43] Similarly, in contrast to claims based on legal positivism and political expediency, the tribunal reaffirmed the central just war principle of military necessity. Although it acknowledged that the customary international law in use during the period permitted the taking of hostages, the tribunal argued that the degree of retaliation against civilians by forces under the defendants' command were criminal due to a lack of proportionality (in some cases 100 civilian lives were taken for every German killed). Rather than shooting hostages "as a last resort," the defendants were shown to have conducted a "campaign of intimidation and terrorism as a substitute for additional troops." The judgment of the tribunal specifically noted that "the German theory of expediency and military necessity *(Kriegsraeson geht vor Kriegsmanier)* surpassed what was allowable under established rules of international law" and reasserted what it considered a correct definition of military necessity. Echoing *General Order No. 100* and Augustinian just war theory, it ruled that:

> Military necessity has been invoked by the defendants as justifying the killing of innocent members of the population and the destruction of villages and towns in occupied territory. Military necessity permits a belligerent, subject to the laws of war, to apply any amount and kind of force to compel the complete submission of the enemy with the least possible expenditure of time, life, and money. In general, it sanctions measures by an occupant necessary to protect the safety of his forces and to facilitate the success of his operations. It permits the destruction of life of armed enemies and other persons whose destruction is incidentally unavoidable by the armed conflicts of the war; it allows the capturing of armed enemies and others of peculiar danger, but it does not permit the killing of innocent civilian inhabitants for the purpose of revenge or the satisfaction of a lust to kill.[44]

Competing Standards of Command Responsibility

Although command responsibility was perhaps contemporaneously one of the least controversial tenets of the Nuremberg principles, there was not one uniform standard utilized throughout the Nuremberg era trails. The IMT was limited in its ability to apply such a standard by the need to simultaneously prosecute senior civilian government leaders and senior military personnel, neither of whose professional responsibility under the Third Reich could be neatly categorized as military, police, or (noncoercive) government functions. One legal scholar, L. C. Green, noted that the IMT was "only concerned with command responsibility in the most indirect fashion, holding the accused liable for having been parties to their framing [of orders], or for issuing or passing on of orders which were of general application."[45] However, the IMT did assist the later trials under *Allied Control Law No. 10* by determining in advance the criminality of specific German military orders. Unlike the IMT, the later trials were not hampered by the most controversial provisions of London Charter, those associated with the Bernays Additions that held individuals responsible for the crimes of collective human entities. Fortunately, the issue of member-ship of criminal organizations was made superfluous by the Allies' ad-ministrative program of *denazification.*

The Yamashita trial is still the most well known and authoritative of the Nuremberg-era trials because of the validation given it by a major-ity ruling of the U.S. Supreme Court. Consequently, the Yamashita precedent was cited as authoritative in the subsequent trials under *Allied Control Law No. 10.* The significance of the "Yamashita Princi-ple" has, however, been a source of debate between legal scholars. On one side, the writings of Telford Taylor, , Capt. Frank Reel (chief counsel for Gen. Yamashita), and Antonio Cassese (former chief justice of the International Criminal Tribunal for the Former Yugoslavia) have held that the Yamashita precedent represents an authoritative, clear, and un-ambiguously affirmative standard of indirect command responsibil-ity.[46] On the other side are conservative legal scholars who claim that the Yamashita trial has been misinterpreted as holding commanders responsible for their subordinate's actions regardless of the circum-stances or the preventive actions undertaken by commanders.[47]

Following the revelation of the My Lai Massacre of March 16, 1968, during the Vietnam War and the subsequent failure of the United States to hold its officers to the same standard that was applied to officers of the defeated nations in World War II, both Taylor and Reel compared the Yamashita precedent to the lesser standards applied to American offi-cers in Vietnam. Later, Justice Cassese based his view of the Yamashita precedent squarely on the working supposition that Yamashita was convicted for crimes for which "he had been kept entirely in the dark" and "could have done little to stop." Cassese utilized the phrase "indi-rect [command] responsibility" (as against the more emotive term "ab-solute" responsibility) and defined it as the culpability of military commanders "for crimes by forces under their command (or at least un-der their control), if they have done nothing to *prevent* or have not taken steps to punish these crimes."[48]

One of the most effective critics of the strict liability standard, Wil-liam Hays Parks, argued that many consequent lessons about command responsibility drawn from the Yamashita case are false and attributed to an "ill-worded opinion prepared *sua sponte* [i.e., on its own initiative] by the lay court," which consisted of a military jury of five American gen-erals "none of whom were lawyers." The High Command and Hostage cases, according to Parks, rejected the strict liability theory identified with Yamashita. Parks also noted that the High Command and Hostage cases have "greater value" for being the products of "judicial minds rather than lay jurors." Parks, now serving as the head of the Department of the Army's operational law division, also holds that Reel's facts were based on popular or bad history and points to the utilization of the word "permitting" in the statement of charges against Yamashita as implying that the tribunal believed Yamashita had had knowledge of the crimes with which he was charged. In his view, the Yamashita precedent is widely misunderstood and the conventional belief that Yamashita was condemned for offenses of which he had no knowledge is erroneous.[49]

The differences between the Nuremberg-era standards of command responsibility have also been utilized to document substantial societal and cultural biases to explain inconsistencies between trials of Europeans and those of Asians. As the Yamashita standard was again utilized in the subsequent conviction of another Japanese officer, Gen. Masaharu Homma, who was executed on April 3, 1943, for his responsibility for the atrocities that occurred during the Bataan Death March, Ann Marie Prevost has claimed that the higher standard of command responsibility utilized against the Japanese military personnel represents the application of a double standard based on racial and cultural prejudice.[50]

While it is not the purpose of the present study to make a legal argument as to the correct legal precedents to be ascribed to the Nuremberg era war crimes trials, a few observations cannot be avoided. First, whether or not one accepts the factual record provided by Gen. Yamashita's defense counsel, it is clear that no other Nuremberg-era trial was reviewed at a higher level of validation. Second, the U.S. Supreme Court, in both the majority and minority reports, clearly acknowledged that Yamashita was charged with crimes committed by his troops, rather than any crime committed directly by himself, regardless of whether or not he had knowledge of or ordered those crimes.[51] Third, in terms of official doctrinal development, the fact that the military panel that tried Yamashita was composed of general officers who were veteran combat commanders and not narrow legal professionals reinforces rather than delimits the significance of the precedent as a formal military-professional norm (as against a mere legal standard). And, finally, even if the High Command case can be said to represent a less rigorous standard of command responsibility, the Hostage case ruling moved back in the direction of Yamashita and toward the "known or should have known" standard that is now associated with current American military doctrine.

International Validation and Codification

The American war crimes program influenced every aspect of the establishment of postwar international institutions. In 1946, the UN General Assembly affirmed the Principles of International Law recognized by the Charter of the Nuremberg Tribunal. Later, other postwar international agreements were undertaken to formalize positions on various problems that were addressed in the preparation and conduct of the Nuremberg-era war crimes trials. As many of the crimes prosecutable under the London Charter occurred prior to declaration of war and were actions by governments against their own citizens, the 1949 Geneva Conventions codified the universality of certain central tenets of international humanitarian law to be applied regardless of the state of belligerency involved. Articles 1–3 of the four Geneva Conventions, also known as the "common articles," bound all belligerents to apply the affirmative obligations embedded in the articles at all times and in "all circumstances," including any "declared war or . . . any other armed conflict" and in all cases of occupation. These obligations appear in a core list of prohibitions under Common Article 3. The prohibitions, which must be upheld in the case of combatants and noncombatants alike, include:

   a. Violence to life and person, in particular, murder, mutilation, cruel treatment and torture.
   b. Taking of hostages.
   c. Outrages upon the personal dignity, in particular, humiliating and degrading treatment.
   d. The passing of sentences and carrying out executions without previous judgment pronounced by a regularly constituted court affording all judicial guarantees which are indispensable by civilized peoples.[52]

With the advent of the global calamity of World War II, noncombatants now comprised the vast majority of casualties in warfare. Accordingly, an entire convention, the Fourth Geneva Convention, was established for the protection of civilians. It included a total prohibition on the taking of hostages (Article 33).[53] Unlike the Common Article 3 prohibitions, however, the Fourth Convention provided no significant advancement in the protection of noncombatants. This was particularly in reference to protections from the aerial bombardment and other tactics utilized by the victors of the war. Also, like other treaties resulting from the initiatives of the International Red Cross (ICRC), the 1949 Geneva Conventions listed only the responsibilities of states (High Contracting Parties), leaving standards of individual and command responsibility to be addressed elsewhere.[54]

The Nuremberg experience in prosecuting crimes against humanity had a direct impact on development of Human Rights Law. Unlike the Geneva Conventions, the 1948 United Nations Genocide Convention, which the United States did not ratify until 1988, directly addressed both indirect and direct criminal responsibility.

> Article 1: The Contracting Parties confirm that genocide, whether committed in time of peace or in time of war, is a crime under international law which they undertake to prevent and punish [italics mine].

> Article 2: In the present Convention, genocide means any of the following acts committed with the intent to destroy, in whole or in part, a national, ethnical, racial or religious group, as such;
>   (a) Killings members of the group;
>   (b) Causing serious bodily harm to members of the group;
>   (c) Deliberately inflicting on the group conditions of life calculated to bring about its physical destruction in whole or in part;
>   (d) Imposing measures intended to prevent births within the group;
>   (d) Forcibly transferring children of the group to another group.

> Article 3: The following acts shall be punishable:
>   (a) Genocide;
>   (b) Conspiracy to commit genocide;
>   (c) Direct and public incitement to commit genocide;
>   (d) Attempt to commit genocide;
>   (e) Complicity in genocide[55]

Not all provisions of the American war crimes program received the same level of international validation. The concept of criminal organizations as originally included in the Bernays Additions was one of the more controversial aspects of the London Charter in that it set a legal precedent for guilt by association. Because the administrative denazification program superseded it, individual Germans were not prosecuted for merely belonging to a criminal organization, even though these organizations included such infamous groups as the SS, the SD, and the Gestapo (Geheime Staatspolizei).

The 1948 United Nations Universal Declaration of Human Rights

(UDHR) also contains principles that effectively mitigate some of the more controversial aspects of the Nuremberg-era trials. Regarding guilt by association, Article 10 required that anyone "charged with a penal offence" has a right to a public trial; and Article 12 required that, in lieu of a public trial, no one shall be subjected to "attacks upon his honor and reputation." Regarding the Nuremberg-era defense claims of ex post facto justice, Article 11 of the UDHR states: "No one shall be held guilty of any penal offense on account of any act or omission which did not constitute a penal offense, under national or international law, at the time when it was committed."[56]

Perhaps the greatest validation of the Nuremberg process took place in Germany itself. By August 31, 1955, the U.S. Army held over 281 German war criminals in custody. Peter Maguire, in his seminal work on the Nuremberg trials, *Law and War: An American Story*, documented that, by 1955, the U.S. Army at the behest of the government of Konrad Adenauer instituted a liberal parole policy that led to the release of 87 percent of prisoners held by the U.S. military. This increasing reluctance of American and German governments to enforce the sentences imposed on German war criminals in the 1950s, contemporaneously criticized by Telford Taylor, was a prime example of what Maguire termed "strategic legalism," the reinterpretation of law in the interest of the changing necessities of American foreign policy.[57] While certainly representative of both official American and German behavior of the first years of the cold war, it is not representative of the official West German conduct over the longer course of the cold war. In fact, the Nuremberg-era trials laid the foundation for the West German government's role in the conviction of over 992 German war criminals between 1958 and 1985, following the resumption of that nation's sovereignty. In 1954, Justice Jackson was prophetic in pointing to the significance of the fact that, "despite German dislike of the [Allied] war crimes trials, Western Germany has embodied in the Bonn Constitution its most basic principles."[58]

Unfortunately, the American tendency to not apply the standards developed by its own officials in the American war crimes program to its own nationals both during and after the cold war cannot be attributed solely to short-term foreign policy requirements. One might use the term "legalism of expedience" to describe this exceptionally duplicitous utilization of the conservative tradition of legal positivism to justify the lack of ethical reciprocity in the application of law. Additionally, it is

standards of individual and command responsibility, rather than definitions of aggressive war, that constitute the central meaning of Nuremberg. No in-depth study of the American war crimes program can
succeed, however, without also acknowledging the existence of the
other competing legacies of Nuremberg. Two major contenders for such
consideration are the outlawing of aggressive war and the rejection of
the tradition of legal positivism.

Of the three types of crimes listed in Principle 6 of the Charter of the
International Military Tribunal, standards of individual and command
responsibilities with respect to war crimes and crimes against humanity
have been incorporated into the four 1949 Geneva Conventions; the
Convention for the Prevention and Punishment of the Crime of Genocide; 1977 Protocols additional to the 1949 Geneva Conventions; the
charters for the International Criminal Tribunal for the Former Yugoslavia (ICTY) and Rwanda (ICTR); and the International Criminal Court
(ICC). Comparatively speaking, the charge of crimes against peace, also
known as planning or waging an aggressive war and associated with the
Bernays Additions, has received far less formal international validation
as an enforceable element of international law. [59]The crime of aggression has not, however, been forgotten by historians and other analysts of
the Nuremberg-era trials, especially by scholars outside of the military
profession.

Former Secretary of War Stimson, writing in *Foreign Affairs* in January 1947, admitted that the charge of crimes against the peace was the
most controversial and novel aspect the American war crimes program.
Nevertheless, he argued that the Nuremberg-era trials "affirmed the
central principle of peace—that the man who makes or plans to make
aggressive war is a criminal"; and this is a standard that places an obligation upon the American government to apply, in turn, to its own citizens.[60] One has to look at the Kellogg-Briand Pact of 1928, and the *jus ad
bellum* doctrine of traditional just war doctrine, to find the pre-
Nuremberg precedents for this charge. Yet, neither of these sources provide sufficient precedents for the adherents of legal positivism to accept
the charge of aggression as valid law.

Brig. Gen. Taylor, in an addendum in his *Final Report to the Secretary
of the Army* dated August 15, 1949, noted that the most common objection of contemporary critics to the Nuremberg trials was that "the act of
planning or waging aggressive war cannot be considered a crime because
there is not a single authoritative definition of aggressive war."[61] Taylor

tried to address the concerns of the critics of the charge by noting that all eight of the defendants at the IMT convicted of conspiracy to wage aggressive war were also convicted for war crimes and/or crimes against humanity, and that in the subsequent trials in Germany the charge failed against all military defendants.[62] The lack of such an authoritative definition in contemporary international humanitarian law was reiterated over a half century later in the final text of the 1998 Rome Statute of the ICC that included the caveat that, even though the Court has jurisdiction over the crime of aggression, it would not exercise such jurisdiction until the crime has been further defined.[63]

While crimes against peace have played a minimal role in American military doctrine, it often is a central theme for civilian critics of a governmental decision to utilize military force for the ends of state, especially when humanitarian concerns are included in a political justification of a particular military action. The result is a lack of shared reference in the discussion of what are in fact divergent Nuremberg legacies. Nevertheless, even the narrowly focused discussion of the impact of Nuremberg on military doctrine and professionalism must include clear delineations of these competing legacies.

Some critics, by considering the central premise of the Nuremberg trial as the outlawing of wars of aggression, understandably have declared the American war crimes program a failure and a "fallacy." Eugene Davidson followed this position when he argued that the Kellogg-Briand Pact "was invoked at Nuremberg as the legal cornerstone of the charges of committing war in violation of treaties." In mentioning the outbreak of the civil war in Greece, Davidson declared that in "the real world of hard events the dissolution of the principles enunciated at Nuremberg began even before the start of the trial [IMT]."[64]

Kranzbuhler, the defense council for Adm. Doenitz and one of the most detailed and nuanced detractors of the Nuremberg project, argued eighteen years after the trial that "Nuremberg was conceived, and can only be understood as, a revolutionary event in the development of international law." In spite of the presence of Soviet jurors, he considered the program trials as consisting of political trials in which a democratic system sat in judgment of a dictatorship. Kranzbuhler recognized two particular aspects of the trial's legacy as revolutionary: (1) the attempt to find a legal basis for the crime of aggression in the Kellogg-Briand Pact; and (2) the challenge to accepted legal premises that an individual "owes primary allegiance to the state" to whom he or she is subject. While he points to the continuing inability of the international community in defining aggression as evidence for the failure of the former, he recognized the latter was in certain cases the "necessary development" of law, specifically in the case of holding individuals responsible for crimes against humanity in spite of its being a "crime of government."[65]

In 1948, Quincy Wright, in his editorial comment in the *American Journal of International Law,* wrote that both the assumptions of the London Charter of the IMT and the later Charter of the United Nations are "far removed" from the underlying assumptions of positive law.[66] The positivist view holds that it is only the sovereign state that is subject to international law. The two central tenets of legal positivism—namely, (1) the "command doctrine" that for a law to be a law it must be posited by someone with authority who has the power to impose sanctions for noncompliance; and (2) the "doctrine of absolute sovereignty," holding that the highest body capable of executing such authority is the nation-state—were articulated in the nineteenth century by John Austin. In 1975, Stanley L. Paulson, a scholar of the philosophy of law, called the rejection of both the defense of superior orders and the tribunal's imposition of ex post facto laws a clear-cut rejection of classical legal positivist doctrines.[67]

Although the present study offers a somewhat narrowly focused analysis of historical developments, such as the Nuremberg principles, in the creation of military doctrine, it is nearly impossible to discuss the American war crimes project without addressing the central issues underlying much of the existing scholarship on the subject. The centrality of such concepts as the outlawing of aggressive war and the rejection of the tradition of legal positivism, as discussed above, is prominent in the existing, legally centered scholarship on Nuremberg because these issues have been so central to the *weltanschauung* of the legal scholars responsible for the majority of that scholarship. For example, scholars associated with the peace movement cannot be expected to comment on any aspect of Nuremberg without the influence of their "wider logic," or the view that Nuremberg was primarily a failed attempt to outlaw aggressive war. In the same way, it is not surprising that conservative legal positivists and others concerned with preserving state sovereignty view Nuremberg, which was in their view a historical anomaly, as a question about the overall legal significance of the trials.[68]

On the fiftieth anniversary of Nuremberg a conference was held at the Judge Advocate General's School, United States Army, in Charlottesville, Virginia. Maj. Mark Martins, the deputy director of the center, noted in his paper that although "no definitive list of Nuremberg principles will ever command unanimous academic support," the trials of military personnel exhibited a conservative focus on the more traditional war crimes charges, and that "Nuremberg's chief contributions to the preexisting body of international criminal law were in setting a standard by which commander's could be held responsible for the war crimes of subordinates [and in] rejecting the defense of military necessity and superior orders." The more "novel criminal theories," those of membership in criminal organizations and criminal conspiracy to wage an aggressive war (both associated with the Bernays Additions), have yet to be incorporated into official military doctrine.[69]

In 1946, Justice Jackson wrote an open letter, published in the leading professional journal of the U.S. Army, discussing the effect of the Nuremberg trial "on the profession of arms." In recognizing that the "armed services are naturally concerned as to what we are driving at in Nuremberg," Jackson reminded his readers that the ideas of Nuremberg "did not originate among theoreticians of the legal profession"; rather, they "originated in the War Department."[70] Specifically, the central tenets of command responsibility and superior orders started as a change in military doctrine, Jackson said, imposed by members of the U.S. military in U.S. military tribunals with U.S. soldiers carrying its capital sentences. It then received international validation and was reincorporated into U.S. military doctrine.

Jackson was a legal realist in the tradition of Oliver Wendell Holmes, a jurist holding an approach to law that views laws not as mere rules but as a body of precedents that were the result of an active, creative, and sometimes expedient process undertaken in the public's interest.[71] Jackson's purpose in his open letter to the American military profession was to convince members that there was nothing foreign to the U.S. military in what was created at Nuremberg. The tragedy for the profession is that, to date, the Nuremberg era "known or should have known" standard of command responsibility has never been successfully applied to an American defendant who has been or is presently a member of the military.

As remarked by Jackson, the standards of command responsibility imposed by senior officers of the United States Military on officers of the Axis Powers cannot be attributed to external influences. The fact that contemporary critics challenged the legitimacy of the Nuremberg-era

tribunals by labeling them victor's justice magnifies, rather than miti-
gates, later charges of institutional hypocrisy, for the victors have failed
to uphold their own standards in cases involving American officers. The
American war crimes program represented an unqualified shift in American war crimes policy. In the aftermath of the First World War, American policy reflected a conservative approach that emphasized legal
positivism and statist concerns over sovereignty. After the Second World
War, U.S. war crimes policy was drafted by the Department of War rather
than by international lawyers on loan to the Department of State from
Wall Street.

With the American war crimes program, the military profession can
be said to have regained control of the issue.[72] The major standards of
command liability associated with the major war crimes trials during
the Nuremberg period were present in the language of the 1956 edition
FM 27–10, which still represents current doctrine ("if he has actual
knowledge, or should have had knowledge").[73] The standards of command responsibility associated with the war crimes program were
drafted by the military, executed by the military, and codified by and for
the military. It could be said that the American military has made its
own bed and now has to lie in it.

The 1956 Edition of Field Manual 27–10

In July 1956, the Department of the Army issued its latest edition of
Field Manual 27–10 (FM 27–10), *The Law of Land Warfare*. This edition
constituted a comprehensive revision of the War Department's 1940
edition of FM 27–10 in that it incorporated material from the four 1949
Geneva Conventions and from the Nuremberg-era war crimes program.
The manual starts from a basic understanding of the laws of war as a set
of obligations placed on combatants regarding the protection of combatants and noncombatants alike from "unnecessary suffering," the
preservation of the "fundamental human rights" of same, and the facil-
itation or restoration of peace. Following the London Charter, the manual divides crimes into: (a) crimes against peace, (b) crimes against
humanity, and (c) war crimes. Following the language of the Genocide
Convention, it expands the field of crimes to include "conspiracy, direct
incitement, and attempts to commit, as well as complicity" as punishable offenses. It is the prevention of war crimes that is of particular concern to military professionals, and the new manual directly refers to

the Grave Breaches of the Geneva Conventions of 1949 as constituting a set of offenses that can be defined as war crimes.[74]

The manual was primarily the result of the efforts of Maj. Richard Baxter, a military lawyer. Baxter was to be later appointed as an American negotiator at the Diplomatic Conference on the Reaffirmation and Development of International Humanitarian Law Applicable to Armed Conflicts (1974–77), which led to negotiations that produced a pair of Protocols Additional to the Geneva Conventions of 12 August 1949 (hereafter referred to as the 1977 Protocols I and II). Baxter was later to be selected to serve as a justice for the World Court at The Hague. In a draft copy of the field manual, Baxter acknowledged his incorporation of the standard of command responsibility associated with the Hostage case and the Yamashita precedent.[75] The passage on the "Responsibility for the Acts of Subordinates" in the final version of the manual provides a clear description of an affirmative standard of both direct and indirect command responsibility:

> In some cases, military commanders may be responsible for war crimes committed by subordinate members of the armed forces, or other persons subject to their control. This, for instance, when troops commit massacres and atrocities against the civilian population of occupied territory or against prisoners of war, the responsibility may rest not only with the actual perpetrators but also with the commander. Such a responsibility arises directly when the acts in question have been committed in pursuance of an order of the commander concerned. The commander is also responsible *if he has actual knowledge, or should have had knowledge* [italics added] from reports received by him or through other means, that troops or other persons subject to his control are about to commit or have committed a war crime and he fails to take the necessary and reasonable steps to insure compliance with the law of war or to punish violators thereof.[76]

CHAPTER FOUR

The American Military Ethic in the Early Cold War

Democracy can be defended only by democrats.

THEODOR BLANK

Despite what Herr Blank had to say, a democratic state is better defended by a professional force than by democratic force.

SAMUEL P. HUNTINGTON

ON JULY 25, 1950, four years, six months, and five days after American soldiers executed his order and placed a noose around the neck of General Tomoyuki Yamashita, Imperial Japanese Army, General of the Army Douglas MacArthur was still serving as the Supreme Allied Commander in the Pacific. The forces under his operational control were now in the midst of fighting a new war on the Korean Peninsula. Over the past month, American forces were in full retreat as the North Korean Peoples Army (NKPA) pushed them into the southernmost tip of Korea, the Puson Perimeter. In attempting to create a viable line of defense against a superior enemy, U.S. Army personnel evacuated 500 to 600 villagers from their homes in the villages of Im Ga Ri and Joo Gok Ri and then drove them down a riverbank. The next morning, after being held overnight without shelter, the villagers were searched and subsequently directed down railroad tracks toward the town of No Gun Ri as retreating columns of American troops passed by. According to the January 2001 Department of the Army Inspector General Review of the incident, American personnel then ordered an air attack on the unarmed villagers, killing approximately 100 with aerial bombing and machine gun fire. The survivors of the aerial attack were then driven by American ground forces into two railroad tunnels. Over the next four days, American personnel, firing into both ends of the tunnels, killed approximately 300 more villagers.[1]

Just as in the case of Japanese forces under Gen. Yamashita during the American liberation of the Philippines, MacArthur's subordinate commanders were facing a chaotic situation that included extremely degraded communications. As with Yamashita, the levels of command with knowledge of the massacre could not, with certainty, be determined. Unlike the case of Yamashita, the massacre at No Gun Ri had a singular character that was not indicative of a wider or systematic lawlessness by adjacent units, and the number of victims was in the hundreds instead of the thousands. However, no contemporary comparisons between No Gun Ri and Manila are to found because, until the Associated Press broke the story on September 29, 1999, the cover-up of the criminal action at No Gun Ri had been successfully maintained for forty-nine years.

In the half decade between Yamashita's execution and the massacre at No Gun Ri, the American War Crimes Program, consisting of trials in Germany and in Japan, had run its course. Although it is impossible, based on the evidence, to make a determination as to whether MacArthur or his subordinate commanders could be found criminally liable for No Gun Ri, it certainly does not point to a rigorous reporting and prosecution of war crimes by MacArthur's subordinates. This inconsistency between official American words and actual American behavior was the first indication of what would become a chronic problem of internal consistency for the American military profession in holding its personnel to the same standards to which it held foreign military personnel at Nuremberg.

Formal institutional policies during the war and in the postwar period found immediate application in the military environment of the early cold war. The American military profession was more integrated into America society and culture than ever before. It was during this triumphant period of institutional standing that some American intellectuals, both military and civilian, would look to foreign models to resolve the inevitable civil-military tensions arising from the establishment of America's first permanently standing military establishment. Competing models of civil-military relations were directly tied to the institutional self-image and chosen worldview of American military professionals.

The institutional legacy and authority of the postwar U.S. war crimes program did not always comport with competing models and worldviews. In particular, as the Prusso-German model of civil-military relations was being rejected in Germany and yet embraced in the United States, the authority of the Nuremberg-era trials was itself standing in the dock of judgment.

The Nuremberg principles, largely the product of the U.S. War Department, received international validation by a United Nations General Assembly resolution in the very same month that the No Gun Ri massacre took place. This resolution also directed the establishment of the International Law Commission to "formulate the principles of international law recognized in the Charter of the Nuremberg Tribunal and in the judgment of the Tribunal, a process that would eventually lead to the incorporation of Nuremberg-era standards of command responsibility for war crimes into international treaties such as the 1977 Protocol I to the Geneva Convention and the Rome Treaty establishing the International Criminal Court.[2] Unfortunately, the United States would eventually decide not to ratify these treaties; nor would American personnel be held to the universal standard of command responsibility that they contained.

Formal and Informal Norms: A Civil-Military Dilemma

The National Security Act of 1947 reorganized the national military establishment from the historical bipolar structure of the Departments of War and the Navy into the triangular structure consisting of the Departments of the Army, Navy, and Air Force operating under the umbrella of the Department of Defense. The Department of the Army inherited the task of revising both the capstone doctrinal publications of the army—such as Field Manual 100–5, which linked military operations to national strategy—and the keystone, subject-specific doctrinal publications utilized across the services. One such keystone publication was the 1956 edition of FM 27–10, *The Law of Land Warfare*, which contained the Nuremberg-era standard of affirmative command responsibility as a formal norm.[3]

While ten editions of FM 100–5 would be issued between 1945 and 2000, the 1956 edition of FM 27–10 would remain in effect into the next century. Consequently, FM 27–10 would remain unchanged over the course of dramatic revolutions in war-making doctrine throughout the early cold war. During the Eisenhower administration, the U.S. Army adapted the "Pentamic concept" of operating on a nuclear battlefield in support of a national security policy centered on massive retaliation, as articulated in the 1956 and 1958 editions of FM 100–5. The Kennedy years saw the introduction of an army role in both conventional and nonconventional warfare as associated with the 1962 FM 100–5 in support of a national policy of flexible response.[4]

While it may appear counterintuitive that there was no doctrinal thread linking the laws of war to the peculiarities of modern nuclear and unconventional war, updating FM 27–10 was not included in the development of national capstone doctrine. The absence of changes may have given FM 27–10 an aura of timelessness and universality, but it also led operationally minded military professionals to regard the laws of war as a field of knowledge not directly relevant to the art of warfare, leaving it merely as a specialized discipline maintained by military lawyers and taught in law schools.

While estranged from national capstone doctrine, FM 27–10's authority as keystone doctrine was without question. Although it was a Department of the Army publication, FM 27–10 also functioned as the Department of Defense's keystone law-of-war publication, the other military departments issuing service-specific law-of-war doctrinal manuals that deferred to the army manual on issues of ground warfare and military occupation. The Department of the Navy issued a naval service doctrinal manual as early as 1944, but the newly created Department of the Air Force did not issue its own manual until 1976.[5]

The settling of formal professional norms in official doctrine does not, however, necessarily trump the influence of less formal factors on professional behavior and worldviews. Unlike formal doctrine, informal cultural and societal norms that influenced the opinions of members of the military profession in the early cold war years remained fluid. As the public reaction to the Nuremberg trial became infected by political partisanship, with Senator Joseph McCarthy and other conservatives coming out publicly against the trials, the officer corps, however apolitical, could not remain completely unaffected by the public debate. Even completely nonpolitical factors cannot avoid triggering informal professional attitudes. For example, the presence of civilian judges on the tribunals, which were otherwise run by American military personnel, provided an excuse for military professionals to look upon the rulings as norms derived from sources external to their profession.[6]

The breadth and scope of unofficial, negative military reactions to Nuremberg would be hard to quantify as military attitudes and opinions are not determined by plebiscite. Such opinions can, however, be gauged by their presence in authoritative semiofficial and unofficial publications. At the time of the sentencing at the International Military Tribunal (IMT) in Nuremberg and the Tokyo Tribunal, the editors of the *Army and Navy Journal* criticized the tribunals for initiating the novel legal proposition "under which professional soldiers, sailors and airmen shall be convicted as criminals on the mere grounds of membership in High Command or General Staffs."[7]

General of the Army and Army Chief of Staff Dwight David Eisenhower publicly acknowledged the authority of the IMT after reports surfaced that appeared to indicate ambivalence on his part toward the trials.[8] Justice Jackson, in his response to the criticism by the editors of the *Army and Navy Journal*, not only responded on the pages of that journal but published his own substantive defense of the trials, "The Significance of the Nuremberg Trials to the Armed Forces," in *Military Affairs*, a journal associated with the War College and with the Army Command and General Staff College.[9]

Military officers were also exposed to criticism of Nuremberg by nonmilitary officials and foreign policy theorists, especially those associated with early cold war political realism. George F. Kennan, a State Department official assigned as a lecturer at the National War College, was categorically dismissive of the American war crimes program. Observing that "the Allied Commanders had standing instructions that if any of these men [the Nazi leaders] fell into the hand of Allied Forces they should, once their intent be established beyond doubt, be executed forthwith," Kennan argued that it was impossible for trials to undo crimes of such magnitude, and that the inclusion of Soviet judges who carried out Stalin's purges made "a mockery" of the trials and any constructive purpose they may serve.[10]

Civil-military influences do not go in one direction only. If the 16.5 million Americans who served in World War II could be said to have democratized the armed forces, their influence also transformed American civil society as they returned to the United States as veterans. Unlike in Europe and Japan, the experience of World War II and the Holocaust did not set off a reaction against everything military within the United States. The Jeffersonian individualistic tendency to remain suspicious of government authority and institutions was, if anything, diminished after the war. In fact, Americans seemed more comfortable with government institutions than ever before, especially with the military. The historian William H. Whyte Jr., in a 1952 *Fortune* magazine article entitled "Groupthink," noted a major shift in American popular values from a libertarian distrust of institutions toward deference to them. Less than seven years after American judges and soldiers placed nooses around the necks of German and Japanese officers for carrying out orders (later deemed unlawful), Whyte noted a shift in American values from admiration for rebellion against the status quo to respect for individual submission to systems and institutions. This dilemma for Whyte was best exemplified by Herman Wouk's 1951 novel, later to be made into a major film, *The Caine Mutiny*, in which a group of young navy officers, just vindicated by a court-martial for their action in relieving an incompetent superior officer, are depicted lamenting their decision.[11]

It was in the midst of this unique postwar harmony between American citizens and governmental authority that America experienced its greatest civil-military controversy since the Civil War. The Truman-MacArthur controversy during the Korean War highlighted the issue of military obedience and civilian control of the military from a new perspective. After being fired as Supreme Allied Commander by President Truman for exceeding his authority, MacArthur articulated a theory of military obedience that extended the range of when it is permissible to disobey orders beyond the Nuremberg principle of not obeying criminal orders. Allowing a military commander to question civilian authority that went against a military commander's personal assessment of the national interest, MacArthur argued that a soldier's "allegiance and loyalty to those who temporarily exercise the authority of the executive branch of government" should be secondary to his or her allegiance to "the country and its constitution," and that military members must be free to "speak the truth in accordance with conviction and conscience."[12] As MacArthur was replaced by less controversial and better-disciplined officers, such as Lieutenant Generals Matthew B. Ridgeway and James Van Fleet, the Truman-MacArthur controversy continued to divide Americans both in and out of uniform.

The American military historian T. Harry Williams, in a 1952 article, "The Macs and the Ikes: America's Two Military Traditions," argued that the so-called Truman-MacArthur debate was just a manifestation of a historical conflict between two irreconcilable "traditions" of civil-military relations in America. The one accepting of direct civilian control of the military, exemplified by Generals Eisenhower and

Marshall, Williams termed "the Ikes;" and the one averse to civilian control, exemplified by Generals MacArthur and McClellan, he termed "the Macs."[13] Williams's concern over recurrent historical episodes of insubordination by leading members of the American military profession would be echoed by other eminent military historians. Russell F. Weigley, in his *Military History of the United States,* notes that MacArthur and his defenders exploited American "misgivings over limited war" to undermine the Truman administration.[14]

The Normal Theory of American Military Professionalism

Williams's thesis concerning an internal division between various leaders of the American military profession initiated the greatest debate on the proper civil-military relationship since the Civil War.[15] Eliot A. Cohen, professor of strategic studies at the School of Advanced International Studies, coined the term "normal theory" to describe a model of civil-military relations that rests on a "conception of professionalism" put forward in 1957 by Samuel P. Huntington in *The Soldier and the State: The Theory and Politics Of Civil-Military Relations.*[16] Distributed to officer candidates in an edited form and remaining on the U.S. Army Chief of Staff's professional reading list for over a half century, *The Soldier and the State* represents the most widely accepted paradigm of American military professionalism during the cold war. Huntington's book, therefore, provides an archetypal example of a publication that is both unofficial yet authoritative.[17]

   The book was a direct response to Williams's article on the Truman-MacArthur controversy that made a case for a conflict model of military professional development in which major military leaders conformed to either a democratic or an aristocratic military tradition. Huntington, in contrast to Williams, argued for a consensus model in which discontinuity exists between American civil society and the increasingly professional American military culture.[18] In his chapter "The Military Mind: Conservative Realism of the Professional Military Ethic," Huntington argues that professional officers maintain a distinctive and persistent *weltanschauung* (worldview) that molds and influences their attitudes and values. Throughout his scholarly career, Huntington has articulated various philosophies related to essentializing the differences between peoples and nations in the language of political conservatism, changing his intellectual foundations to keep pace with changes in the historical currents of American conservative thought.

Huntington designated the modern officer as a professional, in the sense that physicians and lawyers are professionals, owing to the officer's possession of the three distinguishing characteristics: "expertise, responsibility, and *corporativeness.*" The officer's *expertise* lies in his knowledge of the means of warfare. His *responsibility* concerns the management of violence, without the distraction of economic incentives and for a client who happens to be the state. His *corporativeness* results from his ability, or rather that of his profession, to act as an "autonomous social unit" in restricting entrance into the profession based on historically derived universal principles. [19]

The author's more recent writings include the 1996 work *The Clash of Civilizations and the Remaking of the World Order,* which provides a post-cold war model of global conflict that emphasizes civilizational markers between peoples. Similarly, Huntington's 2004 book *Who Are We? The Challenges of American Identity,* offers a rather straightforward defense of an American nationalism based on ethnic and religious homogeneity. Unlike these later works, *The Soldier and the State* emphasizes the centrality of ideological differences typical of the American intellectual and academic currents of the early cold war years.[20]

Huntington's claim of an autonomous worldview possessed by American military professionals, as enunciated in his 1957 work, fit well into the general intellectual current prevalent across postwar American society. Huntington was a contemporary of the Harvard historian Louis Hartz, the leading proponent of the conservative "consensus" school of American political history. Hartz's seminal *The Liberal Tradition in America* appeared just two years before *Soldier and the State.* In the latter, Huntington undertook to portray American society as possessing a persistent ideological bias. Like Hartz, Huntington interpreted American political thought as inherently liberal in the conservative Lockean sense of the term. For a liberal democracy like America to be adequately defended, its liberalism, which included a deep-seated antimilitarism, had to be counterbalanced, said Huntington, by institutions composed of individuals possessing the *weltanschauung* of conservative-realism, such as those belonging to a professional officer corps.[21]

Along with conservative, Hartzian consensus views of American political history, another academic tendency prevalent in postwar aca-

demia was the ascendancy of the "relativistic, social view of man"
inspired by anthropologists like Ruth Benedict. This interpretation
holds that individuals systematically internalize beliefs and norms of
the social and cultural systems in which they operate. Such an approach
fits nicely with William Whyte's conception of the postwar organization man suppressing his individual beliefs in favor of a wider "Groupthink." Whyte maintained that three interrelated ideas sustained this
"groupthink" phenomenon: (1) the relativity of morals and ethics; (2)
the prominence of the need for group harmony in the selection of behavior and opinions; and (3) the utilization of scientific methods for the
study of ethics.[22] Huntington's reduction, in *The Soldier and the State*,
of the proper *weltanschauung* of a military officer to an abstraction he
called "the military mind" is an ideal illustration of a hybrid blend of a
conservative political thought and cultural relativism.

To Huntington, the *military mind* is one that possesses a *conservative realism*, in that it "emphasizes the permanence, irrationality,
weakness, and evil in human nature. It stresses the supremacy of society over the individual and the importance of order, hierarchy, and division of function. It stresses the continuity and value of history. It accepts
the nation state as the highest form of political organization and recog-
nizes the continuing likelihood of wars among nation states."[23] Huntington then asserts a model of civil-military relations that complements
his essentialized distinction between military professionals and their
civilian superiors, in which a so-called objective civilian control of the
military, which maximizes military professionalism by minimizing
civilian interference, is preferable to a so-called subjective civilian control, which maximizes civilian control by constitutional methods.[24] To
do this, Huntington is forced to turn the famous axiom "war is nothing
but a continuation of political intercourse by other means" on its head.
I have already defined this revisionist interpretation of Clausewitz as
neo-Clausewitzian insofar as it inverts Clausewitz's axiom to read:
"political intercourse is nothing but a continuation of war by other
means"—or, in other word, by making foreign policy contingent on
military policy.

The most internally inconsistent aspect of Huntington's model is the
proportion of the American military that it excludes. Not only are
members of the Federal Military Reserve and National Guard forces ex-
punged, but noncommissioned officers and technical officers are
counted among the ranks of the nonprofessionals. In other words, the

vast majority of those who spend the greater portion of their professional lives in the American armed forces are counted out.[25] Huntington's views were antithetical to the value that American military
leaders during the Second World War, especially George Marshall,
placed in enlisted and noncommissioned officers.[26]

The ethical criteria placed on individual members of the profession
of arms found in traditional just war doctrine, in *General Order No.
100*, and in the constitutional oath mandated by Congress after the
Civil War are all extraneous to Huntington's conception of a civil-
military relationship, which he conceives merely as an alliance between a professional whose expertise is the management of violence
and a client who is none other than the state.[27]

The American Rehabilitation of the Wehrmacht

The most troubling point about Huntington's "normal theory" of military professionalism is that, one decade after the Nuremberg trials, it
generally replaced the democratic ideal of the citizen-soldier espoused
by George Marshall with one associated with the military traditions of
Prussia and Germany. Specifically, it challenged the basic Nuremberg
principle that prohibited the defense of superior orders except as mitigation. The disobedience of a soldier, as an example of which Huntington
cites the July 20, 1944, conspiracy by senior German officers to assassinate Hitler, automatically transfers the actor from the realm of military
ethics to the realm of the political. Looking at a case where a soldier is
asked to engage in genocide, Huntington provides the maxim: "As a
soldier, he owes obedience; as a man, he owes disobedience." Like Gen.
Alfred Jodl in the defendant's bench at the IMT in Nuremberg, Huntington placed the July 20 conspirators against Hitler beyond the pale of
military professionalism. This is not to imply that Huntington had any
sympathy for war criminals. Rather, it points out the two oppositional
visions of the military professional ethic, the one held by Huntington
and the one that the United States and its Allies held out to the military
leaders of the defeated Axis powers.[28]

Recognizing the "tragedy of professional militarism" in Germany,
Huntington argued "no other officer corps achieved such high standards of professionalism, and the officer corps of no other power was in
the end so completely prostituted." [29] However, Huntington went far
beyond the qualified statement of Gen. Eisenhower that the Wehrmacht

had not "lost its honor" despite the crimes of many of its leaders or even Justice Jackson's declaration that the "Wehrmacht was a far more decent organization than the more Nazified formations," such as the SS.[30]

The most authoritative historical critique of the German military profession, published in the early years of the cold war, was that of Telford

Taylor. Prior to serving as the chief U.S. prosecutor in the Nuremberg-era trials, Taylor served as the lead military intelligence officer specializing in studying the command structure of the Wehrmacht during the war. In his 1952 encyclopedic history of the German military leadership, *Sword and Swastika: Generals and Nazis in the Third Reich,* Taylor portrayed Germany's prewar and wartime military leaders as lacking the moral discipline to protect their own traditions and as choosing to become pillars of the Third Reich in the "perpetration of atrocities that beggar description."[31]

Taylor dismissed the claim that military leaders are "mere janitors of the military machine" with no interest in the political ends of state policy. Rather, the historical lesson of the German military's failure to stand up to Nazism is to be found in the "cardinal tenet of republicanism that the military are servants of the state, not an autonomous caste." For Taylor, it was not the military defendants at Nuremberg such as Field Marshal Keitel, but Gen. Ludwig Beck and the other General Staff conspirators in the July 20 attempt on Hitler who stood on the right side of military professionalism. Taylor ends his work by quoting Beck:

> History will indict the highest leaders of the Wehrmacht with blood-guilt if they do not act in accordance with expert and statesmanlike knowledge and assurance. Their duty of soldierly obedience finds its limits when their knowledge, conscience and responsibility forbid the execution of the order.[32]

Huntington was far from the only American scholar to challenge negative portrayals of the professionalism of the Wehrmacht such as Taylor's. In 1936, Gen. Albert Coady Wedemeyer, who would later serve on the war plans division in the War Department during World War II and later succeed Joseph Stilwell as commander of U.S. forces in China, attended the prestigious Kriegsakademie in Berlin for two years as an exchange student. He became acquainted with officers who later took part in the plot to kill Hitler, including von Stauffenberg and Gen. Beck, then serving as Oberkommando der Wehrmacht. In his final year in Germany, Wedemeyer was assigned to command a Wehrmacht anti-tank battalion in annual maneuvers. Wedemeyer was very impressed with the German General Staff system doctrine and other German doctrines, which he documented in a 147-page report: "Throughout the instruction at the Kriegsakademie and based upon my observations while serving with troops on maneuvers, I have been impressed with the thoroughness with which the military as a whole is being trained to seize and maintain the initiative. An aggressive spirit is being inculcated in the leaders of all grades."[33]

This report received a favorable notice by Gen. Malin Craig, the army chief of staff, by Gen. George Marshall, then serving as chief of the War Plans division, and by Secretary of War Stimson, who brought it to the attention of President Roosevelt. Wedemeyer served as a conduit for German historical doctrine, especially that of Clausewitz, reaching American military and scholarly professionals both before and after his retirement.[34]

In a 1947 article, the American scholars Edward A. Shils and Morris Janowitz asserted that the wartime officer leadership retained its neo-aristocratic social organization as compared to the SS, whose officers came mainly from the middle class and based their esprit de corps on nationalism and devotion to the Nazi cause.[35] Col. T. N. Dupay, one of America's most prolific military historians and head of the Historical Evaluation and Research Organization (HERO), published research that claimed the Wehrmacht displayed a combat effectiveness of 10 percent superiority over other Allied armies during World War II and 30 percent over British and American forces in the early years of the war. In his *A Genius for War: The German Army and General Staff, 1807–1945,* Dupay observed that the cause of Wehrmacht effectiveness was the fact "that the German Army, uniquely, discovered the secret of institutionalizing military excellence" and that the military was simply the "instruments of policy and the creators of the aggressive aims of their government."[36]

This positive view of the Wehrmacht also found an outlet in American popular culture with the release of the 1965 film "The Battle of the Bulge," produced by Warner Brothers. Made with substantial assistance from the U.S. Army, the film depicts a fictional account of a handsome, apolitical Wehrmacht officer in command of the armored spearhead during the Ardennes counteroffensive, the last German offensive in the western theater. In addressing the sensitive issue of the execution of American POWs at Malmedy in Belgium, this paragon of Huntingtonian virtues is shown lecturing his military superior on how war crimes are militarily disadvantageous because they stiffen enemy resolve. His superior responds by placing the blame for any atrocities on the presence of SS formations in the battle area. In actual fact, the officer who led the armored spearhead during the Ardennes counteroffensive was Waffen SS Gen. Josef "Sepp" Dietrich, who was tried as a war criminal for issuing the orders that led to the Malmedy massacre. The Hollywood rehabilitation of the historical record of this specific campaign and massacre symbolically illustrates the American rehabilitation of the Wehrmacht and the Prusso-German military tradition in general, especially among American military scholars.

What is ironic about all of these Germanophilic sentiments is that they were formally opposed by the modern German Army, the Bundeswehr. Theodor Blank, the first defense minister of the Federal Republic of Germany and an unlikely father of a professional army, was an anti-Nazi labor leader drafted into the Wehrmacht for six years, during which he earned a battlefield commission and the Iron Cross First Class medal for bravery. As head of a planning committee of liberal reformers known as the Amt Blank (which in 1955 became the Federal Republic's Defense Ministry), he provided the legislative foundation for a democratic army based on political integration.[37]

The Wehrmacht veterans leading the new army possessed personal experience of the rapidity with which the hyperprofessional German Army exchanged, in August 1934, its sworn allegiance to the democratic constitution of the Weimar Republic for servility to Hitler. The loyalty of the postwar Bundeswehr was to be based on *Innere Führung*, or "inner allegiance" to the democratic and constitutional principles of the republic. The army was to be organized on the basis of *Inneres Gefuege*, or the "inner structure," of a "democratic army" trained in the lessons of "the Third Reich, the 20th of July 1944, and Nuremberg" to ensure that the demand for strict civil control of the military is met. These doctrines of *Innere Führung*, and *Inneres Gefuege* were formal military doctrines formulated in the early 1950s by Gen. Count Wolf von Baudissin, and they were distinctly and intentionally in opposition to the Prussian civil-military tradition so dear to many American military scholars.[38]

Huntington took issue with Blank's assertion that "democracy can only be defended by democrats." Along with its external critics (i.e., Huntington), *Innere Führung* and *Inneres Gefuege* had to contend with a right-wing opposition within Germany itself. Early resistance to Gen. Baudissin was led by the SS veteran, Gen. Otto Ernst Remer, over the symbolic significance of the July 20 plot. Remer was the officer responsible for arresting the plotters. He then served as a subordinate under Sepp Dietrich in the Battle of the Bulge and became a leader of the neo-Nazi movement after the war.[39] In the late 1960s and early 1970s, Generals Ulrich de Maizière and Eberhard Wagemann fought off a "military counter-reformation" that was spearheaded, initially, by the conservative defense minister, Franz Josef Strauss. Despite successive conservative governments from 1982 to 1998, *Innere Führung* remains the orthodoxy of the armed forces of today's united Germany.[40]

The relationship between the Wehrmacht and the Third Reich, along with the former's conduct during the war and its continuity (or lack thereof) with Prusso-German military tradition, become a central issue in the *Historikerstreit*, or historians' controversy over German national identity in the Federal Republic.[41] Many German and other European scholars painted an even darker picture of the Wehrmacht than did Telford Taylor. Omar Bartov, in his *Hitler's Army: Soldiers, Nazis, and War in the Third Reich*, effectively debunked the claim that the Wehrmacht possessed distinctiveness with respect to the Final Solution, regardless of whether one sees that distinctiveness as based on class or tradition. Bartov also demonstrated that there was no plausibleness to the broadly accepted belief that the Wehrmacht maintained its fighting effectiveness and discipline through the worst wartime conditions, including retreat, owing to its maintenance of prewar traditions of military professionalism, especially within the officer corps. To the contrary, Bartov argued that the Wehrmacht was "the army of the people and a willing tool of the regime," especially in connection with the Final Solution on the Eastern Front. In fact, he agues, Nazi ideology legitimized the barbarism of the Eastern Front along with an unprecedented use of disciplinary terror, including thousands of punitive executions of German soldiers.[42]

In Germany, just as in the United States, public sentiment often clashes with formal doctrine. Between 1995 and 1999, the Hamburg Institute for Social Research rekindled public debate on the issue in a historical exhibition devoted to the crimes of the Wehrmacht,

"Vernichtungskrieg: Verbrechen der Wehrmacht, 1941–1944." In November 2001, about three thousand neo-Nazis held a rally to protest the exhibit's arrival in Berlin. Chanting "glory and honor to German soldiers," they were confronted with over 1,500 counter-demonstrators. A bomb exploded outside an earlier showing of the exhibit in the city of Saarbruecken in 1999 and was blamed on right-wing extremists.[43]

While the appreciation of certain aspects of Prusso-German military tradition, such as the general staff system, should not be taken as an endorsement of the Wehrmacht, the Prusso-German military tradition has received markedly different treatments on either side of the Atlantic. There was, in fact, a switching of legacies between the German and the American militaries during the second half of the twentieth century. In the United States, the emphasis on George Marshall's concept of the citizen-soldier was superseded by a renewed appreciation, at least informally, of the military professional caste, even in the context of a Prusso-German caste of merit. In the Federal Republic of Germany, on the other hand, the aristocratic legacy ending with the Wehrmacht was deliberately and formally exchanged for the ideal of a *democrat in uniform*. Both exchanged "usable histories," as it were, with the legacy of the Nuremberg-era war crimes tribunals being given separate weights by each of the competing *weltanschauung*.

Army Doctrine and the Vietnam War

The legacy of the Wehrmacht sparked two separate historical debates: one in Germany, where the central question concerned what military traditions and doctrines can be an appropriate part of and a *usable history* for the armed forces of a democratic state; and the other in the United States, where the issue was the proper model of civil-military relations in the conduct of ongoing military operations, and the question of when it is appropriate for a commanding general to second-guess civilian authority. At Nuremberg, the question of obedience concerned obeying illegal orders. In the Truman-MacArthur controversy, the issue of obedience concerned obeying the orders of civilians.

While American military professionals in Europe played out set-piece tank battle scenarios on old Wehrmacht training grounds, recovering their equipment in old Wehrmacht motor pools, and returning their troops to old Wehrmacht barracks, the myth of the Wehrmacht lived on. Along with the conflicts between official and unofficial models of civilian control over the military profession, it was part of the cultural baggage that the American military took with it to Vietnam. Actually, veterans of the Wehrmacht preceded American forces to Vietnam. Three years after MacArthur was relived of command, over 1,600 veterans of the Wehrmacht were among Gen. Henri Navarre's French forces as they were overrun by Vietminh forces under Gen. Vo Nguyen Giap at Dien Bien Phu in North Vietnam on May 7, 1954.[44]

As U.S. intervention in Vietnam escalated, two American armies with two separate doctrines deployed to Vietnam. Besides a European-focused mechanized army, the Kennedy administration ordered the creation of an American counterinsurgency capability. The Kennedy doctrine of "Flexible Response" was a reaction to the confining, Eisenhower-era doctrine of "Massive Retaliation," which limited the capability to respond to threats by means other than nuclear (or by threatening to use nuclear weapons). The new policy was officially inaugurated with President Kennedy's National Security Action Memorandum (NSAM) 2, the 1962 edition of FM 100–5, and the expansion of the Special Warfare Center (SWC) at Fort Bragg, N.C.[45]

An informal presentation of the new doctrine appeared in Gen. Maxwell Taylor's book, *The Uncertain Trumpet*.[46] Later serving as chairman of the Joint Chiefs of Staff (1962–64), Taylor was critical of the narrow "professional officer" and called for a realist version of the military professional that was closer to Marshall's idea of the citizen-soldier than it was to Huntington's Prusso-German-derived image. Although defining military service in terms of just war doctrine, Taylor accepted that, in most instances, "an officer has little choice but to assume the rightness of a governmental decision involving the country in a war." "If his side wins," added Taylor, "he knows that there will be few charges of injustice save from the vanquished; if he loses, the victors, following the precedent of Nuremberg."[47]

Rather than a mere expert on the application of violence, Kennedy's and Taylor's ideal counterinsurgent would be more of an ambassador of democracy. Gen. S. L. A. Marshall, the army's seminal official historian, also criticizes the overreliance on nuclear weapons and firepower during the pre-Kennedy years.[48] Both the actual careers of counterinsurgency experts like Sir Robert Thompson and Gen. Edward Lansdale (U.S. Air Force), and the fictional depiction of Lansdale-like characters in the Graham Greene's *The Quiet American* and William E. Lederer's and Eugene Burdick's *The Ugly American*, represented a view of early cold warriors as seeking to win Third World hearts and minds.[49]

In spite of the counterinsurgency initiatives of the Kennedy era, the majority of the leadership of the U.S. Army maintained its historical hostility to constabulary and counterinsurgency operations—even though the U.S. Army had extensive experience in carrying out such functions. This resulted in an army ill prepared to fight a counterinsurgency war or to properly deploy unconventional forces.[50] By the time Kennedy was assassinated, Army Special Forces Alpha Team deployments had been limited to training indigenous tribal militias such as the Montagnards of Vietnam's Central Highlands. Lansdale-like clandestine operators had been superseded by uniformed professionals flying in helicopters as "advisors" in air-mobility operations with the Army of the Republic of Vietnam (ARVN). By 1961, Taylor, along with Kennedy's national security aide Walt W. Rostow, returned form Vietnam with an assessment that the conflict should be regularized to the point of sending an 8,000-man task force to support ARVN operations.[51] On March 8, 1965, the first regular ground forces landed at Da Nang, the initial wave of an eventual 2.5 million troops.

As increasing organizational chaos overtook the American military during the Second Indochina War, many critics of the military policies of the Kennedy and Johnson administrations turned again to the legacy of the Wehrmacht as a positive example of an effective fighting force. During the war, the soldier-scholars Richard Gabriel and Paul Savage compared the conditions faced by the German Wehrmacht in World War II, which they claimed did not undermine the force's cohesiveness and effectiveness until very late in the war, to those faced by the U.S. Army in Vietnam.[52] Gen. William E. DePuy, U.S. Army, who would later take over the army's Training and Doctrine Command (TRADOC), had come to admire the Wehrmacht's efficiency as a combat commander in World War II.[53] He incorporated some German tactical doctrine in the 1968 edition of FM 100–5, the first post-Vietnam overhaul of army doctrine. Dupay also started the tradition at the U.S. Army Command and Staff College (CGSC) and U.S. Army War College (USAWC) of intensive study of the Wehrmacht's retrograde operations on the Eastern Front to provide lessons learned that could be applied to operations in defense of Central Europe (specifically with respect to an attack by Soviet and Warsaw Pact forces). That tradition lasted up until the end of the cold car. At the War College, the superiority of the German General Staff Corps over American staff models is still a popular subject for theses in military studies.[54]

If there was one element of Wehrmacht operations on the Eastern

Front that had direct relevance to the American experience in Vietnam, it was how *not* to conduct constabulary and counterinsurgency operations amid a hostile population whose language and culture is alien to the intervening force. The dark example of the Wehrmacht's counterinsurgency efforts seemed to have escaped the notice of one of its most devoted students, William DePuy, who was assigned as director of special warfare in the Office of the Deputy Chief of Staff for Operations and Plans in 1964 and later, after returning from two assignments in Vietnam, as special assistant for counterinsurgency under the chairman of the Joint Chiefs of Staff. America would go to war in Vietnam as if that conflict were the first in history to feature the problem of partisan irregular tactics. This historical amnesia would exacerbate problems such as discriminating between combatants and noncombatants.

CHAPTER FIVE

Command Responsibility and the My Lai Massacre

I don't think that what is done to a jap hanged in the heat of vengeance after World War II can be done to an American on an imputed theory of responsibility.

F. LEE BAILEY

ON MARCH 16, 1996, I went to the little village of Son My in Vietnam on the 28th anniversary of the My Lai Massacre, the event having been so named because American military personnel incorrectly labeled the village in which the atrocity occurred. After identifying myself as a U.S. Army officer out of uniform, I met and had tea with Phạm Thành Công, the government official in charge of the My Lai Massacre Memorial Park (Khu Chúng Tích Sớn Mỹ). Phạm Thành Công told me that he had been serving in a Viet Cong unit in the area of Son My at the time of the massacre, and then he described finding the dead bodies of his parents, siblings, and entire extended family upon returning to the village that evening. With the help of a translator, over the course of our tea he provided me with the most remarkable assessment of the massacre I have yet come across: "I know what happened here is not what the U.S. Army is about."[1]

It is just as important to note what Phạm Thành Công did *not* say in his assessment. He did not say that he considered the U.S. military intervention in Vietnam a noncriminal policy, although words to that effect were prominent on the museum grounds around us. Neither did he say that the My Lai Massacre was either a representative act or an aberration with respect to the U.S. war effort. By deferring to Phạm Thành Công, a victor in a war whose personal cost cannot be imagined by average Americans, I am intentionally attempting to move the discussion of the massacre beyond the decades-long debate over the characterization of the Vietnam War. While any wider examination of the historical significance of the Vietnam War must include the *jus ad bellum* premises behind American leaders' decision to go to war, such a discussion is beyond the scope of the present work. What is central to any analysis of the institutional breakdown of the American military profession during the period, however, is the *jus in bello* ethical consideration of American military tactics employed during the war, and their relationship to the specific actions of American personnel at My Lai.

Christian G. Appy, a leading scholar of the war, has argued that "atrocity was intrinsic to the very nature of the American intervention in Vietnam, that given the policy of fighting a counterrevolutionary war on behalf of a client state incapable of winning widespread support amongst its people, American atrocities were inevitable."[2] I would argue that such conditions also existed for the Wehrmacht forces serving in the Balkans, and that the standards of command responsibility held out to the leaders of these forces in the Nuremberg-era Hostage case are, therefore, appropriate to apply to American military leaders in the wake of My Lai. The fact that American officers were held to a lesser standard of command responsibility cannot be explained in terms of any distinction between the conditions under which separate criminal acts were perpetrated; rather, it must be explained in terms of the specific identity and/or nationality of the respective perpetrators.

The Vietnam War left the American military with two conflicting standards of command responsibility, a doctrinal standard and a standard representing the latest legal precedent. The Vietnam-era failure of America to hold its own citizens to the same standards it held out to its defeated enemies has contemporary consequences that includes the U.S. possession of a unilateralist legal precedent concerning command responsibility that conflicts not just with its military doctrine, but also with a developing international consensus in humanitarian law.

By the spring of 1968, conventional doctrine (i.e., the doctrine that conventional forces should be built up rather than specialized forces) had largely pushed aside what Gen. William DePuy called Kennedy's and Gen. Maxwell Taylor's counterinsurgency "fad."[3] Conventional American ground forces, rather than specialized counterinsurgency forces, were in the process of mopping up after their tactical victory during the Tet Offensive over both regular North Vietnamese Army (NVA) and Viet Cong forces, and they were now in the process of taking the war to those areas of South Vietnam that were friendly to or under the control of the Viet Cong. Much of what remained of the more covert, *Landsdalean* counterinsurgency operations was conducted by Army Special

Forces Alpha Teams in remote tribal areas and by Operation Phoenix under the CIA station chief, William Colby. Regular forces of the Army had now taken over the bulk of the counterinsurgency effort. The American military increasingly relied on superior firepower, rather than efforts at winning hearts and minds, to bring the war to the enemy. In the words of one of the leading military analysts of the war, Andrew F. Krepinevich: "The Army ended up trying to fight the kind of conventional war that it was trained, organized, and prepared (and that it *wanted*) to fight instead of the counterinsurgency war it was sent to fight," even if the Army's preferences *"maximize[d] the chances of killing civilians."*[4]

Developed for conventional and nuclear environments, rather than counterinsurgency, the standardized conventional tactical operation had become the deployment of airmobile light infantry forces, which was usually characterized by airlifting and insertion of nonmechanized conventional infantry units into a combat zone by UH-1 Huey helicopters. Aimed at depriving enemy units of support areas, these "search and clear operations" had become the norm in anti-insurgency operations by both the ARVN and American forces.

One such operation in the wake of the Tet Offensive was Operation Muscatine, which began on January 26, 1968. The purpose of this operation was to isolate areas of Viet Cong support. Named after its commander, Lt. Col. Frank Barker, the units assigned to Task Force Barker were charged with eliminating the base of support of the 48th Viet Cong Battalion around the provincial capital of Qua Ngai, a coastal city in the central highlands. The operation would have been dismissed as rather routine—except for an assault on a village labeled on American maps as My Lai-4 on March 16, 1968. Although the village included family members of the local Viet Cong forces that operated in the area, no military or insurgent personnel were found in the village, and the American forces sustained no casualties except for one self-inflicted injury. The summary findings of the official Department of the Army investigation, however, documented mass murder of civilians—between 175 and 400 of them—including "individual and group acts of murder, rape, sodomy, maiming, and assault on noncombatants."[5]

Although the "then existing policies and directives" in Vietnam were clear as to the laws of war and their requirements for safeguarding noncombatants and prisoners of war, soldiers in the units involved had not been adequately trained in the Geneva Conventions. The report also found that a criminal cover-up had occurred at "every command level within the American Division." Even command chaplains failed in their obligation to report the truth by, for example, sitting on the statements made by a scout helicopter pilot—Warrant Officer Hugh Thompson—who tried to halt the massacre and who flew several villagers to safety.[6]

The cover-up would be maintained for over a year. In the summer of 1968, one Maj. Colin Luther Powell, the future chairman of the Joint Chiefs and later secretary of state, was assigned as the deputy assistant chief of staff for operations in the 11th Light Infantry Brigade for his second tour of Vietnam. One of Powell's first tasks was to write a response to the Military Advisor Command, Vietnam (MACV) chief, Gen. Creighton Abrams, regarding charges made by an enlisted man, Tom Glen, claiming that members of the American Division had openly discussed violating MACV directives and the Geneva Conventions in connection with the treatment of Vietnamese civilians. In his cursory response in defense of his superiors, Maj. Powell wrote, "In direct refutation of this portrayal [Glen's charges] is the fact that relations between American soldiers and the Vietnamese people are excellent." The cover-up finally fell apart in the spring of 1969 when another soldier, Ronald Ridenhour, sent a letter to his congressman along with copies for other members of Congress and the press. This time Powell was unable to avoid the inconvenient truth.[7]

After commanding American forces in Indochina from 1965 to 1968, Gen. William C. Westmoreland was appointed to the army's senior position—chief of staff—where he would serve his final tour of duty before retiring in 1972. Considering that he was in command in Vietnam in March 1968 when the My Lai massacre took place, Westmoreland was surprisingly supportive of the subsequent investigations, and was responsive to the dark issues it raised in relation to the army's conduct of the war. During his command in Vietnam, Westmoreland stated that he received nothing but routine reports from the American Division regarding operations in Quang Ngai province in March 1968. He initially responded with disbelief to the claims made by Ronald Ridenhour, the former soldier who had written his congressman about the incident. But once the Army Inspector General's investigation substantiated Ridenhour's observations, Westmoreland never equivocated on the issue of the moral responsibility of those in command for failing to prevent and later covering up the massacre. For Lt. William Calley, the only officer the army succeeded in convicting for the massacre, Westmoreland felt "compassion but no sympathy."[8]

In November 1969, Gen. Westmoreland appointed Lt. General William R. Peers to head the official army inquiry into the My Lai Massacre. Westmoreland's choice of Peers, who was not a West Point graduate and who had career experience in nontraditional warfare, gave the investigation greater credibility than it otherwise might have had. Peers had direct command experience in insurgent and guerrilla operations in Burma between 1943 and 1945, and in covert operations with the OSS in China and Korea before being assigned to the CIA in 1949. He stood in stark contrast to many of the senior officers, such as Generals Fred C. Weyend, Edward C. Meyer, and William E. DePuy, who were assigned to counterinsurgency operations and planning in the Office of the Joint Chiefs during the Vietnam War period even though they did not possess a background in counterinsurgency operations. Westmoreland provided Peers with the authority he needed to carry out a competent investigation. Immediately prior to appointing him, Westmoreland successfully resisted pressure, originating in the Nixon White House, to conduct a watered-down investigation. Westmoreland personally informed Peers that he had called Gen. Alexander Haig, special assistant to the president, to Westmoreland's Ft. Myers home to relay an ultimatum to the White House to back off on the My Lai investigation, for if "resistance did not cease" Westmoreland would take the issue directly to the president under his charter as army chief of staff.[9]

Westmoreland received the explosive finding of the Peers Commission report on March 17, 1970. As if the grisly accounts of U.S. Army personnel committing depraved acts of "rape, sodomy, and maiming" before murdering their victims were not enough, the report revealed that these acts occurred in one of the most supervised company-level operations in American military history. Gen. Peers implicated twenty-eight officers, from the ranks of second lieutenant to major general, in the cover-up; the most senior officer, Maj. Gen. Samuel W. Koster, was serving as Commandant of West Point at the time of the report's release. Most damning of all, the Peers report listed preexisting and ongoing attitudes among commanders and staff that contributed to the massacre and its cover-up. These included a "permissive attitude toward the treatment and safeguarding of noncombatants," a climate of racial animosity toward the Vietnamese, and a pervasive willingness among officers to commit perjury in order to protect their superiors.[10]

The Peers Commission and American Military Justice

Although the Nixon administration received numerous requests to establish a special or presidential committee to investigate and prosecute the Americans charged with war crimes at My Lai, the U.S. Army was instead given the chance to validate the integrity of its own judicial process. It failed. Two individuals, Lt. William Calley and Sgt. David Mitchell, were charged respectively with murder and intent to murder following the completion of an initial Inspector General's investigation and the launch of a Criminal Investigation Division (CID) inquiry in June 1965. By the time the findings of the Peers Commission were announced, charges were proffered against two more company-grade officers, including Calley's company commander, Capt. Ernest Medina, and an additional five enlisted men. By this time, of the thirty-three soldiers implicated by the army in the massacre, nineteen were already civilians. The first official American failure to adhere to its own Nuremberg-era precedents was a national rather than a military failure, as neither Article 18 (jurisdiction) nor Article 29 (absence from the military) of the Uniform Code of Military Justice was utilized to return these civilians to uniform for court-martial, and the U.S. Congress did not have the political will to pass enabling legislation to try them as civilians.[11]

The Investigation Subcommittee of the Armed Services Committee the U.S. House of Representatives held hearings on My Lai concurrently with Peers's investigation. Rather than facilitate the army investigation, the committee, chaired by F. Edward Hebert, chose to use its authority to obstruct the application of military justice. Army pilot Hugh C. Thompson, former Specialist Lawrence Colburn, and Specialist Glenn Andreotta, who was killed in action twenty days after the massacre, were crew members of an H-23 reconnaissance helicopter. On the day of the massacre they tried to stop the killings, removed what civilians they could from the path of the rampaging American forces, and reported the crime to their superiors. Testifying before the subcommittee on April 17, 1970, Thompson and Colburn, who were now the chief prosecution witnesses for the government, were intimidated and browbeaten on every detail of their testimony. Rather than the massacre itself, Congressman Herbert and the committee's legal counsel were fixated on (1) the possibility that Thompson ordered Colburn to shoot American soldiers if they continued killing women and children; (2)

the possibility that the level of hostile fire cited on awards processed for Thompson, Colburn, and Andreotta, initiated after the death of the latter, may have been exaggerated; and (3) baseless suggestions that Thompson might be at fault for initiating the massacre by popping the wrong colored smoke grenade to mark the location of civilians needing evacuation.[12] When Capt. Medina, however, provided what he later admitted to be perjured testimony, claiming he was not aware that a large number of civilians were killed on the day of the massacre or of the existence of an investigation immediately after it, he was treated with the utmost deference by Hebert and the committee.[13] With Congress, the White House, southern governors, the American Legion, the Veterans of Foreign Wars, and American public opinion turning against the idea of prosecuting Americans for war crimes, the army was left on its own to uphold its doctrinal standards in the case of My Lai.[14] The first court-martial, that of Sgt. David Mitchell, was compromised by the Hebert Committee's refusal to declassify the testimony of Thompson and other aviators who testified before in Congress. The case therefore ended in an acquittal.[15]

Lieutenant Calley and the Defense of Superior Orders

On November 20, 1970, three days before Sgt. Mitchell's acquittal, Lt. Calley's court-martial was convened at Fort Benning, Georgia. His defense would be simple: Calley, the baby-faced platoon leader who did not understand what all the fuss was about, claimed to have had permission to kill civilians. The defense theory was equally simple: the denial of historical, legal , and doctrinal precedents and principles—as if there never had been Nuremberg-era tribunals and as if Field Manual 27–10 did not exist. Calley's claim of superior orders incriminated another defendant and witness, namely, his commander, Capt. Medina. This claim became the central issue at Calley's trial. The military judge, Lt. Col. Reid W. Kennedy, while not accepting that the defense had met the burden of demonstrating that Calley had received an illegal order from his commander, dismissed the defense's theory in the case by instructing the jury that the lieutenant could not be relieved of responsibility even if the existence of such an order were proven:

> Soldiers are taught to follow orders, and special attention is given to obedience of orders on the battlefield. Military effectiveness depends on obedience to orders. On the other hand, the obedience of a soldier is not

the obedience of an automaton. A soldier is a reasoning agent, obliged to respond, not as a machine, but as a person. The law takes these factors into account in assessing criminal responsibility for acts done in compliance with illegal orders.

The acts of a subordinate done in compliance with an unlawful order given him by his superior are excused and impose no criminal liability upon him unless the superior's order is one which a man of ordinary sense and understanding would, under the circumstances, know to be unlawful, or if the order in question is actually known to the accused to be unlawful.[16]

The American military profession was able at least to uphold one of the major legal precedents of Nuremberg, that is, that superior orders are no defense for war crimes. Calley was sentenced to life imprisonment for premeditated murder. After this first successful trial arising out of the My Lai massacre, the army was subjected to pressures, mostly from outside the military profession, to limit or stop further My Lai prosecutions. The subsequent failure to convict other subordinate soldiers and the lenient treatment, by the Nixon and Ford administrations and the federal courts, of Calley, who ended up serving only three and a half months in a military prison, were an embarrassment not merely for the profession, but for the nation. Herbert Rainwater, the national commander of the Veterans of Foreign Wars (VFW), objected after Calley's conviction that, "There have been My Lais in every war. Now for the first time in our history we have tried a soldier for performing his duty."[17] A study on American public opinion by the sociologists Herbert Kelman and Lee Lawrence, found that 70 percent of the American public disapproved of the Calley conviction following his trial.[18] Considering that it was the American Legion's reaction to the 1944 Malmedy Massacre (Battle of the Bulge) of seventy American POWs by Nazi troops that fostered political support for the establishment of the post-World War II American war crimes program, and *not* the murder of over eleven million noncombatants by the Axis, it is clear that American have shown a consistent disposition to weigh with prejudice the worth of lives of non-Americans vis-à-vis the lives of Americans. American military professionals have always had to be on guard against allowing this ugly aspect of the American character to significantly affect their profession. With the case of My Lai, the United States permitted an unfortunate exception to the precept that a nation's armed forces should be a reflection of the society it protects.[19]

It is to the American military profession's credit that those most outraged by My Lai and the leniency shown to Calley were not members of the peace movement or politicians or even such future human rights luminaries as the sitting governor of Georgia, Jimmy Carter, who defended Calley, but soldiers in uniform. Those who voiced their outrage included Hugh Thompson, who placed his crew between the murder and the victims and threatened to shoot Calley; Col. William C. Wilson and Lt. Gen. William R. Peers, who exposed the cover-up; and Capt. Aubrey Daniel, Calley's prosecutor, who publicly denounced President Nixon's interventions in support of Calley.[20] In the end, the relief Calley eventually received from his sentence was the result of administrative actions by civilian officials, first by the president and then by the secretary of the army. The uniformed military could at least point to the integrity of some of their comrades in uniform in not allowing the superior orders defense. This would, however, not be the case as far as holding Capt. Medina to the same standard of command responsibility as that employed in the Nuremberg-era tribunals.

Capt. Medina's Responsibility

In August 1971, five months after the conviction of Calley, two court-martials were convened to try Calley's commanding officer, Capt. Medina, and the former commander of the 11th Brigade of the American Division, Col. Oran K. Henderson. The trials were held simultaneously, with the former at Fort McPherson in Georgia and the later at Fort Meade in Maryland. Between these officers in the chain of command was Lt. Col. Frank Barker, the commander of Task Force Barker who was killed in a helicopter crash four months after the massacre. Rather than a conspiracy protecting Gen. Westmoreland and President Johnson, it was the death of Barker that left the evidentiary gap that impeded further prosecution up the chain of command. Barker remains a missing and mysterious link in understanding the operation and the sequence of events by which the massacre took place. Although command helicopters of two higher commanders in the chain of command flew above his, he was the counterinsurgency mastermind of Operation Muscatine who gave only informal briefings and left no paper trail. Medina claimed it was Barker who ordered him to "destroy the village, to burn the houses, to destroy the food crop that belonged to the Vietcong, and to kill their livestock." The Bravo Company commander, Capt. Earl A. Michles, responsible for another platoon taking part in the massacre, was also deceased. Medina denied Barker had ordered him to kill civilians. In fact, Medina testified before the Hebert Commission that as "far as Colonel Barker's attitude toward the South Vietnamese, he always wanted us to treat them with proper respect, and to respect them as human beings."[21] As a result of the prosecution's inability to verify Medina's testimony concerning his orders from Barker, no direct responsibility for an illegal order for the massacre itself could be applied to any officer higher in the chain than Capt. Medina.

Unfortunately, it would be the court-martial of Medina that would define the contemporary standard of command responsibility, at least as far as the standard successfully imposed on an American citizen is concerned. The Peers Commission's findings concerning Medina, the sole surviving direct subordinate of a task force commander whose orders were a subject of dispute, were comprehensive. They included, like those for Barker, Henderson, and others above him, information that Medina had suppressed evidence; and, like those for Calley and others below him, information that he had directly ordered and in fact engaged in criminal acts. As the senior commander remaining continually on the ground, Medina was held responsible by the commission for planning, ordering, and supervising "the execution by his company of an unlawful operation against inhabited hamlets in Son My Village which included the destruction of homes by burning, killing of livestock, and the destruction of crops and other foodstuffs, and the closing of wells; and directed the killing of any person there."[22]

By the time of his arraignment, most of these specifics had been dropped against Medina through what the prosecution claimed to be the custom of dropping lesser charges to concentrate on greater charges.[23] The chief prosecutor in the case, Col. William G. Eckhardt, would later write that at the time of the trial the prosecution did not believe that Medina, during his briefing to his company the night before the operation, "intentionally ordered his men to kill unarmed, unresisting, noncombatants." Rather, Eckhardt conceived Medina's involvement as a "classic case of command criminal responsibility" in which the captain had "actual knowledge" that his men were killing unresisting noncombatants and that he had the "communications ability" to ensure that the killing stopped. For three hours, it was stated, Medina was in an area less than ten square kilometers wide in direct proximity with his troops. According to the prosecution's theory of the case, Medina refused to face the obvious evidence of a one-sided firefight because his loyalty was to his career rather than to his immediate duty.[24]

Along with two military attorneys, representation for Medina was supplied by the flamboyant and theatrical F. Lee Bailey. The defense's theory of the case contended that Medina stayed out of the village because of tactical necessity and that he "never became aware of the misconduct of his men until too late." Further, "upon suspecting that his orders were being misunderstood and improper acts [were] occurring, he ordered his men to cease fire [and he] never saw any evidence of suspicious or unnecessary deaths until immediately prior to the cease fire order."[25]

The most critical, precedent-setting event of the trial was the instructions the military judge gave regarding the law concerning what standard of command responsibility the panel (jury) would utilize in considering guilt. The *Prosecution Brief on the Law of Principles* quoted directly from current military doctrine, specifically the paragraph of FM 27–10 on "the Responsibility for the Acts of Subordinates" in which the "known or should have known" standard was articulated.[26] In complete contradiction to the Nuremberg precedent, the military judge instructed the jury that it must establish that Medina possessed "actual knowledge."[27]

Although the prosecution had indeed believed that Medina "knew precisely" what was taking place while the massacre was in process, Medina's acquittal cannot be understood simply as a failure to present sufficient prosecutorial evidence.[28] The military judge's instruction retains the value of precedent regardless of the jury's determination of guilt. The elimination of the phrase "should have known," included in both FM 27–10 and the Opinion and Judgment of the U.S. military tribunal at Nuremberg in the Hostage case, created a new legal standard. In the case of the latter, the phrase "should have known" related to the ability of a commander or staff officer to comprehend the illegal character of an order and the likelihood that dissemination of such an order would result in criminal acts.[29]

Unlike the Hostage case, the Medina precedent creates the possibility that American military commanders could, in the future, avoid being held negligent even in cases where the outcomes of military orders or permissive command climates could be predicted. A year after Medina's trial, one legal analyst wrote that the "actual knowledge test, in a context like My Lai, is an invitation to see and hear no evil."[30] Both Medina and Henderson were, for short periods, on the ground at My Lai in direct proximity to a ditch filled with hundreds of victims after receiving a radio inquiry into possible executions of civilians. If Medina and Henderson had intentionally avoided looking down into the ditch to avoid seeing what they suspected was there, their act of cowardice was rewarded by Judge Howard's novel standard of command responsibility, which abandoned the "should have known" criterion. In an article in the *New York Times* that same year, the American chief prosecutor in the Hostage case, Telford Taylor, argued that the "actual knowledge" requirement in the military judge's instructions to the jury was a directed order for Medina's acquittal. That acquittal took place on September 22, 1971.[31]

On December 17, 1971, Col. Henderson too was found not guilty of being a party to the cover-up and of lying to the Peers Commission. In the nation's newspaper of record, this last My Lai trial ended in the midst of well deserved mockery regarding the inability of careerist officers to recall the actions and statements of their superiors and peers.[32] There are, however, other factors to consider in looking at the failures of the later My Lai trials: the compromising of witnesses by testimony and arrangements made in the earlier trials; witnesses compromised by shrewd legal maneuvers in trial or while awaiting trial, especially in the Medina trial; and, most important, the death of key members of the command, such as task force commander Col. Barker.

There are also factors that cannot be excused, such as the greater likelihood of a defendant being acquitted by a jury of his so-called peers with whom he shares such distinguishing characteristics as rank, race, region, and, above all, nationality. Any officer with combat experience was likely to feel some sympathy for Medina and Henderson in a number of areas: (1) the wretched intelligence briefing by the task force intelligence officer, Capt. Eugene M. Kotouc, indicating that Vietnamese noncombatants would magically disappear from the hamlet when the clock struck 7 a.m.; (2) that Medina and Henderson may have been briefed by Barker about how, against all army doctrine, the task force was about to engage a VC battalion larger in size than the attacking American forces; and (3) that the company had suffered a casualty, albeit a single one, in the days prior to the operation. It takes more than a small amount of courage for officers to turn their heads to look, or admit to looking, into ditches containing bodies that demonstrate the extent to which they had lost control of their subordinates during a combat operation.

Considering the lack of successful convictions based on command responsibility in the My Lai trials, the U.S. Army's decision not to acquiesce to Gen. Taylor's call to convene a special war crimes tribunal, as in the Nuremberg-era trials, was obviously a mistake.[33] When asked during an Army War College oral history program interview prior to his retirement if he thought the army's legal effort had adequately enforced his commission's findings, Gen. Peers bemoaned the fact that so many offenses listed in his report were never brought to trial and were instead dealt with administratively:

> I think they [the administrative actions] were totally inadequate. These sentences were so mild, that in a way it simply says that we don't like this kind of activity but in a way condone it. I believe the Army Corps, the Officers Corps, and the NCO Corps and the American public would have been better satisfied if those people had been brought to trial. Now, if they were found not guilty that is one thing, but I am not sure they would have been found not guilty. And I think it would have provided a much better precedent for something that may happen in the future. Now that we have this precedent, I would ask, if we have another conflict, what the hell are we going to do with the people who commit war crimes or related actions?

When asked whether the army put its "best foot forward" in the individual cases that made it to trial, Peers responded he did not feel that the army had adequately manned either the prosecution teams or the members of the court-martial itself, especially in consideration the defense had lawyers of the caliber of F. Lee Bailey with major staffs to support of the defense's case.[34]

The most fundamental legacy of the My Lai trials was the severance of the doctrinal standard of command responsibility from the contemporary legal precedent associated with the Medina court-marshal. Nowhere is the significance of this discontinuity better expressed than in the racist comment by Medina's attorney, F. Lee Bailey: "I don't think that what is done to a jap hanged in the heat of vengeance after World War II can be done to an American on an imputed theory of responsibility."[35]

The Taylor Thesis

On January 6, 1971, Dick Cavett introduced an unusually serious guest on his television talk show, which was otherwise known for lighthearted banter with celebrities. This guest was a very somber Telford

Taylor. In the wake of the convening of the Calley court-martial two months earlier, Taylor stated, in reference to a book he just authored, *Nuremberg and Vietnam: An American Tragedy,* that if Dean Rusk, Robert McNamara, McGeorge Bundy, Walt Rostow, and 'Gen. William Westmoreland were tried for war crimes under the same standards applied in the case of Gen. Yamashita at the Tokyo Tribunal, they would likely "come to the same end" as the Japanese general. Carried the next day in the *New York Times,* the quote became a critical weapon to those claiming that the U.S. intervention in the Second Indochina War was criminal.[36]

Through the course of the My Lai trials, Taylor authored one book and wrote three editorials for the *New York Times* that addressed the Vietnam war in general and My Lai in particular in the context of the Nuremberg-era war crimes trials. His first article, printed on January 10, 1970, discussed the wider conduct of the war, especially the bombing campaigns, and discussed the concept of command responsibility in the context of the Yamashita standard. He accepted the premise of Yamashita's defense as articulated in the U.S. Supreme Court ruling, namely, that Yamashita, as a commander, was condemned to death "not for what he himself did, but for failing to give and enforce orders to check the excesses of his troops." His second article, on November 21, 1970, came out on the fourth day of the Calley trial, which went unmentioned in the text of the article. For this article, Taylor had gained access to an abridged release of the Peers Report. He noted that the environment and the assets available to the U.S. military command in Vietnam were far more favorable than what was experienced by the German army in occupied Europe and called for the creation of special military tribunals to try the My Lai cases so as to ensure that Americans accused of war crimes would be handled in the same manner as foreigners were handled by Americans in the Nuremberg-era trials. His 1970 book, *Nuremberg and Vietnam,* provides a more detailed exposition of themes addressed in his *Times* articles. After a two-year break, Taylor followed up with a final *Times* entry. Printed on February 2, 1972, after the acquittal of Capt. Medina, Taylor's article addressed the general failure of the My Lai prosecutions to enforce the standard of command responsibility found in both army doctrine and the Nuremberg and Tokyo tribunals. [37]

It was not in his articles, book, or even in the numerous panels on the war in which he participated or chaired that Taylor articulated the "come to the same end" thesis, however. This so-called Taylor thesis, rather, was based on a poorly summarized statement attributed to Taylor by the journalist Neil Sheehan in a January 9, 1971 *Times* article under the caption "Taylor Says by Yamashita Ruling Westmoreland May Be Guilty." Sheehan interviewed Taylor after being granted pre-broadcast access to a screening of a taped episode of the Dick Cavett Show. The journalist misleadingly summarized Taylor's statement regarding Westmoreland in the first line of the article: "Telford Taylor, former Chief prosecutor at the Nuremberg trials, has declared that Gen. William Westmoreland, the Army Chief of Staff, might be convicted as a war criminal if war crimes standards established during World War II were applied to his conduct of the war in Vietnam."

However, later in the article Sheehan paraphrases the Cavett-Taylor dialogue as follows:

> Taylor: Well I certainly suggest very strongly in the book, and would be quite prepared to say it a little more explicitly, that if you apply to the people you've mentioned [or to the high commanders at Nuremberg] like General Westmoreland, if you were to apply to them the standards that were applied in the trial of General Yamashita, there would be a very strong possibility that they would come to the same end as he did.
>
> Cavett: Then you imply they would be found guilty?
>
> Taylor: Could be found guilty. It was not the purpose of the book to say that "X" is guilty, or "Y" is guilty or "Z" is guilty. That's for some court to decide if you have the evidence there and look at it. But it is the function of the book to say that these principles were applied before and if you applied them now, such and such results might follow. And the American people cannot face their own past and cannot face the principles that they laid down and applied to Germans and Japanese unless they're to have the principles work the other way. [38]

It is obvious from both Taylor's actual words in the interview and in his published writings that he never tried to put forward a factual case against Westmoreland. Taylor's words, in reference to My Lai specifically or the conduct of his command of U.S. ground forces in Vietnam in general, never directly equated the words or actions of Gen. Yamashita during the Japanese defense of the Philippines to Westmoreland's conduct in Vietnam. In fact, in his 1970 article, Taylor admitted lacking any detailed knowledge of the My Lai Massacre, the event having been "obscured by the fog of war." In fact, Taylor characterized the military directives issued by Westmoreland's command regarding the humanitarian treatment of the Vietnamese as "impeccable."[39] In his book, Westmoreland is scarcely mentioned by Taylor except to make two separate and distinct points: (1) Westmoreland certainly possessed superior assets to monitor and supervise the activities of his forces, unlike Gen. Yamashita; and (2) Westmoreland could be identified as a supporter of the strategy of massive firepower, a violation of the just war doctrine of proportionality.[40] The tone and thesis contained in Sheehan's headline and introductory statement are not those that Gen. Taylor would have employed.[41]

It was only after the end of the My Lai trials that Taylor made a direct comparison between the conduct of Yamashita and that of an American officer; and that officer was Capt. Medina.[42] Even then, Taylor never claimed to be making or putting forward a formal legal argument. As a professor of international law at Columbia University and a noted authority, he could have chosen from any number of prestigious law reviews to publish his views. Instead, Taylor chose the medium of newspaper op-eds and current affairs in order to make a non-legalist, ethical challenge regarding the conduct of the war to the nation at large. The massive number of law review articles and legal dissertations written in response to a misleadingly phrased newspaper headline was an obvious literary example of "asymmetrical warfare" that missed the target of Taylor's central non-legalistic argument. Thirty years later, it is far easier to appreciate the changes in Taylor's attitudes toward the war, from general support prior to 1965 to later criticism regarding the overuse of firepower.

In his 1970 book, Taylor recognized the important distinction between the competing interpretations of the legacy of the Nuremberg trials. While dismissive of some of the more radical legal theories associated with Nuremberg, he was tolerant of the fact that the Nuremberg legacy includes "both what happened there and what people think happened," the latter at times being more prominent than the former. Taylor was specifically critical of the so-called "Nuremberg defense," one claiming that a soldier can refuse military service on the *jus ad bellum* argument that the war was manifestly aggressive. He also doubted that a "judicial decree" could be utilized to nullify the legal resort to military actions by the president and the U.S. Congress.[43] As a result, more radical critics of American policies, such as Princeton's Richard A. Falk, considered Taylor's "minimalist indictment" of America's involvement in Vietnam as too conservative.[44]

Criticism of Taylor by conservatives was far less deferential and at times bordered on linguistic hysteria. Waldemar A. Solf, chief of the international affairs division of the army's Office of the Judge Advocate General, was Taylor's most ferocious critic. The functional successor of Richard Baxter as far as developing official army doctrine on the laws of war is concerned, Solf, in an unofficial law review in 1972, charged that Taylor's thesis, so considered, elevated "Professor Taylor to the status of a first magnitude star among scapegoat mongers" and that there were so many demonstrable errors of law and contradictions" in his (pre-1972) writings that Taylor "thereby forfeits the opportunity to assume a place" among those qualified to discuss "what international law really is."[45]

Solf noted that any comparison between the Yamashita and My Lai trials had to address the procedural discontinuity between a special military commission, on the one hand, and a military court-martial, on the other. If it can be shown that military commissions are weighted *against* defendants while military court-martials are weighted in the *interests of* defendants, it is fair to point out possible ethnocentric, racist, or national biases in the treatment of foreign defendants as against the treatment of one's own nationals. Solf branded Taylor's call for fairness in trying the My Lai defendants before a special military tribunal a "nostalgic preference for Post World War II procedures." He noted three major distinctions between military commissions and court-martials: "procedural limitations, exclusionary rules of evidence, and due process standards." This placed Yamashita in the position of being a passive victim of bad timing in not being granted the same procedural protections given later to American officers tried by the United States. Solf was the first of many legal critics of Taylor who associated Taylor's criticism of the outcome of the Medina trial with a so-called "absolute liability" standard or secondary liability standard. These critics utilized the concepts of *substantive* standards or norms, related to formal legal precedents, and *procedural* standards or norms, related to the less rigorous demands placed upon the Nuremberg-era prosecutors. This had the effect of playing down the significance of the contrasting instructions concerning the standard of command responsibility given by the respective judges in the Yamashita and Medina trials.[46]

In summary, the attempt to attribute categorical support for a theory of absolute command responsibility to Gen. Taylor, based on his wartime writings, is a classical example of the "straw man" fallacy in which one posits a counterfactual description of one's opponent's position (the straw man), attacks it, and proclaims victory, even as the real position of that opponent remains untouched.

Another authoritative critic of Taylor was Solf's successor as America's top doctrinal authority on the law of war. William Hays Parks ascended to the dual leadership of both the offices the Law of War Branch of the Department of Defense and the International and Operational Law Division of the Office of the Judge Advocate General of the Army immediately prior to Ronald Reagan's accession to the White House. A retired colonel in the U.S. Marines with combat experience in Vietnam, Parks marked his entrance to the profession of law with his 1973 thesis, "Command Responsibility for War Crimes," which challenged Taylor's characterization of the Yamashita precedent. Except for classifying the My Lai Massacre as an "aberration" in the first sentence, Parks undertook to challenge the concept of absolute command liability that he associated with Taylor, among others, without utilizing the My Lai trials as a comparison. Unlike other contemporaneous critics of Taylor who used the straw man of "absolute" liability, Parks, to his credit, did not attempt a justification of the Medina acquittal in terms of the Yamashita precedent.

While Parks was critical of the dominance of non-lawyers in the Yamashita trial, as a former combat officer he appealed to what he considered the sentiments common to the combat arms in his writing. In his thesis, Parks utilizes a non-legalistic tactic of laying out subjective criteria to determine whether or not a commander possesses a sufficient "means of knowledge" to be charged with war crimes, a criteria more likely to be appreciated by officers having combat command experience. Parks requires one to consider the following:

(a) The rank of the commander.
(b) The experience of the commander.
(c) The training of the men under his command.
(d) The age and experience of his men.
(e) The size and experience of his staff.
(f) The comprehensiveness of his duties.
(g) The "sliding probability ratio" of unit-incident-command.
(h) The duties and complexities of the command by virtue of the command held.
(i) Communications abilities.
(j) Mobility of the commander.
(k) Isolation of the commander.
(l) Composition of the forces within the command.
(m) Combat situation.[47]

Parks utilized these criteria to make a case that Yamashita was not held to an absolute standard of liability as a commander and could well have been convicted under the standards of the later Hostage and High Command cases. If, however, one were to use these criteria to compare the words and actions of Gen. Yamashita with those of Capt. Medina, Taylor's specific claim that Medina was held to a completely different legal standard from Yamashita (or any other Nuremberg-era defendant) appears obvious.[48] Let us examine each in turn:

(a, b) *Rank and experience:* General Yamashita was proclaimed a national hero for his capture of Singapore from the British. He was the commander of Japanese forces in Manchuria prior to being given command of the Philippines. Captain Medina was an experienced soldier who came up from the ranks after excelling as a noncommissioned Officer (NCO). He graduated fourth in a class of two hundred at Officer Candidate School, and the men of his company respected him. His company was considered the best in the battalion.

(c, d) *The training, size, and experience of his command:* Ten days before Yamashita's arrival in the Philippines on October 20, 1944, the United States began its reconquest by a decisive victory in the Battle of Leyte Gulf. Half of the forces Yamashita assigned to the campaign were killed. Yamashita described the soldiers of his "Army Group" as poorly trained and with low morale. The size of Yamashita's forces were approximately 100,000 personnel. In contrast, Medina's command consisted of 105 men on the day of the massacre. Charlie Company was considered average and differed "little from the Army as a whole." Two days prior to the massacre, a patrol member stepped on a mine, killing one NCO and injuring two other soldiers. On that same day Medina's soldiers murdered an unarmed wounded woman, an act the captain failed to report or act upon. Numerous soldiers of Medina's command reported that Charlie Company had stopped the practice of taking prisoners, military or civilian, well prior to My Lai.

(e) *The size and experience of his staff:* In the later trial of Adm. Toyoda, the Army Group under Yamashita was noted as being capable only of a "limited command function" as a result of Toyado, the senior officer in charge of the defense of the Philippines, having removed the Japanese theater staff from Luzon prior to Yamashita's arrival. In contrast, at My Lai, the division, task force, and battalion commanders were all physically present in helicopters above their company. The My Lai Massacre was one of the most supported and supervised operations of its type in the history of American warfare.

(f) *The comprehensiveness of his duties:* As Yamashita felt his command scattered across hundreds of miles of terrain, incapable of decisive action, he ordered the evacuation of Manila, an action opposed by his subordinate commanders, who were simultaneously questioning his authority for the order. In contrast, Medina's mission was to "make contact and destroy" enemy forces in one specific location. However, the forces of the 48th VC Battalion, approximately 500 personnel, were falsely reported by intelligence to be at My Lai.

(g) *The "sliding probability ratio" of unit-incident-command:* When U.S. forces landed on Luzon on January 9, 1945, the Japanese forces, refusing to surrender the capital of Manila engaged in murdering and torturing between 60,000 and 100,000 civilians. Medina's 105 soldiers murdered between 300 and 500 unarmed men (many of them elderly), women, and children in four hours. While the scale of the operations are not in any way comparable, each soldier under Medina killed three to four times the average number of civilians that the soldiers in Yamashita's army group killed.

(h) *The duties and complexities of the command:* The Philippines were written off by the Imperial Headquarters by the time Yamashita took command. Yamashita's counterattack to enable the forces in Manila to withdraw failed, and by March all Japanese forces in the city had been killed. In contrast, the American forces at My Lai received no hostile fire from the village and sustained no casualties except for one self-inflicted injury.

(i) *Communications abilities:* Yamashita's communication with the forces in Manila was lost immediately upon the landing of U.S. forces on Luzon. In contrast, Medina maintained a company command post position with his radioman in a direct physical proximity of My Lai 4 for the entire four-hour duration (except for when he entered the village proper to have lunch with his men).

(j) *Mobility of the commander:* Yamashita was held up in a remote mountain region until he surrendered on August 15, 1945. His supplies were low and dispersed throughout the island. In contrast, Medina's company conducted a state-of-the-art air-mobile operation.

(k) *Isolation of the commander:* As opposed to Yamashita, Medina's forces could not approach anything resembling the isolation experienced by Yamashita. Medina's three higher-echelon commanders tried to avoid colliding with one another directly overhead of his company.

(l) *Composition of the forces within the command:* Yamashita possessed an army group with virtually no naval or air support. Medina possessed an infantry company with artillery, helicopter gunships in direct support, and had massive air-support assets available.

(m) *Combat situation:* Yamashita conducted retrograde operations, having neither control of the air nor functional communications. In contrast, Medina conducted a search-and-destroy operation that was standard for American ground forces in Vietnam.

It becomes obvious from the facts presented in the above comparison, which utilizes Parks' own "subjective criteria," that Yamashita would not have been sentenced and hanged by Capt. Medina's jury had he come before it wearing the same uniform as the captain. One does not have to be a lawyer to appreciate Taylor's obvious conclusion. The contrast between these two trials is not the result of differing interpretations of legal sufficiency. Rather, it is a clear example of the lack of consistent institutional moral standards over time.[49] The results of the official My Lai investigations, and the subsequent failure to convict any officers on the basis of command liability, demonstrate that the United States government failed to adhere to the standard of command indirect responsibility affirmed both at Nuremberg and at the trial of Gen. Yamashita.

The Legacy of My Lai

It is not the reaction of lawyers, military or otherwise, that is central to an analysis of the doctrinal response to My Lai. Rather, it is the actions of senior members of the military profession. If one were seeking a comfortable and undemanding last tour of duty before retirement, serving as Chief of Staff of the U.S. Army for four years would hardly be a tempting choice. After commanding American forces in Indochina from 1965 to 1968, Westmoreland was appointed to the army's senior position.

Only three days after his staff completed its review of the Peers report, Westmoreland directed the Army War College Commandant, in a memorandum dated April 18, 1970, to initiate a study in response to "several unfavorable events" that brought into question the "state of discipline, integrity, morality, ethics, and professionalism of the Army." Westmoreland specifically requested the development of a concise and understandable "Officer's Code" to enable officers to recognize and resist institutional pressures that could compromise their integrity. Officers at the Army War College completed the report in less than ninety days. After extensive interviews with company-grade officers at various training installations, the study's authors bluntly concluded that within the Officer Corps there was a "strong, clear, and pervasive" perception that a barrier existed between the ideal values of military service and the actual and operative values of military leaders.[50]

The group of officers who administered the 1970 Army War College study had been selected by the Department of the Army for grooming for eventual service as general officers. Although they found that the West Point cadet code of "Duty, Honor, Country" was "espoused" by officers at all levels, this choice group of officers found it necessary to draft a more affirmative and comprehensive Officer's Creed to reaffirm the principle of "selfless" service:

> I will give to the selfless performance of my duty and my mission the best that effort, thought, and dedication can provide.
>
> To this end, I will not only seek continually to improve my knowledge and practice of my profession, but I will exercise the authority entrusted to me by the President and the Congress with fairness, justice, and restraint, respecting the dignity and human rights of others and devoting myself to the welfare of those placed under my command.
>
> In justifying and fulfilling the trust placed in me, I will conduct my private life as well as my public service so as to be free both from impropriety and the appearance of impropriety, acting with candor and integrity to earn the unquestioning trust of my fellow soldiers—juniors, seniors, and associates—and employing my rank and position not to serve myself but to serve my country and unit.
>
> By practicing physical and moral courage I will endeavor to inspire these qualities in others by my example. In all my actions I will put loyalty to the highest moral principles and the United States of America above loyalty to organization, persons, and my personal interests.[51]

It is significant that these officers, the majority of whom commanded American forces in Vietnam, were clearly convinced of the need to include a categorical affirmation to protect human rights (paragraph 2) in an oath that they believed should be added to the standard code of conduct. Unfortunately, the Department of the Army never promulgated the oath.

In July 1970, one month after personally testifying before the House of Representatives' Armed Services Investigating Subcommittee on the My Lai incident, Westmoreland held a stormy meeting with the army's disbelieving top leadership to discuss the findings of the War College's *Study on Military Professionalism*. The most striking and central conclusion of the study, which exposed the army's leadership to scrutiny, was that there was "no direct evidence that external fiscal, political, sociological, or managerial influences" were causative factors in the army's fall from professional grace. After a heated discussion, it was decided not to release the damning study to the public.[52]

In the remaining months of 1970, more troubling disclosures on laws-of-war violations by U.S. Army personnel in Vietnam appeared in the press. A criminal investigation into the murder of an alleged Vietnamese double agent involving a Special Forces contingent was conducted. The investigation was brought to the attention of the media by a civilian defense lawyer. In another incident, television interviews of the most decorated veteran of the Korean War, Lt. Col. Anthony B. Herbert, broadcasted his claim that he was relieved of his duties as an inspector general in Vietnam for reporting on the mistreatment of enemy prisoners.[53] With these new scandals following on My Lai, Westmoreland ordered the deputy chief of staff for personnel, Lt. Gen. Walter T. Kerwin Jr., to organize the United States Army Vietnam War Crimes Working Group, which eventually analyzed 246 separate allegations relating to the conduct of the war. In his memorandum to Kerwin, Westmoreland ordered an examination of all the Department of the Army procedures for handling war crime allegations. Included in that mandate was a review of the adequacy of the Army's definition of war crimes and the need, if present, to modify the military, inspector general, and legal structures. The selection of Kerwin was, however, a potential embarrassment, since the very war crime directive that was in force at the time of the My Lai massacre bore his signature.[54]

Starting in the early 1970s, criticism of the soundness of the army as an institution became pervasive in academia. Following the lead of the army's own *Study on Military Professionalism*, civil and military scholarly analyses emphasized a crisis in army professionalism.[55] British Lt. Gen. Sir John Winthrop Hackett, perhaps the greatest non-American fan of the American military tradition, delivered a lecture in October 1970 at the U.S. Air Force Academy that provided an alternative model in the debate over military professionalism. The cadets listening to Hackett were probably well aware that they were aspiring to a profession that had already lost the faith of society regarding its integrity. In contrast to Huntington's model of professionalism as developed in *Soldier and the State*, Hackett made a critical distinction between the military and other professions. Where other professionals—

in law, medicine, or business, for example—can achieve expertise and behave in a collegial manner while, at the same time, being selfish, cowardly, and false, "what the bad man cannot be is a good sailor, soldier, or airman." [56] Hackett's speech concluded by invoking the fundamental importance of the ethical dimension in military institutions: "The highest service of the military to the state may well lie in the moral sphere." [57]

Unfortunately, this post My Lai military reformation did not survive Westmoreland's tenure as army chief of staff. The men who succeeded Westmoreland began openly criticizing the Peers Commission report on My Lai. Gen. Edward C. Myers, in his memoir *Who Will Lead* (1995), cast doubt on the judgment of the "so-called Peers Board" for its readiness to publicly "point the finger of indictment all the way up to the division commander" [58] Although that commander, Gen. Koster, was never indicted, despite the recommendation of the Peers Commission, he was forced to resign in disgrace from his subsequent assignment as Commandant of West Point. Gen. Bruce Palmer, who took over as acting army chief of staff at Westmoreland's retirement, charged that the "so-called" Peers report "lacked objectivity and balance" and was "considered by many observers to be highly improper." Palmer asserted that the Peers Commission had taken on the guise of a "star chamber," denying witnesses the benefit of cross-examination or access to legal counsel.[59]

During the Army's soul-searching in the early 1970s, the United States had not yet been definitively defeated in Vietnam. Westmoreland and the authors of the *Study on Military Professionalism* were willing to be quite critical about the army. After it became apparent that the United States had been defeated, however, the call for ethical reform faded, and army professionals again turned to a disciple of Carl von Clausewitz to provide a model for the future of their profession.

Col. Harry G. Summers, one of the nation's leading commentators on military affairs until his death in 1999, was a lecturer at Fort Leavenworth when news of the My Lai massacre first broke in 1969. Years later, he remembered his reaction when he first heard of the atrocities: "What they ought to have done with Calley and Medina was to have hung them, then drawn and quartered them, and put their remains at the gates of Fort Benning, at the Infantry School, as a reminder to those who pass under it of what an infantry officer ought to be." [60] Summers had no sympathy for the two officers in command at the scene of the My Lai massacre. Yet Summers's subsequent analysis of the war proved to be extremely influential in reframing the debate on Vietnam. It shifted attention away from the idea of My Lai as an ethical failure.

Summers's rise to prominence as a spokesperson on military issues began when he took over the Vietnam "lessons learned" course at the U.S. Army War College in Carlyle, Pennsylvania. By the early 1980s, interest in the class had been waning and enrollment was becoming sparse.[61] Summers set a new tone by replacing the critique of military failure with a more upbeat approach emphasizing the U.S. military's tactical superiority in Vietnam and then attributing the actual American defeat to civilian strategists. Probably more than any other scholar and commentator on military affairs in the post-Vietnam period, Summers furthered the accommodation of the U.S. military to its defeat in Southeast Asia. By shifting the major blame to civilian strategic errors, the military establishment finally had an opportunity to abandon the type of analysis that focused on specific military failures such as My Lai.

Summers and former army chief of staff Gen. Fred C. Weyand were the co-authors of *Vietnam Myths and American Military Realities,* an officially sanctioned study issued by the Department of the Army and intended to incorporate the definitive lessons of the Vietnam War into a strategy assessment. Summers subsequently developed the theme into his book, *On Strategy: A Critical Analysis of the Vietnam War* (1982).

In that work, the author admits that mistakes were made by the armed forces in Vietnam. He argues, however, that the war was lost because of the military's deferral to civilian leadership on war strategy. If only the military had been allowed to fight the Vietnam War the way it wanted to, his argument goes, the U.S. would have been victorious. That interpretation coincides with the theory of military professionalism advocated by Samuel P. Huntington and other realists that called for the separation of military and civilian authority. In this perspective, it is not difficult to dismiss the My Lai massacre as "an aberration"—which is precisely what Summers does.[62]

The influence of this Vietnam War revisionist school began to push aside any significant effort to displace the Huntingtonian model of professionalism, which remained influential despite never having attained the imprimatur of official doctrine. The important messages of the 1970 War College study and the Peers Commission were left behind as blame for the defeat in Vietnam shifted from how the ground war was conducted to the errors of the civilian policy makers. The ethical disintegration of the officer corps and the darkest day of the army's history—March 16, 1968—receded into memory. The views expressed by Summers at a 1994 Tulane University conference on the My Lai massacre illustrate the trend. After admitting that the war was fought with "great stupidity," and that practices like obtaining body-counts were "barbaric," Summers insisted that the war "was driven from Washington . . . driven from Washington!"[63]

If the army could deny responsibility for how the war was fought, it was well on its way to marginalizing the significance of a moral disaster such as My Lai. The debate over how the Vietnam War was lost became increasingly fixated on the decisions made to engage the army in the first place. At two major conferences held at the Fletcher School of Law and Diplomacy (Tufts University) in 1973 and 1974, the focus drifted away from the military toward civilian politicians and society.[64] Discussions involved questions such as cultural clashes between Americans and Vietnamese, and the soon-to-be mantra of post-Vietnam revisionism, namely, that the civilian leadership lacked clearly defined goals in Vietnam. The My Lai massacre, according to one conference participant, Brig. Gen. S. L. A. Marshall, was an aberration not only in scope but also in kind. Marshall measured that exception against the regular sacrifice of American soldiers' lives in the interests of avoiding civilian causalities.[65]

Another major revisionist was Gen. Palmer. Aside from his harsh criticism of Peers, Palmer was in many ways a softer revisionist than Summers. His *The 25-Year War*, published just two years after Summers's *On Strategy*, is critical of the trend to place blame solely on U.S. civilian leaders for what went wrong in Vietnam.[66] Palmer denounces army leadership for deficient training and orientation on the Geneva Conventions and on the kind of war they would face in Vietnam. Unlike Summers, Palmer does not blame the defeat on civilian leadership's emphasis on counterinsurgency operations, as opposed to conventional warfare.[67] The corollary to Summers's extreme revisionist perspective, of course, is the depiction of My Lai as the unfortunate but predictable outcome of throwing soldiers into unconventional, confusing situations where it is difficult to identify the enemy.[68] Yet, even if the ahistorical argument that it was new or unusual for soldiers to operate in those kinds of circumstances was valid, the focus on strategy and pitting the military's choice of conventional warfare against the civilian government's coun-

terinsurgency framework displaces the fundamental ethical issue. Whatever kind of war soldiers are waging, killing babies and raping women
does not constitute legitimate military conduct.

The revisionist thesis of America's tactical inviolability in Vietnam
even has a "revealed" mythology to support it. In the introduction to *On
Strategy*, Summers describes a conversation in 1975 in Hanoi with Colonel Nguyen den Tu of the North Vietnamese Army. Summers writes
that when he told the Vietnamese officer "you know you never defeated
us on the battlefield," Tu replied that "that may be so, but it is also ir-
relevant." Retired U.S. Army Colonel David Hackworth gives a different version of that exchange, however, in his 1989 book *About Face*. In
Hackworth's account, Tu is quoted as responding that the U.S. Army
was "routed militarily" and that tactical rather than strategic failures
were "the main cause that led to the tragic U.S. defeat."[69]

In 1977, the Department of the Army published its next version of
Field Manual 100–5. The manual promoted a very conventional doctrine
of "active defense," signifying the return of the defense of central
Europe as the center of gravity for the armed service. Prepared to fight a
conventional war consisting of slow, elastic withdrawal toward the
Rhine, the new army doctrine emphasized mechanized conventional
operations in support of NATO forces in a conflict involving superior
Warsaw Pact numbers. The era of anti-insurgency and irregular force
structures was over, at least doctrinally.[70]

Michael Walzer, in his *Just and Unjust Wars*, the most quoted and
authoritative contemporary work in on just war theory, persuasively argues that soldiers "are not responsible for the overall justice of the wars
they fight; their responsibility is limited by the range of their own activity and authority." The responsibilities of officers, on the other hand,
are "unlike anything in civilian life." For Walzer, My Lai can have no
justification. In his formulation, the My Lai incident is not merely an
indicator that there was something wrong with the *jus ad bellum* premises that American leaders used to justify their decision to go to war.
Rather, it is an indicator of the institutional breakdown of *jus in bello*
military ethics.[71] Tragically, with the end of the military draft in 1973,
an increasingly conservative military leadership found other excuses for
the American military failure in Vietnam other than a breakdown in institutional ethics.

The Vietnam War left the American military with two conflicting
standards of command responsibility, a doctrinal standard and a stan-

dard representing the latest legal precedent. The Medina Standard, far from representing better law, has not received international validation. Rather, the standards generally associated with the Yamashita trail, the Hostage case, and FM 27–10 are those that have been adopted internationally, in Additional Protocol I, in the statute of the International Tribunal for the Former Yugoslavia, in the statute of the International Tribunal for Rwanda, and in the Rome Statute for the International Criminal Court.

The Vietnam-era failure of the United States to hold its own citizens to the same standards it applied to its defeated enemies has contemporary consequences. The maintenance of a de facto unilateralist legal precedent concerning command responsibility does not mitigate the concerns of the nation's traditional allies over the rising tide of American unilateralism. With the scandals related to the improper handling of detainees by U.S. military authorities in Guantánamo, in Afghanistan, and in Iraq, the U.S. Army is again dealing with incidents that, like My Lai, are neither "aberrations" nor true representations of the American military professional. Those investigating these incidents and the corrective actions that should be taken would probably be better served by a review of the Peers Report and the 1972 Army War College *Study on Military Professionalism* than by efforts to brush up on their Clausewitz.

CHAPTER SIX

The 1977 Geneva Protocol I and Post-Vietnam Military Doctrine

It is not, what a lawyer tells me I may *do; but what humanity, reason, and justice, tell me I ought to do.*

EDMUND BURKE

OVER THE COURSE OF THE DECADE and a half following the end of the Second Indochina War, the U.S. military profession underwent doctrinal and organizational revolutions as it reassessed the nature of its association with American civil society and its image of itself. Specifically, the attitudes of official and military authorities toward developments in international humanitarian law underwent a substantial transformation, as documented by the sequential negotiation, endorsement, and later rejection of the Additional Protocol to the Geneva Conventions of August 12, 1949 (otherwise known as Protocol I). While adjustments to formal keystone doctrine relating to the laws and customs of war remained relatively nuanced and subtle, the negotiations and evaluations of Protocol I signified a transformation in formal norm for that period.

Both the wider reorientation of capstone doctrine, as represented in the 1982 and 1986 editions of FM 100–5, and the growing official American antagonism toward developments in international humanitarian law were expressed in the language of a conservative realism that grew among American military professionals in the wake of America's defeat in Vietnam. Clausewitzian realism, the preference for Prussian military structures, and a distrust of civilian decision makers were, to be sure, nothing new for American military officers. Yet attitudes once held informally now entered formally into official policy for the first time on a major scale. The development of keystone doctrine concerning the laws and customs of war cannot be separated from the dynamics of the changes affecting capstone doctrine.

The Department of the Army, as the direct successor to the Department of War, continued in its role as the traditional entity responsible for the development of interservice doctrine, specifically "keystone" doctrine upon which the other services would establish their own supplemental doctrines. Following the American military withdrawal from Vietnam, the 1956 edition of Army Field Manual 27–10, *Law of Land Warfare*, continued to be the keystone publication on the laws of war. On November 5, 1974, the Department of Defense (DoD) issued Directive 5100.17 designating the secretary of the army as the executive agent for the administration of the DoD law-of-war program. Formalizing the primacy of the Department of the Army for law-of-war matters organizationally as well as doctrinally, the bulk of the document concerned assigning responsibilities and implementing guidance within the Department of Defense. The central policy statement of the DoD directive stated, "The Armed forces of the United States will comply with the law of war in the conduct of military operations and related activities in armed conflict, however such conflicts are characterized."[1] This statement reflected continuity within the military in accepting a broad interpretation of the applicability of international humanitarian law.

Although a specific task was not addressed in DoD Directive 5100.17, the negotiation and review of international treaties on the laws of war and humanitarian law would be a major activity of the personnel tasked under the DoD law-of-war program and assigned component services offices. However, beginning with the first session of the Diplomatic Conference on the Reaffirmation and Development of International Humanitarian Law Applicable in Armed Conflicts (called hereafter the Geneva Diplomatic Conference), which met in Geneva, Switzerland, on February 20, 1974, diplomatic negotiations would be a major activity of the personnel tasked under the DoD law-of-war program.

U.S. Position on the 1977 Protocols Additional to the Geneva Conventions of 1949

Common Article 3 to the Geneva Conventions of 1949 imposed, for the first time, universal prohibitions and affirmative responsibilities on combatants regarding the protection of noncombatants. By the end of the 1960s, however, it had become apparent that civilians still comprised a disproportionate number of the victims of contemporary conflicts and that revisions and/or additional conventions would be required to provide a more effective regime of protections for noncombatants. Consequently, the United Nations General Assembly, in 1969, passed two resolutions requesting the Secretary-General to undertake a study to identify areas of international humanitarian law regarding the protection of civilians that should be revised or expanded. This action was undertaken in the midst of the Second Indochina War and the final wars of national liberation across Africa.[2]

After the 21st Convention of the Red Cross in Istanbul in 1969, Richard R. Baxter, the author of the 1956 edition of FM 27–10 and future World Court Justice, represented the United States at the conference of government experts held prior to the convening of the Geneva Diplomatic Conference. Assisting Baxter was Waldemar A. Solf, chief of the international affairs division at the Office of the Judge Advocate General of the Army and the person who became Baxter's functional successor as the Department of the Army's doctrinal authority on the laws of war. These meetings resulted in two draft Protocols to the Geneva Conventions of 1949: Draft Additional Protocol (Protocol I) to the Geneva Conventions of Aug 12, 1949, Relating to the Protection of Victims of International Armed Conflicts; and Draft Additional Protocol (Protocol II) to the Geneva Conventions of August 12, 1949, and Relating to the Protection of Victims of Non-International Armed Conflicts.[3]

The Geneva Diplomatic Conference met in four sessions between 1974 and 1977. The American delegation was led by State Department Legal Advisor George H. Aldrich and assisted by Baxter along with eight additional representatives, seven of whom represented either DoD or the component military services. Besides Solf, who had served in combat as an artillery officer during World War II, the DoD/military representatives included Brig. Gen. Walter D. Reed, future Judge Advocate General of the Air Force; and Maj. Gen. George S. Prugh, Army Judge Advocate General and someone who had served under Gen. Westmoreland as the MACV staff Judge Advocate (1964–66). During his MACV tour, Prugh had been successful in persuading the government of South Vietnam to view the insurgency in the south as an international conflict and, consequently, grant Geneva prisoner-of-war status to Viet Cong and North Vietnamese soldiers. This came about to stop the retaliatory mistreatment of American prisoners in the north over conditions inside South Vietnamese prison camps—such as the tiger cages at Con Son Island, which remained in operation for most of the duration of the conflict. During the first two sessions of the diplomatic conference, Prugh was in the midst of publishing the major statement on the laws of war consequent to the Vietnam conflict, *Law at War: Vietnam 1964–1973*.[4] In 1980 Prugh and Westmoreland, each retired, would coauthor a major legal brief that did not avoid the "dark side of the record" of the breakdown of military law, for which they were both personally responsible. In particular, it gave a damning assessment of the army's failure to prosecute successfully the perpetrators of the My Lai massacre.[5]

In view of the military membership of Ambassador Aldrich's team, it would be hard to imagine a more authoritative and imposing delegation, or one more qualified to deal with the most controversial issues addressed by the Geneva Diplomatic Conference, the application of Protocol I to wars of national liberation.[6] From the beginning of the process, the United Sates agreed to support the ICRC's effort with "considerable misgivings." The conference was divided between the major Western states on one side and socialist and emerging states on the other. Besides the obvious ideological polarization of the international community at the height of the cold war, the experience of war in the Third World led the United States to an outlook very different from that of the developing nations. In the *Report of the United States Delegation*, Aldrich recognized the fundamental conflicting interests between nations whose military effectiveness relies on "technology, modern equipment and firepower," such as the United States, and developing countries that were more dependent on sheer manpower to achieve their military ends. Even though he viewed the conference as "more of a hazard than an opportunity," Aldrich felt that an acceptable outcome could be attained. The conference plenary sessions were to be run on a consensus basis (requiring a two-thirds supermajority), by means of which the major areas of North-South disagreement could be (and was) precluded from the final instrument.[7]

Issues relating to the status and representation of national liberation organizations and the controversy of whether Protocol I should apply to wars of liberation dominated the first session. By early 1974, traditional colonialism was in its death throes, as Portuguese rule in Angola, Mozambique, and Guinea Bissau collapsed. President Ould Dada of Mauritania set the tone of the session with an opening speech that included remarks in favor of national liberation groups in general and the conflicts in Palestine and Southeast Asia in particular.[8] Only a few months prior to the conference, the United Nations General Assembly adopted

Resolution 3103, which defined armed resistance to colonial rule, alien occupation, and "racist regimes" as international armed conflicts requiring the application of the Geneva Conventions.[9] It was, therefore, not surprising that the nations that supported this resolution would support similar language in an international instrument such as the Protocols.

The United States delegation also brought with it the baggage of America's particular experience with Third World insurgencies. Gen. Reed observed, "the Vietnam War had a particularly disproportionate effect on the first session."[10] The hostile atmosphere was clearly apparent as the North Vietnamese delegation introduced a provision to prohibit methods used by the United States in the war, such as use of napalm and defoliants, free-fire zones, and an expansive use of aerial bombardments. The U.S. delegation kept in mind the refusal of the North Vietnamese to afford full prisoner-of-war status to U.S. prisoners as it supported codification of provisions to ensure the granting of such status to all prisoners, regardless of the nature of the conflict. The American delegation was voted down by the committee majority on several issues: the decision to invite members of national liberation movements, such as the Palestine Liberation Organization (PLO), to participate (except for voting); the invitation to the Provisional Revolutionary Government of South Vietnam (PRGSV); and, most important, the decision by the majority of states to recognize wars of national liberation as international armed conflicts requiring the application of both Protocol I and the 1949 Geneva Conventions. Not surprisingly, at the end of the first session, Ambassador Aldrich considered the likelihood of American accession to the protocol as threatened.[11]

The protocols were not intended to supplant the Geneva Conventions, but rather to extend and direct their reach. As such, they would lack the foundational weight of the four 1949 Geneva Conventions, even if the protocols were to be universally ratified. Additionally, from the beginning, it was foreseen that Protocol I would be considered more authoritative than the more novel Protocol II. The reason that the latter has been relatively ignored in comparison with the former is that Protocol I extends applicability of Common Article 3 of the Geneva Conventions of 1949 in reference to grave breaches, which is considered the most fundamental provisions of international humanitarian law concerning the protection of noncombatants. This is why the North-South debate over extending humanitarian law to wars of liberation took place during the negotiations over Protocol I and not Protocol II. The tendency to apply the more authoritative standard when possible or when in doubt was drawn from the de Martens Clause found in the 1899 Hague Convention, the opposite of the tendency to find the most minimalist standard—the tendency that I labeled earlier in this book the *legalism of expedience.*[12]

According to Baxter, the delegations of the United States and its allies were not prepared for the determined support by developing nations for the inclusion of wars of national liberation as conflicts covered by Protocol I.[13] When Argentina, Honduras, Mexico, Panama, and Peru submitted an amended Article 1, it was approved by a vote of 70 to 21 along a North vs. South polarization. Article 1(4) explicitly conferred protections on "peoples [who are] fighting against colonial domination and alien occupation and against racist regimes [e.g., South Africa's apartheid government] in the exercise of their right of self-determination."[14] The American opposition consisted of submitting a position statement that argued that treating wars of national liberation as international armed conflicts introduces just war doctrine into modern international law. The American position statement utilized the term *bellum justem* in the derogative sense of being an inferior concept compared to the more modern (and Western) laws of war by attributing to just war tradition a lack of impartiality of treatment toward the victims belonging to the side of lesser justice (the side in opposition to the national liberation movements).[15]

Following the first session of the conference, many articles were published in various law journals that commented on the first session in general and on amended Article 1 in particular. Three members of the American delegation also published articles as private citizens.[16] Baxter, in a 1975 article, explained the context of the U.S. delegation's pejorative use of just war doctrine. Baxter described the U.S. action in opposition to the amended Article 1 in terms of a thesis put forward by Georges Abi-Saab in an article published two years before the first session of the conference. A professor of international law at the Graduate Institute of International Studies in Geneva, Abi-Saab argued that nonstate actors should be regarded as international entities under the UN Charter when they or those that they represent are denied self-determination. As such, liberation movements have a valid *jus ad bellum* claim for resorting to armed action and are likewise then bound by *jus in bello* restrictions on their own operations.[17]

While admitting that insurgencies, such as those contemporaneously directed against Portugal, may fall in line with Abi-Saab's logic, Baxter countered that the struggles between domestic minority groups and majority groups, such as in South Africa, Rhodesia, and Israel/Palestine, did not so fall in line because they were not directed against foreign occupying powers. Additionally, to be considered international conflicts, noted Baxter, such national liberation groups had to become parties to the Geneva Conventions of 1949. Except for the example of Algeria, none of the resistance groups in question had formally done so at that time. Consequently, granting such groups rights under the conventions would represent a declarative affirmation of the *justness* of their cause, and the requirement of impartiality in treatment of victims associated with the modern laws of war would be compromised.[18] It was this issue of the lack of impartiality in treatment in just war doctrine that would be utilized as a point of demarcation between the modern laws of war and just war by those defending and those challenging the protocols.[19]

Unfortunately, Baxter used the general term *bellum justum* instead of the more specific *jus ad bellum* in his article in response to Abi-Saab; by doing so, he created a false opposition of concepts. Baxter, along with his fellow delegates who also wrote articles for law journals in 1974 and 1975, had engaged in a liberal use of *jus in bello* terminology, such as the just war principles of military necessity, distinction, and proportionality, in describing the delegation's positions during the session. These *jus in bello* concepts are just as much a part of just war doctrine as the *jus ad bellum* concept of just cause that Baxter was addressing. When he wrote, "the idea of just war has in the past been productive of some of the worst offenses against victims of war," Baxter was likely referring to the crusades of the Middle Ages and the religious wars generated by the Reformation rather than to the traditional just war doctrines laid down by Saint Augustine in the fifth century.[20]

The most notable modern affirmation of the *jus ad bellum* principle is the UN Charter itself. Articles 2(4), prohibiting the use of force in a "manner inconsistent with the Purposes of the United Nations," and 51, on the "right to individual self defense," have been recognized by many authors as a modern codification of the "just cause" principle of traditional just war doctrine.[21] The codification of the right not to recognize the humanitarian rights of specific individuals serving in so-called unjust causes received no codification in the UN Charter, the Geneva Conventions of 1949, the 1977 Protocols, U.S. General Order 100, or

Augustinian just war doctrine. It is, however, to be found in the actual behavior of individual states. North Vietnam's treatment of American prisoners in the 1970s serves as an example, as does U.S. treatment of detainees in the so-called war on terror under President George W. Bush.

Although the United States and its Western allies would eventually agree to the inclusion of amended Article 1, the delegation report noted a number of actions during the final session introduced to address Western concerns. The Preamble to the Protocol, echoing Article 153 of U.S. General Order 100, acknowledged a distinction between the application of the Protocol's humanitarian provisions and the recognition of the legitimacy of a party's resort to arms. Article 96 mandated that no special status in regard to *jus in bello* obligations would be given to liberation groups. In other words, they could have "no rights without corresponding obligations."[22] The question of whether national resistance movements would be allowed to sign the Final Act resulted in the adoption of a compromise formula that allowed national liberation forces to sign the Final Act on a separate attached sheet to the final instrument under a clause that stipulated, "it is understood that the signature by these movements is without prejudice to the positions of participating States on the question of precedent." Aldrich asked for the article to be adopted by consensus, but Israel asked for a vote. The Final Act was then adopted by 87 votes in favor, one nation (Israel) voting against, and 11 abstentions, the United States included.[23]

Later, writing in support of ratification of the protocols in 1985, Solf would use more precise language to sum up the American delegation's initial "just war" concerns. Solf listed four concerns related to the introduction of *jus ad bellum* into modern law: (1) Article 1(4) introduced a specifically *jus ad bellum* subjective element that could conflict with the more specifically *jus in bello* neutral and objective standards associated with modern international law; (2) this change of emphasis could allow the forces on the so-called "just side" of the conflict to not respect the *jus in bello* "prohibitions and restraints of humanitarian law; (3) equal application of protections of civilians in all conflicts, regardless of the justness of any one side, would be threatened; and (4) the "non-state parties" in whose behalf Article 1(4) was submitted are "not likely to have the resources to fulfill their *jus in bello* obligations" anyway. The American position entailed a rather absolute interpretation that refused to recognize the common-sense understanding that the principle of reciprocity is always to some degree compromised by the fact that the treatment of protected persons and prisoners is dependent upon the resources available to captors or occupying powers.[24] In any conflict, the principle of reciprocity places the side with more resources in a position of deciding whether to provide better protection to protected persons associated with the other side, or accept that its own protected persons will be treated according to the lowest "shared" common denominator. Two questions must be asked, (1) whether the side with more resources will allow itself to be answerable to other parties regarding its treatment of protected persons; and (2) should standards be codified on the basis of the ability of the weakest party, in terms of material resources, to comply with them? The operating principle of just war is that with power comes responsibility, and it follows that unequaled power should entail unequaled responsibility.

Solf was aware of the irony that he was a delegate of a nation founded by military leaders who also utilized badly uniformed "part-time combatants" who also would readily blend into the noncombatant population between engagements. He was also aware that with the adoption of U.S. Army *General Order No. 100* during his country's Civil War, the attitude of the U.S. Army toward the irregulars had changed. The U.S. military's attitudes toward the tactics of Viet Cong (PRGSV) irregulars had much in common with the U.S. military's attitudes toward irregular Confederate formations a century earlier.[25] Solf recognized that greater protections against the actions of regular forces affecting civilians in irregular conflicts would naturally be sought by "governments and authorities that employ guerrilla warfare," just as it was natural for the United States to emphasize the difficulties in distinguishing between enemy combatants and noncombatants in such conflicts. Finally, Solf characterized the delegation's eventual acquiescence to Article 1(4) as merely the "Western willingness" to accept the symbolism of the justness of wars of liberations against "racist regimes," for Article 1(4) was "for all practical purposes a dead letter." Solf believed the article "would never be implemented" because the targets of the article, Israel and South Africa, were not likely to become parties to the protocol anyway.[26]

What may be a "dead letter" in the operation of a treaty, however, is not necessarily dead when it comes to engendering domestic support for or opposition to a treaty. After the passage of the Final Act, the leading members of the American delegation became active in support of the signing and ratification of the protocols by the United States. Unfortunately, as far as the issue of wars of liberation was concerned, the damage had been done. The poor utilization of just war terminology by Baxter and other members of the legal profession, whose direct knowledge of the sources of just war theory might be limited, is understandable. The utilization of imprecise terminology, however, did facilitate the creation of a derogatory just war "black legend" that would be used by conservative critics of Protocol I in their opposition to ratification. One of the earliest critics was Capt. David E. Graham, a U.S. Army lawyer, who argued that the U.S. acceptance of amended Article 1 would "hasten the world's return to the eleventh century," and maintained that the nations representing the majority at the Geneva Diplomatic Conference had revived the concept of the just war in order to discredit existing international law.[27] Later supporters of ratification, even those with a far better understanding of Augustinian just war doctrine, would still be haunted by the specter of a return to "medieval *jus ad bellum*" when in fact, there was no major treatise on just war written between Augustine's in the fifth century and Aquinas' rearticulation of Augustinian doctrine in the thirteenth century.[28]

The *jus ad bellum* aspect of Article 1(4) was far from the only aspect of just war doctrine of relevance to Protocol I. In his statement to the final plenary session of the conference, Aldrich, while making no mention of issues surrounding Article 1(4), stated that his "delegation believes the conference can take satisfaction in having achieved the first codification of the customary rule of proportionality" and in "setting minimum, humanitarian standards that must be accorded to anyone who is not entitled to better treatment."[29] The central just war doctrine of proportionality has always been associated with the related doctrine of discrimination that includes the modern principle of noncombatant immunity. Article 51, the Protection of the Civilian Population, lists noncombatant protections that include not being the intended "object of attack," not being subjected to an indiscriminant attack resulting from the inability to direct an attack at a legitimate military target, and not being the subject of a reprisal attack. Like earlier codifications of noncombatant protections in humanitarian law and just war theory, these protections are not absolute. Because legitimate targets are almost never completely free of noncombatants, the weighing of the principles of proportionality, involving collateral damage, and the principle of decisive action, involving the military worth of the target, still must be made. The question of whether the rigorous standards found in the protocol places too much weight on noncombatant immunity at the expense of military decisiveness—and, thereby, places too great a burden on superior forces—has been the subject of much discussion and scholarship.[30]

Command Responsibility and Protocol I

The controversial issue of standards of command responsibility was not actively discussed until the fourth session. The two conferences of government experts meeting in 1971 and 1972 prepared three major articles to address the concept of an affirmative command responsibility: draft Article 76, Failure to Act (final Article 86), draft Article 77, Superior Orders, and draft Article 74, Repression of Breaches (final Article 85). The wording of the second paragraph of the draft article followed the text of the affirmative standard of command responsibility associated with the Hostage case and FM 27–10 (see Chapter 3).

> The fact that a breach of the Conventions or of the present Protocol was committed by a subordinate does not absolve his superiors from penal responsibility if they *knew or should have known* [italics mine] that he was committing or would commit such a breach and if they did not take measures to prevent or repress the breach.[31]

In the discussion on Article 86, it was noted that the article did not create a new law and that it codified customary law established by the Charter of the International Military Tribunal at Nuremberg and the Yamashita case. The Syrian delegate, however, put forward an amended version that removed the "or should have known" Hostage case wording from the second paragraph as too vague; and agreement was reached by replacing "or should have known" with "knew, or had information, which has enabled them to conclude in the circumstances at the time that . . ."[32] The West German delegate to the conference considered the new language as a more rigorous standard than even the Yamashita case, in that it included a subjective requirement of being able to conclude something regarding the future actions of subordinates.[33]

Draft Article 77, Superior Orders, was discussed next. As the United States had successfully applied this principle in the trial of one of its officers during the Vietnam War (see Chapter 5), the American delegation could negotiate from a position of credibility. However, a number of nations argued that to codify provisions against following superior orders would undermine military discipline. A compromise was put forward to restrict the application of the article to grave breaches only. The U.S. delegation considered that concept already a part of customary law and refused to support the compromise. With the U.S. delegation in opposition, the amended article failed to obtain the required two-third majority in the session's plenary session.[34]

The U.S. delegation responded to the defeat of Article 77 by putting forward a new article to clarify the duties of military commanders vis-à-vis their subordinates. Listed as Committee Article 76 *bis*, Duty of Commanders, the American proposal required commanders not only to prevent, suppress, and report grave breaches committed by their forces but to ensure, "commensurate with their level of responsibility," that their subordinates are aware of the provisions protecting noncombatants, that steps are initiated to prevent violations where they are likely, and that penal actions are taken against violators. The American article was passed without opposition and was redesignated as Article 87 in the final instrument.[35]

Unlike the American position on failed draft Article 77, the United States could not claim that it had itself enforced this more rigorous standard of command responsibility on its own officers. Despite this discrepancy, the American delegation successfully pressed for the expansion of the principle of command responsibility. Unlike the debate over Article 1(4), the United States, in this instance, was pushing for an expansionist rather than a minimalist interpretation of provisions of humanitarian law.

The U.S. Military Evaluation of Protocol I

After Ambassador Aldrich signed the final act in Geneva on June 9, 1977, the next step toward ratification was to prepare for the signing of the protocols by the United States six months later. According to Solf, the protocols were "closely scrutinized by the military services and by the Joint Chiefs of Staff (JCS), as well as the Ministries of Defense of our allies."[36] Aldrich argued that the secretary of defense and the JCS had approved the delegates' positions papers throughout the conference and that any defects found in further review of the protocols were "curable by means of understandings or reservations."[37]

While the level of Pentagon participation in the evaluation of the protocols has been a matter of debate, the DoD's Law of War Working Group undertook a cursory analysis of the protocols in late October. The effort involved the JCS, the service staffs of each of the military branches, and the worldwide regional commands over a two-week period. Upon review of the working group's assessment, the JCS, in executive session on November 2, 1977, approved a decision memorandum in support of signing, under the understanding that a more thorough military analysis of the protocols would be undertaken prior to the decision by the executive to refer them to the U.S. Senate for ratification.[38]

Prior to the U.S. signing of the protocols on December 12, 1977, a North Atlantic Treaty Organization (NATO) staff-level review resulted in a determination that the provisions of the protocols would not significantly degrade NATO operations. Except for the subject of reprisals, NATO's political and legal experts succeeded in addressing interpretive differences regarding the protocols among member states.[39] In the late 1970s, even future critics of the protocols described them rather benignly as "not being without fault"—but also as an overdue codification of customary law on proportionality. Nothing indicated the ferocious neoconservative assault on the protocols that would follow the election of Ronald Reagan.[40]

On August 5, 1978, Lt. Gen. E. C. Meyer, then deputy chief of staff for operations and plans (later army chief of staff) issued a directive to the Strategic Studies Institute of the U.S. Army War College to "examine the protocols with a suspense date of November 30, 1978." On October 18–19, subject matter experts from throughout the services attended a workshop to clarify and discuss the protocols' provisions in order to provide impact guidance on specific articles (i.e., their potential effects on land/air operations, joint operations, and coalition warfare) in addition to identifying areas of interest for doctrinal development.[41]

The group was specifically charged with recommending reservations and understandings that could be submitted to the U.S. Senate by the executive branch with the overall executive recommendation on ratification. Besides the U.S. understandings expressed at the time of signature, the study recommended only one formal understanding relative to the ratification process. This understanding concerned the need for encryption equipment on medical evacuation aircraft (possibly prohibited by Article 28 of Protocol I). Nineteen other possible understandings for further analysis were referred to the army chief of staff with the recommendation that changes in training and doctrine would be necessary in order to ensure successful integration of the designated articles of the protocols into U.S. military operations. Included in the discussion of the latter were pragmatic recommendations that emphasized the increased difficulty of preventing "intermingling of military and civilian activities" and "separat[ing] and protect[ing] civilians on the modern battlefield." One solution found in the report was the introduction of the word "feasible" in specific articles dealing with combat operations (Articles 41, 42, and 44). The report also addressed the weighing of the growing U.S. emphasis on force protection with the more traditional norm of minimizing civilian casualties. The report endorsed rather than reintroduced reservations already put forward by the U.S. delegation at the Geneva Diplomatic Conference, such as the reservation concerning the articles dealing with reprisals (Articles 51–56) to ensure that the United States reserved the right to reprisal in the specific incidences where ". . . massive and continuing attacks directed against the civilian population, to take reprisals against the civilian population or civilian objects of the State perpetrating these illegal attacks for the sole purpose and only to the extent necessary to end illegal attacks. These measures shall not include any of the actions that are otherwise prohibited by the Geneva Convention of 1949 or this Protocol."[42]

Despite the participation of future opponents of ratification, the report's overall assessment of the protocols was favorable. While acknowledging that the main effects of Protocol I related to national strategy and plans, it considered the probable impact on the common combat soldier as negligible. Overall, the report considered such major advances as increased protections for civilian populations and the extension of Prison of War status to irregular combatants as positive features. However, the primary concern of the authors of the report lay elsewhere. The study was completed with the participation of American military professionals who were mostly veterans of World War II and the early cold war. This generation of officers and officials tended to be functioning internationalists, as compared to the generation of officers who experienced their initial service in Vietnam. It is not surprising, therefore, that as the major voice of "general concern for the military," the report addressed the consequences of non-ratification from an internationalist perspective:

For the United States, a nation that has participated willingly, fully, and competently in Protocol development and refinement, it appears that the

greatest significance of the Protocols will be at the national level, where
ratification will express U.S. goodwill and intentions. In light of the U.S.
leading role in their development, U.S. failure to eventually ratify the Protocols might tend to denigrate U.S. credibility and lesson our present or
future influence in the world.[43]

The next—and what ended up being the last—stage in the review of
Protocol I was the DoD Law of War Working Group's review, initiated
and directed by William Hays Parks under his dual role as special assistant for law-of-war matters and chief of the Law of War branch of the
DoD's law-of-war program). Also participating was the international
and operational law division of the Office of the Judge Advocate General of the Army. Parks was critical of what he called the "chameleon-
like" approach of the U.S. proponents of the protocol, and accused the
American delegates at the Geneva Diplomatic Conference of changing
their interpretation of the meaning of some provisions to facilitate U.S.
military approval of the protocol.[44] Parks started the process of a military reevaluation of the protocols by issuing a memorandum on June 19,
1980, to the effect that the "work accomplished to date was not regarded
as constituting a military review of the 1977 Protocols." In 1982 he convened a "Worldwide Military Operations review" in order to carry out a
"responsible military review" of the 1977 protocols.[45]

This second military review of Protocol I was not competed until
May 3, 1985, well into the second Reagan administration. The final
product was a 110-page document without a table of contents or summary attached. The working group classified each article of Protocol I
and grouped each into categories according to whether they were too
categorical, too ambiguous, or already included in existing law. As each
of these three categories tended to run against the need for ratification,
the result was predictable: formal understandings were drafted for
thirty-one articles, many of the articles falling under multiple understandings. In even the critical area of command responsibility and
criminal liability, where it was the American delegation to the Geneva
Diplomatic Conference that initiated the effort to codify an *expanded*
principle of applicability, the review suggested an understanding on its
applicability in regard to apartheid practices in South Africa. The most
striking features of the report, however, was its total lack of acknowl-
edgement of any previous review, such as the U.S. Army War College
Study or the understandings prepared by the U.S. delegation at the time
of signing.[46]

Although Parks denied that his working group labored under any assumption of nonratification, the comprehensiveness of the report's rejection of the protocol was remarkable: it would have made any attempt to salvage the protocol by another branch of the executive impossible.[47] The entire report was attached as an enclosure to a two-page memorandum to the secretary of defense from Gen. John S. Vessey, Chairman of the Joint Chiefs of Staff. The chairman's memo listed the following problems as outweighing any advantage to the United States from ratification:

1. Some nations may reject the U.S. nuclear understanding.
2. Guerrillas, in many situations, would be granted a higher legal status than regular forces.
3. It would eliminate most uses of reprisals, even as a deterrent against the humanitarian violations by an enemy.
4. The level of protection given to civilian persons and property would impede military operations and result in indecisive, and therefore unjust, results.
5. Attacks against infrastructure targets, such as damns, dikes, and nuclear power stations would be "unreasonably restricted."
6. Article 1(4) and other articles would introduce "political criteria" into humanitarian law.
7. The restrictions on operations in urban areas were "ambiguous."
8. Soviet Block countries may not reject the Article 75 fundamental guarantees given to persons "who do not benefit from more favorable treatment" under the Protocol.[48]

Behind many of the points of divergence between the War College study and the Law of War Working Group effort was the latter group's insertion of and stress on the allegation that Article 1(4) would introduce a "just cause" principle into humanitarian law. The report's first four pages put forth an argument that the protocol would be binding only on Western nations, because developing and socialist nations would deny prisoner status depending on the lack of "justice of the cause for which they fight."[49]

The large number of reservations in the report left challenging the approach or tone of the report by a member of Reagan's cabinet the only remaining option if the protocol were to advance. This was unlikely, for the protocol had ferocious critics at both the State Department, in the person of Aldrich's successor, Abraham Sofaer, and the Defense Department, in the person of Douglas Feith, a deputy assistant secretary of defense for negotiations.[50] Both Sofaer and Feith were representative

of the only competing worldview that could challenge the Clausewitzian realist assumptions that dominated the Pentagon's uniformed
leadership. Unfortunately, this other worldview was that of neoconservatives whose practice of the legalism of expedience would be far more
provocative than would be the tactful application of Clausewitzian realism by leaders of the military. As far as the protocol was concerned,
nothing could be further from the neoconservatives' belief in American
exceptionalism, their unequivocal support of Israel, and their distrust
of all international bodies and treaties than this document. Between
the finalization of the report on May 3, 1985, and the transmittal of the
protocols to the Senate on January 29, 1987, Feith cut his neoconservative teeth by writing a barrage of articles in opposition to the ratification of Protocol I. Most emphasized the so-called just war provision of
Article 1(4).[51]

The White House letter of transmittal, which formally recommended
the ratification of Protocol II and explained why Protocol I was not being
referred for advice and consent, mirrored the basic neoconservative argument: "Protocol I is fundamentally and irreconcilably flawed. It contains provisions that would undermine humanitarian law and endanger
civilians in war. One of its provisions, for example, would automatically
treat as an international conflict any so-called 'war of national liberation.' Whether such wars are international or non-international should
turn on objective reality, not on one's view of the moral qualities of each
conflict. To rest on such subjective distinctions based on a war's alleged
purposes would politicize humanitarian law."[52]

Accusations of a politicized review process within the Pentagon reflecting the foreign policy priorities of the Reagan administration, especially concerning South Africa and Israel, came from many quarters.
The American Journal of International Law, between 1987 and 1991,
became the forum for both those who criticized the decision and those
who defended it. Hans Peter Gasser, a senior ICRC humanitarian law
authority, criticized the lack of any legal argument in the U.S. decision
against ratification and the "unprecedented" language of the White
House letter, which he said injected "political and partisan controversy"
into the process. Ambassador Aldrich argued that "President Reagan's
decision resulted from misguided advice that exaggerated certain laws
in the Protocol" and misconstrued a humanitarian and antiterrorist instrument as one that could give aid and comfort to terrorists. The inability of the administration to recognize the difference between basic

principles and the claims of a few states and organizations in the Middle East and elsewhere that the protocol lent support to their policies, led the United States to disingenuously adhere to a minority characterization of the protocol that was rejected by the vast majority of nations endorsing it. Sofaer defended the president's decision by framing it as a stand against Third World states that, by underwriting the causes of the Palestine Liberation Organization and southern African "liberation movements," had chosen "not to respect our strong views and those of our European Allies."[53]

The American decision against ratification did not create a North-South or East-West split as envisioned by Sofaer, but rather a split in the Western Alliance as 162 nations became parties to Protocol I. Although Parks and Sofaer undertook an effort to dissuade allied nations from ratification, nearly all of the United States' major Atlantic-Pacific rim allies later became parties to the protocol, while the Unites States continues to be a nonparty in the company of Sudan, Somalia, Iran, Afghanistan, and Israel.[54] By 1993, the pretense that the military review of Protocol I was based on the merit, or lack thereof, of its provision as international law, was dropped by the one antiratification official remaining in his position during the Clinton administration. Parks, in a book review, admitted that the "principal reason for the Reagan administration's decision against ratification of Additional Protocol I was political," and that the new status of the Palestine Liberation Organization and African National Congress in talks with Israel and the South African government allow for a reevaluation of the "negative values" of Article 1(4) and other articles in the protocol.[55]

In 1997, with the deaths of Baxter and Solf and the retirement of Generals Prugh and Reed, Ambassador Aldrich noted that it was the "the passage of time" and the replacement of the team he had led in negotiating the protocols by "skeptics and individuals with different political agendas" that were the major factors in the failure of the ratification effort. Even with the passage of time, the support for the protocol by authoritative experts had to be addressed and played down by those opposed to ratification. Parks, for example, pointed out that no member of the American delegation to the Geneva Diplomatic Conference "had dropped a bomb in anger in the quarter century preceding the conference" to explain the delegation's willingness to incorporate a higher threshold of proportionality and noncombatant immunity into the protocol than what might have been the case if the delegation had been

staffed with personnel having more professional experience in aerial
bombardment.[56]

A Neo-Clausewitzian Critique of International Humanitarian Law

The defeat was not owing to the replacement of individuals as much as
it was owing to the replacement of one generation's professional outlook and worldview with another. Ten years had passed between the
United States' signing of Protocol I and President Reagan's final decision not to submit the document for ratification by the U.S. Senate.
During this period, the U.S. Army underwent a revolution that was celebrated as the great American Military Renaissance of the 1980s, when
disillusioned Vietnam veterans turned wizened sages, such as Colin
Powell, Barry McCaffrey, and Norman Schwartzkopf, rebuilt an all-
volunteer professional army that achieved Clausewitzian glory in the
Gulf War of 1991.[57]

An example of process in which Clausewitzian realism finally
achieved the status of formal military doctrine is found in the career of
Parks, who served as the leading doctrinal expert on the laws of war in
the departments of both the Army and Defense through three presidential administrations—and is now serving under a fourth.[58] The study of
Parks's career and opinions affords the student of U.S. policy an opportunity to observe, over an extended period, the balancing by one high-
level, nonpolitically appointed official of official policy, collectively and
authoritatively derived, with private opinion, as formed by personal experience within the context of broader cultural and institutional forces.
The fact that an officer or an unelected high civilian official is in a position to carry out policies he or she happens to be in ideological agreement with is not necessarily an indicator of a professional conflict of
interest, although, in a democracy, policy should at least have the appearance of bearing executive or legislative authority. The correspondence between Parks's private and official positions, such as his
published personal opposition to the concept of international humanitarian law and, especially, Protocol I, indicate his preeminence in his
field of expertise for more than a quarter of a century.[59]

Parks utilized the story of an encounter between his predecessor
and a senior ICRC official as his point of departure for offering a detailed neo-Clausewitzian critique of Protocol I and of international humanitarian law as a concept envisaged by the ICRC. During the 1971

conference of government experts, Solf discussed the tension between the American desire to increase noncombatant protection and the American concern regarding the difficulty of identifying legitimate noncombatant activities in modern warfare. The late Jean S. Pictet, the senior ICRC authority on international humanitarian law, was reported by Solf to have replied, "If we cannot outlaw war, we can make it too complex for the commander to fight"! One does not have to be a Clausewitzian or any other type of realist to appreciate the condescending antimilitary essentialism contained in such a remark. Solf, a World War II combat veteran, never published an account of this encounter, but passed the story on to his young successor.[60]

Parks accused the ICRC, in its replacement of the term "law of war" with "international humanitarian law" in its twentieth-century treaty codifications, of having "borrowed a page from the Marxist-Leninist lexicon" in order to blacklist anyone that resisted the adoption of ICRC rules as being antihumanitarian. Parks, as a combat veteran who had engaged in the self-avowedly unhumanitarian act of killing "at ranges as close as three meters," considered the use of the term "humanitarian" for the legal conduct of military operations as "singularly inappropriate." Like many in his generation, Parks was a self-proclaimed disciple of Clausewitz who considered the great Prussian's words as "timeless and (of) greater value today than they were when they were written 150 to 200 years ago." For Parks, the main problem with Protocol I was its relation to the Clausewitzian tenet of friction in war. The ICRC, by its "unrealistic interpretations of the Just War principle of proportionality" and its obsession with limiting aerial bombardment, created friction by limiting the natural tendency of war to expand toward its natural maximum intensity.[61]

The ICRC has been criticized for its overemphasis on the principles of proportionality and discrimination (noncombatant immunity) at the expense of the principle of probability of success (decisiveness). Even from the perspective of just war doctrine, given historical examples of the suffering of noncombatants caused by the many indecisive wars experienced in the Third World both during and after the cold war, it can be argued that undermining military decisiveness places noncombatants at greater, not lesser, risk. On the other hand, it is very hard to view the neo-Clausewitzian celebration of wars unlimited by friction as a balanced alternative in a nuclear era. Parks's solution was to divorce the law of war conceptually from the ICRC and its antimilitary ideology of international humanitarian law. The result was a new legal discipline Parks christened "operational law." Parks devised the term in 1980 for two reasons: (1) after the American defeat in Vietnam, military instruction on international law had been noted as ineffectual in the Peers Report; and (2) many combat arms officers were under the impression that international law, as they understood it, had kept them from winning the war in Vietnam. By including all legal aspects connected to military operations, the term "operational law" avoided associations that would turn off military professionals.[62] The negatives of creating a new terminology are obvious: an increase in the insulation of military professional vis-à-vis other professionals in general and from the humanitarian law and human rights community in particular.

Clausewitzian Realism as Formal Military Doctrine

In the 1980s and 1990s, it was not unusual to see students at the U.S. Army Command and General Staff College (CGSC) carrying beautifully bound copies of Clausewitz under their arms as they went from class to class like monks carrying their breviaries. Parks's choice of the term "operational law" for his neo-Clausewitzian enterprise to sever the laws of warfare from international humanitarian law was calculated to complement such Clausewitzian mantras as "operational art." Officially defined, "Operational art is the use of military forces to achieve strategic goals through the design, organization, integration, and conduct of strategies, campaigns, major operations, and battles."[63] Or, in simple non-Clausewitzian terms, it is the skill and competence of military command.

Over the course of the 1980s, three milestones documented the establishment of Clausewitzian realism, for the first time, as a formal norm for the American military profession: (1) the introduction of a new capstone doctrine, (2) the organizational restructuring of the U.S. military, and (3) a new model of civil-military relations relating to the decision to deploy military forces.

First, the new capstone doctrine was introduced in the 1982 and 1986 editions of FM 100–5. Known as the doctrine of Air-Land Battle, it represented a doctrinal change in emphasis away from the tactics and strategies associated with active defense and close battle, which focused on firepower, to those associated with a deep multi-echelon offense, which put a greater emphasis on maneuver and interservice or joint operations.[64]

In the 1980s, the NATO strategy for the defense of central Europe (West Germany) consisted simply of a limited conventional blocking capability against a Warsaw Pact thrust across Germany, with a guarantee of a nuclear strike when the Soviets approached the Rhine River.[65] The main purpose of the force-on-force bloodletting that was expected to take place in the Fulda Gap and the northern German plain was to steel the allied political resolve to execute the nuclear trigger that was the true basis of the NATO deterrent. This became a problem for the Americans driving their new M-1 tanks and M-2/M-3 armored vehicles around the old Wehrmacht training ranges—Americans who were now wedded to a doctrine that was more operationally "artsy" than that centered on a soldier's dying in place. The U.S. Army had worked out the kinks of its new doctrine for the defense of Europe in the new National Training Center (NTC) deep in the uninhabited Mojave Desert at Fort Irwin, California, a place where the friction of war, especially concerning the presence of a civilian population, could be kept to a minimum.

The second milestone in the formalization of Clausewitzian realism in the 1980s was the realization of a "Prusso-German" inspired reorganization of the American military by the Goldwater-Nichols Department of Defense Reorganization Act of 1986. It replaced the convoluted system of administrative authority by the service chiefs with a centralized management process through the chairman of the Joint Chiefs of Staff. Although the chairman and service chiefs remained outside the formal chain of command, the chairman was designated as the principal military advisor to the president, National Security Council, and secretary of defense. The formal operational chain of command was restructured to have the four unified commanders reporting directly to the secretary of defense and then to the president via the National Military Joint Operations Center (NMJOC) in the Pentagon. It was not the Prussian General Staff Corps, but it was a major, and needed, step in that direction without formally challenging the constitutional provision for actual civil control of the military.

Finally, the most neo-Clausewitzian of all the initiatives of the 1980s was the Weinberger Doctrine in opposition to humanitarian interventions. In a speech at the National Press Club on November 28, 1984, Secretary of Defense Caspar Weinberger argued that civilian leaders should meet six major tests before committing U.S. forces to any over-seas combat mission.

1. Is the mission vital to U.S. interests?
2. Have sufficient resources been allocated to guarantee victory?
3. Are the objectives clearly defined?
4. Will commitment be politically sustained?
5. Will there be a sufficient guarantee of the American public's commitment to the operation?
6. Have other options been exhausted?

The Weinberger or Powell Doctrine (after Colin Powell, the sitting Chairman of the Joint Chiefs of Staff, who was also a protégé of Summers), comprised a list of demands of civilian leadership unprecedented in history. This doctrine had its intellectual origins in neo-Clausewitzian theorists such as Summers.[66]

In spite of the doctrine, the U.S. military became engaged in operations that clearly did not meet Weinberger-Powell tests: first in Operation Restore Hope in Somalia, then in Operation Restore Democracy in Haiti, and then in various operations in the Balkans.[67] All these operations were conducted under Chapter VII, "Action with Respect to Threats to the Peace, Breaches of the Peace, and Acts of Aggression," of the UN Charter, as was utilized by UN Security Council at the start of the Korean War, rather than Chapter VI, the "Pacific Settlement of Disputes," which was usually associated with "blue helmet" UN observer missions. However, both "humanitarian purists" at the UN and Clausewitzian realists like Summers interjected the inappropriate model of traditional peacekeeping operations to undermine the doctrinal rationale for these operations.[68]

On October 7, 1994, Summers testified before the Committee on Armed Services, U.S. House of Representatives, against the ongoing deployment of a United States military task force to Haiti as violating the principles of Presidential Decision Directive (PDD) 25, the Clinton Administration's policy on multilateral peace operations. PDD 25, Summers argued, was a restatement of the preconditions laid out by the Weinberger Doctrine concerning the limitations that the civilian leadership of the armed forces should observe, "before America commits forces to combat overseas."[69]

In March 1996, U.S. forces under the command of Adm. Leighton Smith, head of NATO's Southern Command and the Implementation Force (IFOR) in Bosnia, stood passively by as Bosnian Serb forces took advantage of the evacuation of seventy thousand residents of the Serbian section of Sarajevo, of which thirty thousand were forced from their homes by violence or threats of violence by fellow Bosnian Serbs, to burn that section of the city to the ground. As the Bosnian government sent its "antiquated fire-fighting equipment into the city," state of the art fire-fighting equipment stayed in the U.S. controlled military compounds. All requests for IFOR assistance were ignored.[70] Richard Holbrooke, President Clinton's chief negotiator responsible for the Dayton Agreement that led to the transfer of the sector to Bosnian government control, called the American military commander's inaction contrary to the president's intent:

> However, in the wake of Vietnam and Somalia, the military had a tremendous aversion to using its force beyond a very limited mission. And they call this mission creep. And it really inhibited us and the great crisis; the greatest tragedy came in the 90 days after Dayton when the military simply refused to do anything except the narrowest articulation of its own mandate. . . . NATO forces stood by. The NATO commander and American admiral refused to take the fire trucks out of the barracks. He refused to do anything to stop the burning until the very last minute, when he did too little too late. . . . And people who were there are ashamed at what they saw that day. And I think there's no excuse for it. I'm sure what I'm saying now is going to provoke some reaction on the part of the commanding officers in Sarajevo, British and American and French, but I have to tell it the way I saw it, and this was not what the President of the United States or his senior civilian advisers had in mind. And they had the authority. These military men had the authority to arrest the arsonists and put out the fires. They simply chose not to do so.[71]

The passive performance of IFOR in Bosnia does not stand alone. The initial phase of Operation Restore Democracy, eighteen months before in Haiti, was criticized in the major official professional journal of the U.S. Army, *Military Review* (July-August 1997), and by the U.S. Army War College Strategic Studies Institute.[72] Operation Restore Democracy began in September 1995 with the wrenching internationally televised images of soldiers, tears streaming down their faces, being forced by their superiors, incorrectly it turned out, to stand by as noncombatants were beaten and even bludgeoned to death. The dead Haitians lying before these tearful soldiers only hinted, however, at the even greater atrocity that had taken place a continent away, when three months before 800,000 noncombatant Rwandans were massacred and placed in mass graves as U.S. military aerial intelligence platforms flew overhead providing detailed reports of the daily progress of the genocide to both the Pentagon and the UN. The hysterical reaction of the American public to televised scenes of a couple of American bodies being dragged through the streets of Mogadishu in Somalia in the fall of 1993 is not a sufficient explanation for the dishonorable American official inaction in Rwanda, Haiti, or Bosnia.

After the end of the cold war, one of the problematic legacies of Air-Land Battle doctrine was in its character as the extreme manifestation of the U.S. Army's 200-year-old refusal to provide a sufficient doctrinal base for constabulary operations. Morris Janowitz, in the conclusion of his essential *The Professional Soldier* (1960), insisted that "the worth of the military profession has been deeply rooted in the importance of its non-military functions."[73] The obvious importance of operations that fall somewhere between full combat operations and police duties, which Janowitz classifies as "constabulary," is not belied by the fact that they have been more frequent in the history of the armed forces of the United States than have full combat operations.

In the 1982 edition of FM 100-5, the amount of space provided such operations was a mere four pages. They were similarly ignored in the 1986 edition, and were not incorporated into FM 100-5 until the 1993 edition that replaced Clausewitzian Air-Land Battle doctrine with a doctrine that addressed "what the Constitution and U.S. Code Title 10, Section 3062 demanded of the Army: to fight and win wars and perform every other mission that the civilian leadership assigned."[74] This effort came too late and was too disorganized to affect the unsuccessful American interventions in Haiti and Rwanda in 1994. In Haiti, for example, planners were confused as to which doctrines to apply to the operation order: the Military Operations Other Then War (MOOTW) concept in the 1993 edition of FM 100-5; the concept of Military Operations in Low Intensity Conflict (LIC) found in the 1990 publication of FM 100-20; or the new ultra anti-Clausewitzian concept of Peace Operations found in the new FM 100-23 (1994).[75]

The operational experience of the 1990s consisted of failed, or at best, marginally successful operations carried out for humanitarian purposes. the United States' lukewarm military efforts in Operation Restore Hope (Somalia, December 1992), Operation Restore Democracy (Haiti, Fall 1994), as well as the nation's abject failure to make a responsible effort to prevent the recurrence of the practice of genocide in the former Yugoslavia and Rwanda, demonstrated a lack of political will on the part of the Clinton White House and tolerance of failure for these specific operations by military leaders. It was not until the U.S.-led NATO war in Kosovo in 1999 that American and NATO prestige was imperiled enough to ensure that the mounting political price of another indecisive military engagement was too high to bear, even if the mission was merely humanitarian.

After a decade of executing unenthusiastic security operations in support of humanitarian objectives, the legacy of the "we are not the world's policeman" mantra of the 1990s would manifest in Operation Iraqi Freedom in 2003 as the U.S. military failed to secure the civilian population and infrastructure of Baghdad (excepting the Oil Ministry), which is proximate cause of the success of the ongoing insurgency in Iraq. As thousands of U.S. citizens lose their lives in an irregular conflict that is increasingly reminiscent of the Vietnam War—the type of war that the Clausewitzian military renaissance was supposed to ensure would never be fought again—the United States is now paying in spades for the military's post-Vietnam pattern of extreme force protection and its Clausewitzian contempt for noncombat functions. Unfortunately, the cost in Iraqi life is in the tens of thousands.

While formal capstone doctrine underwent substantial changes over the last quarter of the twentieth century, as neo-Clausewitzian realism was formalized in U.S. military doctrine for the first time, formal keystone doctrine has remained relatively constant in comparison. The 1956 edition of FM 27–10, *The Law of Land Warfare*, remains the operative doctrinal manual on the law of armed conflict. For the past twenty-four years, Parks has been tasked to draft an updated manual. This manual will be published under the new Joint Doctrine Publication System, which will apply to all services and will eventually supplant all field manuals. Parks has been working with his counterparts in "English-speaking nations and some of our NATO allies" to reach a consensus on doctrine, in spite of the United States' unique position as a nonsigner of Protocol I. As of this writing, this undertaking has yet to be accomplished, for good or ill.[76]

However, DoD Directive 5100.17, *The Department of Defense Law of War Program*, has undergone subtle changes in this period that are probably indicative of the changes to be expected in the new joint manual. The 1974, post-My Lai edition of the directive expanded humanitarian principles from narrow legal norms focused on declared norms toward a professional military ethic encompassing all military operations affecting noncombatants. "The Armed Forces of the United States will comply with the law of war in the conduct of military operations and related activities in armed conflict, however such conflicts are characterized."[77] The 1998 edition of the manual interjected a notable qualification, namely, that the law of war will be complied with during "all armed conflicts, however such conflicts are characterized, and with the *principles and spirit* [italics mine] of the law of war during all other operations."[78] This minimalist wording reflects Parks's expert testimony in the trials of both Gen. Manuel Noriega of Panama and the present author regarding how the Geneva Conventions did not "technically" apply to Operation Just Cause in Panama in 1989 or to Operation Restore Democracy in Haiti in 1994.[79]

In the direct aftermath of the U.S. failure to apply the Nuremberg-era standards of command responsibility in the trials following the massacre disaster at My Lai, the United States took the lead in successfully negotiating the inclusion of an affirmative definition of command responsibility in Article 86 of Protocol I. The more rigorous standard of command responsibility was not specifically a major issue in the Department of Defense's and the Reagan administration's overturning of the Army War College recommendation for ratification. However, the tendency in America's recent contribution to the development of international humanitarian law position, limiting the applicability of international humanitarian law in general, narrowed the actions for which a commander, or at least an American commander, could be held liable. The general consolidation of a more conservative *weltanschauung* within the American military profession in the 1980s affected U.S. military capstone doctrine in general and professional attitudes toward the concept of international humanitarian law in particular. The promulgation of the Air-Land Battle doctrine, the Goldwater-Nichols Act, and the Weinberger Doctrine documented the formal codification of conservative realism in American military doctrine. Despite these developments, the 1956 FM 27–10 and the affirmative Nuremberg-era standard of command responsibility contained within it remains the official keystone doctrine concerning the law of armed conflict.

Drinking from the Poisoned Chalice

Sinful man hates the equality of all men under God and, as though he were a God, loves to impose his sovereignty on his fellow men. He hates the peace of God which is just and prefers his own peace which is unjust.

AUGUSTINE

IN THE FIFTH CENTURY, Augustine individually addressed military professionals on the proper or "just" conduct of their profession without deference to the concepts of either political realism or legal positivism. Many modern authorities echo Augustine's antagonism toward mere legalism or the mere "sovereignty" of the state as foundations for the proper conduct of armed conflict. World Court Justice Richard Baxter, the author of FM 27–10, *The Law of Land Warfare*, lamented the "triumph of legalism over humanitarianism" in the contemporary discussions of international humanitarian law; and Antonio Cassese, the president of the International Criminal Tribunal for the Former Yugoslavia, used the Kantian term *leidige Tröster*, or "irritating comforters," to describe the influence of practitioners of political realism on the development of international humanitarian law.[1]

On June 30, 1995, a little over a half century after Supreme Court justice Robert H. Jackson was appointed by President Truman to be the American chief prosecutor at the International Military Tribunal at Nuremberg, the president of the International Committee of the Red Cross (ICRC), Cornelio Sommaruga, issued the first apology for that "institution's moral failure with regard to the Holocaust, since it did not succeed in moving beyond the limited legal framework established by the States."[2] Two weeks later, a Serb army and militia units captured the Bosnian town of Srebrenica and proceeded to conduct a mass-execution of over 8,000 Muslim men and boys. Only a year before, the Rwandan Genocide in which over 800,000 noncombatants was undertaken in the full view of the United Nations and U.S. intelligence assets.

In 1999, UN Secretary-General Kofi Annan signed two fact-finding reports accepting responsibility for the UN's and the international community's failures in Rwanda and Bosnia. In the case of Rwanda, the Secretary-General admitted that in 1994 the UN and the entire global community "failed to honor" the obligation it undertook after World War II to "prevent and punish" the crime of genocide; and that, in the case of Bosnia, the UN should have taken "more decisive and forceful action to prevent the unfolding horror."[3] If one accepts the maxim that with unequal power comes unequal responsibilities, it is the United States that bears, at least in the case of Rwanda, a primary responsibility. On a trip to Rwanda in 1998, even President Bill Clinton accepted responsibility for the United States' not doing what "we could have and should have done to try to limit what occurred in Rwanda in 1994."[4]

Like so much else as far as U.S. reactions to atrocities are concerned, the attack on 9/11 changed nothing. The main contribution of the American hyper-reaction to 9/11 is to clearly illuminate how a nation, after its official inaction in the face genocide (in Rwanda, and before that in Cambodia under the Khmer Rouge), can explain to the international community that history, for America, started over with murder of 3,500 Americans. The prevention of genocide remains, even after 9/11, a low priority in the new epoch's crusade against evil. In February 2006, after the loss of hundreds of thousands of lives in Darfur in the Sudan, a meeting of NATO diplomats resulted in a consensus to provide more support to the inadequate 7,000-strong African Union (AU) deployment; the use of NATO's own forces to bring up troop strength on the ground was ruled out. Groups such as Human Rights Watch and the International Crisis Group say that a ground force of up to the 20,000 is needed to end the three-year civil war that no one now denies is a genocide. President George W. Bush also wants his NATO allies to do more in Darfur—at least more than what he is doing as the leader of the sole remaining military superpower.[5]

Undeniably, the human rights of certain human populations remain less consistently enforced than others. Thanks to the work and discussion generated by Samantha Powers's *A Problem from Hell: America and the Age of Genocide*, we now understand the banality of those who are willing to do by inaction what Hannah Arendt's Adolf Eichmann was willing to do by deliberate action.[6] We cannot avoid the fact that military commanders still often answer to political leaders and are representatives of societies that are hostile or functionally indifferent to the lives of the noncombatant populations that come in contact with their forces. In spite of that, some commanders are still being held responsible for the lives of noncombatants in areas in which their forces operate or operated. Along with the "never again (and we really mean it this time)" sanctimony and regret, the international community, over the past few decades, has introduced enforcement mechanisms to apply international humanitarian law, although applicable only to particular conflicts or, more important, particular nations.

Current Standards of Command Responsibility

Three tribunals were created to address the issue of enforcement. Two of the tribunals, the International Criminal Tribunal for the former Yugoslavia (ICTY) and the International Criminal Tribunal for Rwanda (ICTR), also known as the ad hoc tribunals, addressed past and current crimes for a specific geographic region over a specific time span. The third tribunal, the International Criminal Court (ICC), was established by the Rome Treaty of 1998 to address future crimes on the basis an international reciprocity of application. The preamble of the Rome Treaty recalled that it is "the duty of every State to exercise its criminal jurisdiction over those responsible for international crimes."[7] The court would only take jurisdiction if, in future conflicts, a state proved it did not have the integrity or competence to do so on its own. One such historical example was the unsuccessful record of the United States in prosecuting cases of war crimes committed by its personnel in Vietnam.

The Ad Hoc Criminal Tribunals

In each of the tribunals, the texts of the articles on individual responsibility, on ruling out the defense of superior orders, and on the standard of command responsibility to be applied is the same. Specifically, language closely approximating the Nuremberg-era's "known or should of known" (regarding law-of-war violations) was incorporated in Article 7(3) of the statute of the ICTY and Article 6(3) of the statute of the ICTR. Also, the provisions on superior orders, which failed to make it in Protocol I, was incorporated into Article 7(4) of the statute of the ICTY and Article 6(4) of the statute of the ICTR:

> 3. The fact that any of the acts referred to in articles 2 to 4 of the present Statute was committed by a subordinate does not relieve his or her superior of criminal responsibility if he or she knew or had reason to know that

the subordinate was about to commit such acts or had done so and the superior failed to take the necessary and reasonable measures to prevent such acts or to punish the perpetrators thereof.

4. The fact that an accused person acted pursuant to an order of a Government or of a superior shall not relieve him or her of criminal responsibility, but may be considered in mitigation of punishment if the International Tribunal for Rwanda determines that justice so requires.[8]

Thus far, the tribunals have been successful in a number of prosecutions under these provisions. In the ICTY's *Celebici* decision, the tribunal successfully prosecuted the Bosnian Serb administrator of the Celebici prison-camp, Zdravko Mucic, for the systematic rape of women and other crimes by his subordinates under the theory that "the crimes were so frequent and notorious" that Mucic's claims of ignorance could be dismissed.[9] In its *Blazkic* decision, the ICTY found Croatian colonel Tihomir Blazkic guilty for having known or having had reason to know that subordinates were preparing to commit crimes against noncombatants, for not having taken the necessary and reasonable measures to prevent these crimes; and for, following the completion of the acts, failing to report and punish the subordinates concerned.[10] Additionally, under the tribunals, command responsibility has for the first time been applied to a head of state. While the trial of former Yugoslav president Slobodan Milosevic at the ICTY ended prematurely with Milosevic's death, the ICTR successfully prosecuted the former prime minister of Rwanda, Jean Kambanda, for genocide and crimes against humanity; he is now serving a life sentence for crimes committed by his subordinates.[11]

The presence of American prosecutors and judges serving the ICTY has undermined the credibility of the court, especially with respect to the enforcement of a standard of command responsibility that has never successfully been enforced against American citizens. Rather, the presence and the leadership of Americans at the ICTY lends great credence to the tribunal's critics, such as former U.S. Attorney General Ramsey Clark, who argue that the ICTY and ICTR "are inherently discriminatory, evading the principles of equality in the administration of justice"; in contrast, the ICC is recognized as having been "created by treaty" and having universal jurisdiction.[12] ICTY and ICTR, no matter how responsibly conducted, can never escape the risk of standing as historical examples of power preaching to the vanquished, as Nurembergs lacking their Jacksons. Fortunately, the ICC has instituted protections against defendants being prosecuted or judged by citizens of a nation that does not hold itself bound by the very provisions that form the basis of a prosecution.

The International Criminal Court (ICC)

The genocidal conflicts in Rwanda and the Balkans reignited interest in a 1953 UN draft statute for a standing, permanent international tribunal. The onslaught of the cold war destroyed the possibility of obtaining the consensus needed to negotiate a final statute and proceed with the establishment of a permanent war crimes tribunal. Fifty years later, however, the cold war was over and foreign nationals were again sitting in docks awaiting judgment according to the rules first crafted by American War Department officials during World War II. The United States put forward no objection as the Nuremberg-era standards on individual and command liability for war crimes found their way into the charters of both of the ad hoc criminal tribunals. It did, however, as in the Medina case, draw the line at the prospect of allowing American citizens to be judges by the same standards. There was a great deal of consistency between the provisions of the Rome Statute for an International Criminal Court and the provisions of the ICTY and ICTR. In Article 33 of the Rome Statute, "Superior Orders and Prescription of Law," the prohibition of a defense based on superior orders was maintained. Article 28, "Responsibility of Commanders and Other Superiors," applied two distinct standards of responsibility: one specifically for military commanders and another for civilians holding authority over military or police formations. For the former, military officers officially assigned to a command position were liable if they "either knew or, owing to the circumstances at the time, should have known that the forces under their command were committing or about to commit" war crimes. For the latter, an even more rigorous standard applied in cases where a civilian "superior either knew, or consciously disregarded information which clearly indicated, that the subordinates were committing or about to commit such crimes."[13]

One major distinction between the ad hoc tribunals and the ICC was that the Rome Treaty placed, for the first time, American citizens in jeopardy of being held to the same standards of command responsibility that American judges had applied and are at present applying to foreigners. If the United States had ratified the Rome Treaty establishing the ICC, the lack of American constancy in the application of standards of command responsibility between trials of an American citizens and foreign nationals would have been resolved. Unlike the case of Protocol

I, where neoconservatives played a supporting role in the defeat of a treaty, neoconservatives in the case of the Rome Treaty would frame and execute the opposition to ratification. Subsequently, this time, the opposition would be more overtly political and venomous.

Just as in the case of the Geneva Diplomatic Conference and the Geneva Protocols of 1977, the UN General Assembly adopted a resolution on December 19, 1995, calling for the establishment of a conference to review a draft statute for a permanent international war crimes tribunal, this times drafted by the International Law Commission (ILC). Between June 15 and July 17, 1998, United Nations Diplomatic Conference of Plenipotentiaries on the Establishment of an International Criminal Court (otherwise known as the Rome Conference) negotiated The Rome Statute of the International Criminal Court (ICC).

David J. Scheffer, the ambassador-at-large for War Crimes Issues during the second Clinton administration, led the American delegation. The American attempt to reserve for itself, either directly or through the Security Council, a right to veto the jurisdiction of the court over American citizens failed. However, as in the case of Ambassador Aldrich's delegation at the Geneva Diplomatic Conference, Scheffer was able to negotiate subsequent provisions that would at least partially address the legitimate American concerns that its military personnel would be disproportionably targeted for prosecution owing to the American material capability and willingness to support international humanitarian operations: Article 8 of the statue specified that the court would deal only with serious and systematic violations of the law of war rather than with isolated incidents; Article 15 dealt with the concern that the statue could create "an international Ken Starr" who would prosecute American citizen out of political-ideological zeal, a concern that was addressed by the requirement of a standing three-judge pretrial panel that would have to approve the initiation of an investigation by the ICC prosecutor; and Article 16 allowed the Security Council to vote for a renewable twelve-month postponement, actually granting a "de facto" veto to permanent members of the security council.[14]

Despite the inclusion of these provisions, the United States voted against the final adoption of the Rome Statute of the International Criminal Court on July 17, 1998.

Unlike the multigenerational review of Protocol I, the opposition to the ICC was carried out on the floor of the U.S. Congress. In a hearing of the Senate Foreign Relations Committee on June 23, 1998, Senator Jesse Helms, the Committee's ultra-conservative chairman, laid out a five-point plan of opposition to the ICC:

1. Withdrawal of U.S. troops from any country that ratifies the ICC.
2. Mandating the Executive Branch veto any Security Council referral of any case to the ICC.
3. The blocking of funding to the ICC by any international organization of which the U.S. is a member.
4. Renegotiation of "status of forces" agreements and extradition treaties to proscribe host nations from complying with extradition requests by the ICC involving American war criminals.
5. Prohibit any U.S. military personnel from engaging in any humanitarian or regional action that may fall under the jurisdiction of the ICC.[15]

Unlike the Reagan administration, which openly opposed the ratification of Protocol I, Bill Clinton formally signed the Rome Treaty at the very end of his administration. In one of the clearest examples of disingenuousness and political cowardice by any president, Clinton had given his neoconservative employees in his own State Department every opportunity to kill the treaty and then signed it knowing full well that it would never be sent to the Senate for ratification by his successor. It would be wrong, even, to call the signing an empty gesture, for that would imply a passivity on the part the Clinton administraion that was not, in fact, part of its calculations.

Despite the efforts of the Clinton administration and subsequent efforts on the part of the second Bush administration, the Rome Treaty went into force on April 30, 2001, after the sixtieth country ratified it. Again, the United States stood out from its traditional allies who ratified a major treaty extending human rights protections and instead stood in the company of Sudan, Yemen, North Korea, Iran, and Israel, which did not. In one of the last political efforts of his career, Helms, with the assistance of Tom DeLay in the House of Representatives, pushed his program, in a slightly modified form, through Congress. This legislation, misleadingly entitled the *American Service-Members' Protection Act of 2002* (ASPA), was not simply a rejection of the Rome Treaty; it was a plan for the destruction of the ICC. Just as arch neoconservative Douglas Feith worked with Abraham Sofaer in opposition to the 1977 Geneva Protocols during the Reagan administration, so again Feith, appointed as undersecretary of defense for policy by President George W. Bush in July 2001, worked with John R. Bolton, Undersecretary of State for Arms Control and International Security, to undermine the operation of the ICC. Unlike the case with the Protocol I, where the United States' position was to respect its allies' adoption of the protocols and even to accept some articles as international customary law, the ASPA in effect drafts the entire U.S. government as an agent provocateur to undermine the court and penalize those nations that did not sign Bilateral Immunity Agreements (BIAs), which acknowledge the immunity of American personnel charged with war crimes from extradition to or prosecution by the ICC.[16]

Command Responsibility and the Road to Abu Ghraib

In February 2004, the ICRC presented a report to American officials that documented systematic abuse of prisoners of war and other detainees by American military personnel in Iraq. The most serious of the ICRC findings was the charge of "brutality against protected persons upon capture and initial custody, some causing death or serious injury" and the "excessive and disproportionate use of force against persons deprived of their liberty resulting in death or injury" during later periods of confinement.[17] After Army Specialist Joseph M. Darby discovered and turned over evidence (photographs) of the sexual degradation and other systematic abuse of detainees, which initiated an Inspector General's investigation, and after this evidence found its way onto a *60 Minutes* television broadcast on April 28, 2004, the American ground forces commander, Lt. Gen. Ricardo Sanchez, appointed Maj. Gen. Antonio Taguba to conduct a special investigation (Article 15–6) into the reports of abuse. The "Taguba Report" confirmed "numerous incidents of sadistic, blatant, and wanton criminal abuses" at the Abu Ghraib Confinement Facility between October and December 2003.[18] Finally, after a public uproar both in Western countries and the Arab world, a four-member panel, led by former Secretary of Defense James R. Schlesinger and assisted by former Secretary of Defense Harold Brown, found that both the commanding general of the 800th MP Brigade, Brig. Gen. Janis Karpinski, and the commanding general of the 205th MI Brigade, Col. Thomas Pappas, *"either knew, or should have known,* abuses were taking place and taken measures to prevent them [italics mine]."[19]

What is the significance of the existence of over 300 charges of incidents of prisoner abuse? Regardless of equivocations taken by officials in the Department of Defense's law-of-war program and the army's International and Operational Law Division regarding the application of international humanitarian law to U.S. operations, nothing in U.S. military doctrine authorizes soldiers to commit human rights violations of the type documented at Abu Ghraib prison in Iraq. Many studies have focused on how our society is habituated toward violence by our military and martial history.[20] Far too often, the opposite is in fact the case. The military is corrupted by an American human rights hypocrisy on the societal scale. One does not have to look further than major motion pictures to document the obvious fact that American soldiers are sent to war with mixed messages.

Although one can find examples humanitarian norms in warfare being held in derision in American popular culture as far back as World War II, the depiction of American soldiers violating the laws of war has become a staple in post-Vietnam American films depicting war.[21] Director Steven Spielberg, actor Tom Hanks, and historian Stephen E. Ambrose recently collaborated on a ten-part popular miniseries, *Band of Brothers*, that celebrated our World War II veterans by showing them engaging or tolerating the abuse of enemy prisoners of war in almost every episode—and the same can be said of Spielberg's epic movie, *Saving Private Ryan*.[22] If the "color of the corpses" were changed and Americans instead of German soldiers were depicted being summarily executed after being disarmed, these films would have sparked a public outrage. The abuse of prisoners in Iraq, Afghanistan, and Guantánamo was no secret that was diligently kept from the press. It was only the wont of sensational pictures that kept the stories off the front pages. In fact, just a few months prior to the leaking of the Abu Ghraib images, Fox News's Bill O'Reilly and Sean Hannity went on a crusade to try to pressure the army out of disciplining one Lt. Col. Allen B. West for mistreating a POWs during interrogations in Afghanistan. When this officer chose not to face a court-martial and settled for an administrative fine and separation from the military, O'Reilly and Hannity called on their viewers to contribute to a fund to pay the colonel's fine.[23]

American military professionals should not be blamed for the societal and cultural baggage that citizens bring with them upon entry into the military. However, the military can be blamed for not identifying when action needs to be taken to address doctrinal inconsistencies that affect good order and discipline. They can be blamed for not placing a greater emphasis on the secondary battle functions, such as the proper handling of detainees, and for failing to ensure that such sensitive and critical functions are carried out by the most competent, trained soldiers available (regardless of whether or not such functions are emphasized in Clausewitzian scripture). And, finally, they cab be blamed for sending mixed messages regarding the laws of warfare that are internal to the profession.

The Independent Panel Review, the only functionally independent review of Abu Ghraib, cited "both institutional and personal responsibility at higher levels" for the failure of military personal in maintaining proper discipline, which resulted in the failure of whole units in following known standards. The report emphasized how the legalist efforts to limit the application of Geneva Conventions in regard to one group of detainees, the so called illegal combatants, resulted in the denial of humanitarian treatment to those clearly under the protections of the Conventions. On February 7, 2002, President Bush signed a memorandum that documented his determination that detainees associated with al Qaeda are not protected under the Geneva Conventions.[24] Subsequently, detainee operations at Guantánamo became an operational model for the treatment and interrogation of prisoners worldwide regardless of the status of the prisoners. While the presidential memorandum and other orders regarding the treatment of detainees did not authorize the acts depicted in the photos of abuse at Abu Ghraib, it sent an informal message that indicated that the national command authority was more concerned with minimizing the application of the laws of warfare than with extending their application.[25]

In simple terms, the presidential memorandum and other Guantánamo-derived policies facilitated a climate of impunity that spread to other operational regions. What was a formal norm for a specific condition became an informal predisposition on the part of military professionals seeking guidance on the application of humanitarian obligations. One must ask what type of climate has been facilitated by the historic tendency of the United States (1) to be in constant opposition to new codifications of the law of warfare; (2) to be out of alignment with the closest allies as to what provisions of law of warfare to apply to multinational operations; (3) to have no action on the part of the legislative and executive branches of government in drafting legislation that would allow the prosecution of its own citizens under the same standard of command responsibility it held and holds foreign nationals.

Even if the command climate in Guantánamo, Afghanistan, and Iraq reveals factors internal to the American military profession, including a disposition to set a low priority for humanitarian concerns and a professional bias against international humanitarian law, the initiatives that led directly to abuses via were derived from external sources. If the road to Abu Ghraib went through Guantánamo, the road to Guantánamo appears to have started not in the Pentagon, but in a clique of conservative lawyers in the Department of Justice and the White House with little or no military input.[26]

It would be very convenient to point to Abu Ghraib as the logistical consequence of the present thesis, namely, that the American military profession slowly backed away from the very standards of command responsibility that it was historically responsible for developing. However, the most significant internal indicator for the military profession, to which this thesis can be fairly applied, is the lack of successful prosecution of the military intelligence and military police commanders directly responsible for the "command climate" under which their subordinates in Abu Ghraib prison acted. Even if many of the political and societal factors that led to that command climate was beyond their control, these commanders should have been held responsible under the *known or should have known* standard for failing to ascertain that criminal acts were being perpetrated or about be to perpetrated by their subordinates. That was, after all, the burden that their American professional predecessors placed on German and Japanese officers in the era of Nuremberg.

More generally, the revered Clausewitzian prodigal sons of the so-called American Military Renaissance of the 1980s and 1990s proved incapable of protecting their internal professional ethics in the face of external political and societal interference. They should have put down their Clausewitz long enough to study the example of Gen. Westmoreland standing up to the Nixon White House in the case of the My Lai prosecutions. If they are not directly responsible for the road to Abu Ghraib, they are directly responsible for the road back. And let them build a highway—if not for their god, then for suffering humankind.

Justice Jackson's "Poisoned Chalice" challenge regarding how all nations were to be equally bound by the same standards of responsibility is now laid at the door not only of the American profession of arms but of the nation itself:

> We must never forget that the record on which we judge these defendants is the record on which history will judge us tomorrow. To pass these defendants a poisoned chalice is to put it to our lips as well.[27]

How can command responsibility be consecrated as a simple and common-sense military principle if it falls short of the basic mandate that military commanders have an affirmative duty to protect the civilians and prisoners in the territory their forces occupy or control, and that this mandate extends to all military operations—limited only by clear and decisive military necessity. The supposition that the states that had signed the Nuremberg Charter would themselves fail to refrain from the defenses of absolute national sovereignty, absolute obedience, and claims of political prosecution as proffered by the Nuremberg defendants, their councils, and other contemporary critics of the IMT, is still unanswered. The incorporation into contemporary treaties of a standard of command responsibility higher than the one the United States is willing to apply to its own officers makes the cynics' case stronger. Even if one accepts the legitimacy of the case against the ratification of Protocol I and the Rome Treaty, that does not make the official position of the United States any less duplicitous in the context of the great biblical maxim "Judge not that ye be not judged." This dilemma brings us to Saint Augustine's conundrum of positing the justice of imperfect men to take up arms in defense of others. Either we must stop holding others to a higher standard or stop holding ourselves to a lower one.[28]

NOTES

Introduction: Nuremberg, Germany, November 20, 1945

1. Quoted in Telford Taylor, *The Anatomy of the Nuremberg Trial* (New York: Little, Brown, 1992), 168.

2. U.S. Army Field Manual 27-10, *Laws of Land Warfare* (Washington, D.C.: GPO, 1956). 178–179.

3. Joint Chiefs of Staff (JCS) Publication No. 1, *Terms and Acronyms* (Washington, D.C.: GPO, 2000), s.v. "doctrine."

4. "The Army's doctrine lies at the heart of its professional competence." See Department of the Army, Field Manual 100-5, *Operations* (Washington, D.C.: Department of the Army, 1990), 3. This manual describes itself as the U.S. Army's "keystone warfighting doctrine" as it "links Army roles and missions to the National Military Strategy" and describes how commanders are "to think about the conduct of campaigns, major operations, battles, engagements, and operations other than war."

5. Virgil Ney, *The Evolution of the United States Army Field Manual: Valley Forge to Vietnam* (Fort Belvior, Va.: Combat Operations Research Group, 1966). For unofficial works claiming that drill manuals should be considered as capstone doctrine, see William O. Odom, *After the Trenches: The Transformation of U.S. Army Doctrine, 1918–1939* (College Station: Texas A&M University Press, 1999), 3; and Walter Edward Kretchik, "Peering through the Mist: Doctrine as a Guide for U.S. Army Operations, 1775-2000," Ph.D. diss., University of Kansas (2001), 1–3.

6. Stanley L. Paulson, "Classical Legal Positivism at Nuremberg," *Philosophy and Public Affairs* 4 (1975): 133–135. See also Jeffrie G. Murphy and Jules L. Coleman, "The Nature of Law," in *Philosophy of Law: An Introduction to Jurisprudence*, rev. ed. (Boulder: Westview Press, 1990), 6–33.

7. Joint Publication 1–02, *Department of Defense Dictionary of Military and Associated Terms* (Washington, D.C.: GPO, April 12, 2001, as amended May 7, 2002), 62, 82.

8. See FM 22–100, *Military Leadership*, chap. 4. The draft 2000 version drops the concept of an ethical dilemma as a result of the adoption of Aristotelian virtue ethics as the base model of ethics.

9. Justice Robert Jackson, "The Significance of Nuremberg to the Armed Forces," *Military Affairs* 10 (1946): 2–15.

10. William V. O'Brien, "The Law of War, Command Responsibility, and Vietnam," *Georgetown Law Review* 60 (1972): 606.

11 There were six lawyers sitting in the dock at the IMT alone. In addition to Hans Frank, former president of the Academy of German Law, other leading members of the Third Reich's legal profession included Wilhelm Frick, the father of the legal

concept of race; Hans Frank, the former minister of justice for Bavaria; Constantin von Neurath; Ernst Kaltenbrunner; and Artur Seyss-Inquart. For Frank's declarations regarding "the majesty of law," see Eugene Davidson, *The Trial of the Germans: An Account of the Twenty-two Defendants before the International Military Tribunal at Nuremberg* (1966; reprint, Columbia: University of Missouri Press, 1997), 441. One of the trials held under Allied Control Law No. 10 was the "Justice Case," in which fourteen leading members of the Nazi judicial system were tried for crimes against humanity and the legalization of extermination.

1. Just War Doctrine and *General Order No. 100*

1. *Instructions for the Government of Armies of the United States in the Field* (1863), originally published as *General Orders No. 100*, War Department, Adjutant General's Office, April 24, 1863, cited hereafter as *General Order No. 100*. Quote taken from the title of World Court justice Richard R. Baxter's article on the origins of this document, "The First Modern Codification of the Law of War," *International Review of the Red Cross* 25 (April 1963): 171–189, and 26 (May 1963): 235–250.

2. See Telford Taylor's foreword to *The Law of War: A Documentary History*, ed. Leon Friedman (New York: Random House, 1972), xvii–xviii.

3. The definitive biography of Francis Lieber, although somewhat dated, remains Frank Freidel, *Francis Lieber* (Baton Rouge: Louisiana State University Press, 1977). Substantial biographical information is also available in Charles R. Mack and Henry H. Lesesne, eds., *Francis Lieber and the Culture of the Mind* (Columbia: University of South Carolina Press, 2005); John Catalano, *Francis Lieber, Hermeneutics, and Practical Reason* (Lanham, Md.: University Press of America, 2000); and Richard Shelly Hartigan, *Lieber's Code and the Law of War* (Chicago: Precedent, 1983).

4. In 1821, Lieber's party of volunteers were not only refused the right to fight the Turks, they were robbed and denied sustenance before escaping their Greek allies turned captors. See Baxter, "The First Modern Codification," 172.

5. Francis Lieber, *Manual of Political Ethics* (Philadelphia: J. B. Lippincott, 1838–1839), reprinted 1876. In addition to this work, which served as a basic text for American law students until the end of the nineteenth century, Lieber's political and legal philosophy may also found in his *On Civil Liberty and Self Government*, 3d ed. (Philadelphia: J. B. Lippincott, 1877), and *Legal and Political Hermeneutics; or, Principles of Interpretation and Construction in Law and Politics*, 3d ed., ed. William G. Hammond (St. Louis: F/H Thomas, 1880). For a discussion of the relationship between Lieber's philosophical hermeneutics and his political ethics, see Catalano, *Francis Lieber.* Judith Shklar defined legalism as "the ethical attitude that holds moral conduct to be a matter of rule followings," and the moral relationship to consist of duties and rights determined by rules. See her *Legalism: Laws, Morals, and Political Trials* (Cambridge: Harvard University Press, 1964), 1.

6. Lieber, *On Civil Liberty*, 270–346. While Calhoun's "concurrent democracy" stressed the balance of power between minorities and majorities, Lieber's "institutional democracy" emphasized the balance between individual liberty and social/institutional responsibilities.

7. Francis Lieber, *Amendments to the Constitution, Submitted to the Consideration of the American People* (New York: Loyal Publication Society, 1865).

8. Francis Lieber to Henry W. Halleck (November 13, 1862). The Lieber-Halleck correspondence found in the Lieber Papers at the Huntington Library, San Marino, Calif., is reprinted in Hartigan, *Lieber's Code and the Laws of War*, 79–84.

9. See note 1.

10. War Department Document No. 467, *Rules of Land Warfare* (Washington, D. C.: Office of the Chief of Staff, 1917). Baxter argued that this document "preserved much of Lieber's language." See "The First Modern Codification," 249, n. 26. The document was later superseded by Department of the Army, Field Manual 27–1, *Rules of Land Warfare* (Washington, D.C.: GPO, 1940), subsequently replaced by the present edition of the manual of which Baxter himself was the primary author. See note 22.

11. For a discussion of foundational or "keystone" doctrine, see the Introduction, note 4.

12. See H. W. Henry Wagner Halleck, *Elements of Military Art And Science: or Course of Instruction in Strategy, Fortification, Tactics of Battles, etc., Embracing Actions of Staff, Infantry, Cavalry, Artillery, and Engineers adjusted to the use of Volunteers and Militia*, 3d ed. (New York: D. Appleton, 1862) and *International Law; or, Rules regulating the Intercourse of States in Peace and War* (New York: D. von Nostrand, 1861).

13. See letter from James A. Seddon, Confederate War Secretary, Richmond, to Robert Ould, Agent of Exchange, June, 24, 1863, denouncing *General Order No. 100*. Reprinted in Hartigan, *Lieber's Code*, 120–130.

14. John Keegan, *A History of Warfare* (New York: Knopf, 1993), 3.

15. Augustine to Boniface, Letter 189 (6). Except for those from the *City of God*, all citations for the writings of Augustine are from *Augustine, Political Writing*, ed. E. M. Atkins and R. J. Dodaro (Cambridge: Cambridge University Press, 2001).

16. Cicero, *Pro Milone* (Oxford: Clarendon Press, 1956), 4, 11. Although, following the Roman practice of *bellum Romanum*, or unlimited war, Cicero placed no constraints on the conduct of war, he distinguished a just war from an unjust war as one waged for the sole purpose of repelling or punishing aggression. See *De officiis* (Cambridge: Harvard University Press, 1968), 1, 11.

17. For a general overview of Saint Augustine and just war doctrine, see R. A. Markus, "Saint Augustine's Views on the Just War," in *The Church and War*, ed. W. J. Shields (Oxford: Published for the Ecclesiastical Society by B. Blackwell, 1983), 1–13; Paul Ramsey, "The Just War According to St. Augustine," in *Just War Theory*, ed. Jean Bethke Elshtain (New York: New York University Press, 1992), 8–22; and Simon Chesterman, *Just War or Just Peace?* (Oxford: Oxford University Press, 2001), 9, n. 13.

18. Class given by Col. Glenn Weidner, U.S. Army, the last commandant of the U.S. Army School of the Americas during Human Rights Week in January 1999 and February 2000. Weidner was formerly a student of the preeminent just war theoretician J. Bryan Hehir while a Fellow attending Harvard University's Center for International Affairs.

19. Though leading pacifist theorists such as Henry David Thoreau, Mahatma Gandhi, and Martin Luther King Jr. argued that pacifism required an affirmative requirement for an individual to renounce and forswear the benefits received from

unjust state action or commerce with unjust states, such ethical consistency is less stressed among many contemporaries who claim to be pacifists.

20. See Richard J. Regan, *Just War, Principles and Cases* (Washington, D.C.: Catholic University of America Press, 1996), 4–7.

21. Augustine, *City of God*, trans. Gerald G. Walsh et al. (New York: Image Books, 1958), xix, 12.

22. Hannah Arendt's doctoral thesis on the centrality of social obligations in Augustine's ethical writings is contained in *Love and Saint Augustine*, ed. Joanna V. Scott and Judith C. Stark (Chicago: University of Chicago Press, 1996), 100.

23. Aristotle *Politics* 1, 3–5.

24. Augustine, *City of God*, xv, 4.

25. Ibid., xv, xviii, 2, 6.

26. On the prohibition against self-defense, see Regan, *Just War*, 17. For a critique of the myth of Augustine as the progenitor of holy war ideology, see Markus, "Saint Augustine's Views," 10–13.

27. National Conference of Catholic Bishops, *The Challenge of Peace: God's Promise and Our Response: A Pastoral Letter on War and Peace* (Washington, D.C.: United States Catholic Conference, 1983).

28. Augustine, *City of God*, xix, 7.

29. Paul Ramsey: *The Just War: Force and Political Responsibility* (New York: Scribner, 1968), 143.

30. See NCCB, *The Challenge of Peace*.

31. "War is always judged twice, first in reference to the reasons states have for fighting, second with reference to the means they adopt. The first is adjectival: we say that a war is just or unjust. The second is adverbial: we say a war is being fought justly or unjustly." Michael Walzer, *Just and Unjust Wars: A Moral Argument with Historical Illustrations* (New York: Basic Books, 1977), 21.

32. This was the former view of the author, as found in Captain Lawrence Rockwood, U.S. Army, "Apology of a Buddhist Soldier," *Tricycle, A Buddhist Review* (Spring 1996): 70–77. Others holding this position include William V. O'Brien, "The International Law of War as Related to the Western Just War Tradition," in *Just War and Jihad*, ed. John Kelsey and James T. Johnson (New York: Greenwood Press, 1991), 165; and Homes, "St. Augustine and the Just War Theory," 338. The opposite is the present view of the author, and is also found in Paul Ramsey, *War and the Christian Conscience: How Shall Modern War Be Conducted Justly?* (Durham: Duke University Press, 1961).

33. See Steven Runciman, *A History of the Crusades* (New York: Harper Torchbooks, 1964), 1: 39–40, 86, 107, 108–109.

34. Thomas Aquinas, *Summa theologiae*, II–III.

35. Bartolomé de Las Cases, quoted in Tzvetan Todorov, *The Conquest of America: The Question of the Other* (New York: Harper Perennial, 1992), 162.

36. Regan, *Just War*, 17–18.

37. Francisco de Vitoria, *On the Law of War*, 3, 3–4, v. 43. All citations from the works of Vitoria are from *Vitoria, Political Writings*, ed. Anthony Pagden and Jeremy Lawrence (Cambridge: Cambridge University Press, 2001), 319.

38. Bryan J. Hehir, "Kosovo, A War of Values and the Values of War," *America*, May 15, 1999, 17, 7.

39. Vitoria, *On the Law of War*, v. 60.

40. Aquinas, *Summa theologiae*, I–II. Grotius later combined the law of nations into positive law, leaving the division of law into the categories *lex divina, lex naturalis,* and *lex humana*. See Grotius in the "Prolegomena" to *De Jure Belli ac Pacis*, trans. Francis W. Kelsey (Indianapolis: Bobbs-Merrill, 1962).

41. In reference to Augustine's application of just war criteria to non-Christians, see note 37.

42. Two authors who utilized these four principles to characterize Grotius's contribution to the laws of warfare are Robert A. Kahn, "The Law of Nations and the Conduct of War in the Early Times of the Standing Army," *Journal of Politics* 6 (1944): 87, and Cornelis van Vollenhoven, *Grotius and Geneva* (Leiden: E. J. Brill, 1926), 13–16.

43. See note 2.

44. Hobbes, *Leviathan*, bk. 1, chaps. 8 and 9.

45. Ibid., chap. 15.

46. Kahn, "Law of Nations" 90–100.

47. Grotius cited by Arthur Schopenhauer, *On the Basis of Morality*, trans. E. F. J. Payne (Oxford: Berghahn Books, 1995), 70, n. 19.

48. Emerich de Vattel, *Le droit des gens.*, trans./ed. Joseph Chitty (Philadelphia: T. & J. W. Johnson, 1879), bk. 2, art. 150, and bk. 3, art. 103.

49. As quoted by Lieber, *Political Ethics*, 56.

50. This was the position of a critic of both Kant's and Grotius's ethics, the nineteenth-century German philosopher Arthur Schopenhauer, who countered with a universal ethic basic to the natural foundation of human interconnectedness. As the foremost advocate integrating ancient Indian and modern philosophy, Schopenhauer posited what he considered a truly universal ethic that mandated an affirmative intervention, as found in the teachings of Vedic Hinduism, Buddhism, and early Christianity. Schopenhauer tried to further universalize Kant's passive imperative of *neminem laede* ("injure no one") into an affirmtaive imperative of *neminem laude immo omnes, quantum potes, iava* ("injure no one, on the contrary, help everyone as much as you can"). See *On the Basis of Morality*, 70.

51. For just war elements in Islamic sources, see Said El-Dakkak, "International Humanitarian Law Lies Between the Islamic Concept and Positive International Law," *International Review of the Red Cross* 782 (March/April 1990): 101–116. For Buddhist sources, see Rockwood, "Apology of a Buddhist Soldier," 70–77. Other non-Western sources—for example, Hindu texts such as the Mahabharat and Ramaajan, the ethical guidelines of the Hindu Kshatria warrior caste; Sun Tzu's Chinese classic *The Art of War*; and several African sacred traditions—place more on the conduct of war and the mitigation of its "harmful consequences" than on the just or unjust causes of wars. A review of the 1988–1994 volumes of *International Review of the Red Cross* on the international origins of humanitarian law reveals that the emphasis on *jus ad bellum* is not a universal characteristic of the discussion of the morality and ethics of violence in war. See especially L. R. Penna, "Written and Customary Provisions Relating to the Conduct of Hostilities and Treatment of Victims of Armed Conflict in Ancient India," 778 (July/August 1989): 333–48, and Mutoy Mubiala, "African States and the Promotion of Humanitarian Principles," 776 (March/April 1989): 93–110.

52. Hegel defined the state as the "concrete manifestation of the 'ethical whole' " and the "essential being, the unity of the subjective will and the universal." See *Lectures on the Philosophy of World History*, trans. H. B. Nisbet (Cambridge: Cambridge University Press, 1975), 93.

53. For Augustine and other classical writers, the basic political unity was the city. "The source of blessedness is not one thing for a human being and another for a city: a city is indeed nothing other than a like-minded mass of human beings." See Augustine to Macedonis, Letter 155. For Lieber, the state is a society composed of those "who have the same interest and strive unitedly for it." See *Political Ethics*, 147.

54. For a discussion of the East/West dichotomy in the debate on human rights universalism, see Daniel A. Bell, *East Meets West: Human Rights and Democracy in East Asia* (Princeton: Princeton University Press, 2000); Thomas M. Frick, "Are Human Rights Universal," *Foreign Affairs* 80 (2001): 191–204; and Peter R. Baehr, "Controversies in the Current International Human Rights Debate," *Human Rights Review* 2 (October/December 2000): 7–32.

55. Samuel P. Huntington, *The Clash of Civilizations and the Remaking of World Order* (New York: Simon & Schuster, 1996), 69–70, 187.

56. R. Niebuhr, "Augustine's Political Realism," in *The City of God: A Collection of Critical Essays*, ed. Dorothy F. Donnelly (New York: Peter Lang, 1995). Niebuhr reached "conclusions about the propriety of war not substantially different from those of traditional just war theorists." See Regan, *Just War*, 18.

57. For just war doctrine and Protestant denominations, see Regan, *Just War*, 19.

58. Department of the Army, Field Manual 27-10, *The Law of Land Warfare* (Washington, D.C., GPO, 1954), hereinafter cited as FM 27-10.

59. Baxter, "The First Modern Codification," 176.

60. Lieber, *Political Ethics*, 446.

61. Works cited by Lieber include Halleck's *International Law* as well as Grotius, Bymkershoek, Pufendorf, and von Martins among many other lesser known authors on the laws of war. See Baxter, "The First Modern Codification," 224.

62. "Peace is their normal condition, war is the exception. The ultimate object of all modern wars is a renewed state of peace," *General Order No. 100*, art. 29. Grotius wrote, "war is undertaken for the sake of peace"; see *De Jure Belli ac Pacis*, bk. 1, chap. 1.

63. For Vitoria's defense of limited slavery, see note 39. For Aristotle's unlimited defense of slavery, see note 23.

64. Lieber, *Political Ethics*, 81.

65. Grotius, *De Jure Belli ac Pacis*, bk. I, chap. 2, art. vii.

66. Augustine wrote to the renegade Boniface that, "if Roman Empire provides you with good things, even if they are ephemeral and earthly (for it is an earthly, not an heavenly, institution and can only provide what is in its power); if then it has bestowed good things upon you, do not return evil for good." See Augustine to Boniface, Letter 220 (8).

67. Edward M. Coffman, "The Army Officer and the Constitution," *Parameters* 17 (September 1987): 2–12.

68. See Augustine to Macedonis (a Catholic official), Letter 153. Augustine's po-

litical writings are peppered with supplications to Christian officials to meditate on their own imperfection in the context of their judgment of others by constant referrals to the Gospel passage in which Jesus cautions the would-be executioners of the woman caught in adultery: "If any of you are without sin, let him be the first to cast a stone at her." See Augustine, "Commentary on the Gospel of John," 33, and "On the Feast of St. Lawrence," Sermon 302 (7).

69. Augustine to Boniface, Letter 189 (4).

70. Arthur Schopenhauer wrote that "there are actions whose mere *omission* is a wrong, and they are called duties." He coined the term *doppelte Ungerechtigkeit*, or "double injustice," to describe the "non-fulfillment of an obligation" that leads to the injury of another person. See *On the Basis of Morality*, 156.

71. Robert L. Homes, "St. Augustine and the Just War Theory," in *The Augustinian Tradition*, ed. Gareth B. Matthews (Berkeley: University of California Press, 1999), 336.

72. Vattel, *Law of Nations*, bk. 3, art. 39.

73. Augustine to Nectarius, Letter 91 (9).

74. *General Order No. 100*, art. 21.

75. Augustine to Boniface, Letter 189 (6).

76. For both Augustine and Lieber, the basis for ethical action is a selfless love (Augustine, see note 31) or the possession of "sympathy or fellow feelings" toward others (Lieber, *Political Ethics*, 20) that must be expressed by a constructive engagement with the world as it is rather than as it ought to be. While Lieber admired the universal tone of Kant's categorical imperative, he dismissed the intentionalism, passivity, and otherworldliness of Kant's ethics when he wrote "Laws and institutions are nothing more than dead forms of words, unless they operate." See Lieber, *Political Ethics*, 78.

77. The famous case, of Yolanda Huet-Vaughn, a U.S. Army Reserve captain who served eight months in prison for refusing to serve in the Gulf War, involved a soldier who declined to serve in what she considered an unjust war. Her critics emphasized that she accepted a commission and served actively in the reserves during a period in which the U.S. military was involved in similar operations, albeit on a lesser scale. The army's Court of Military Review later overturned her conviction, ruling that she was denied the opportunity at her trial to present evidence that the Gulf War was illegal and immoral. See Colman McCarthy, "Anti-War Doctor Under Fire," *Washington Post*, November 30, 1993.

78. Saint Augustine, *The City of God*, xix, 7.

79. Augustine to Darius, Letter 229 (2).

80. Sun Tzu, *The Art of War*, trans. Samuel B. Griffith (London: Oxford University Press, 1963), 76.

81. In future wars, the United States Army would continue to engage its adversaries with the advantage of greater material resources but not always with the moral determination to accept the costs that resorting to war entails. That was not the case for the U.S. Army in 1863, as it finally started accepting the costs required to win a war of military attrition.

82. James A. Seddon to Robert Ould, June 24, 1863.

83. Saint Augustine, *The City of God*, xv and 4.

84. Augustine to Boniface, Letter 189 (4).

85. Ibid., 6.

86. Lieber's doctrinal longevity is also related to his avoidance of maneuver. Lieber's purpose, in spite of his direct experience of war, was not to provide regular forces with tactical and strategic principles to defeat other regular forces in set battles. Although he intended his code to be applicable to such, in fact his code emphasized the very aspects that regular force commanders have always tried to avoid and never have succeeded in avoiding, constabulalary function and the handling of irregular forces.

87. See Walzer, *Just and Unjust Wars*, 251–283; O'Brien, "The Challenge of War: A Christian Realist Perspective," in Elshtain, *Just War Theory*, 169–196; Regan, *Just War*, 100–121; and Ramsey, *The Just War*, 211–258. It is ironic, now that the necessity for such means has diminished, that the issue of proportionality has all but ceased being a central concern.

88. Augustine to Boniface, Letter 189 (6).

89. For a discussion on contemporary views of *General Order No. 100* in reference to reprisals and denial of quarter, see Theodor Meron, "Francis Lieber's Code and the Principles of Humanity," *Columbia Journal of Transnational Law* 36 (1997): 269–274.

90. The prominent civil rights attorney and Harvard Law School faculty member Alan Dershowitz equivocated on a categorical prohibition against torture to extort information from those he considered terrorists, first in the case of Israel in 1988 and then in the case of the United States after September 11, 2001. See Ken Gewertz, *Harvard Gazette*, December 13, 2001, 8. For other contemporary equivocations of the prohibition of torture, see William V. O'Brien, "The Law of War, Command Responsibility and Vietnam," *Georgetown Law Journal* 60 (1972): 648; and Michael Levin, "The Case for Torture," *Newsweek*, June 7, 1982, 13, reprinted in *The Norton Reader*, 6th ed. (Ontario: Penguin Books Canada, 1988), 364.

91. Frank Newman, ed., *International Human Rights: Law, Policy, and Process*, 2d ed. (Cincinnati: Anderson Publishing, 1996), 3.

92. One of the greatest critics of the ICRC's doctrine of neutrality and silence is Médicins san Frontières. See Michael Ignatieff, *The Warrior's Honor: Ethnic War and the Modern Conscience* (New York: Metropolitan Books, 1997), 124. The most authoritative critic of the international community's and his own office's problematic observance of neutrality and voluntarism in humanitarian operations is former undersecretary-general for peacekeeping operations Kofi Annan, now secretary-general of the United Nations. See UN Press Release SG/SM/7263 AFR/196, 16 December 1999, "Report of the Secretary-General Pursuant to General Assembly Resolution 53/35" (1998), "Srebrenica Report" (1998), and "Report of the Independent Inquiry into the Actions of the United Nations During the 1994 Genocide in Rwanda" (1999).

93. The ICRC continues to operate under the protocol that it will only inspect confinement facilities upon invitation of national authorities. On June 23, 1944, the Nazi *Schutzstaffel* (SS) voluntarily allowed the neutral ICRC to inspect Theresienstadt. On September 27, 1944, Dr. Maurice Rossel, the ICRC delegate, attempted to inspect Auschwitz and was refused by its commandant. A positive effort by the

ICRC to press the Third Reich would have violated the organization's protocols. The ICRC now requires an invitation to inspect all confinement facilities within a prison system. See *ICRC Action on Behalf of Prisoners* (Geneva: ICRC, November 1, 1977).

94. See Howard Zinn, "A Just Cause, Not a Just War," *Progressive* 65 (December 2001): 12.

95. See Louise Doswald-Beck and Sylvain Vite, "International Humanitarian Law and Human Rights Law," *International Review of the Red Cross* 293 (1993): 94–119.

96. Taylor, foreword to *Laws of War*, xvii.

97. U.S. House of Representatives, 40th Cong., 2d sess., House Executive Document (The Andersonville Trial), vol. 8, no. 23 (1865), 19–20.

98. The most notorious example of falsely comparing Sherman's March to later war atrocities is the habeas corpus ruling by Judge Robert Elliot in a district court in Columbus, Ga., in which Sherman's March was used as a historical example to justify his ruling that U.S. Army Lt. William Calley should be freed from confinement for the murder, rape, sodomy, and mutilation of over 500 noncombatants at My Lai in Vietnam in 1968. See Michael Bilton and Kevin Sim, *Four Hours in My Lai* (New York: Viking Penguin, 1992), 356. While there was an unquestionable massacre against noncombatants by Federal forces during the period of the Civil War, it was not against citizens of the Confederacy. On November 29, 1864, the Sand Creek or Chivington Massacre involved the slaughter of hundreds of friendly and disarmed Cheyenne Indians in southeastern Colorado Territory by a force of 1,200 Federal militia under Col. John M. Chivington, a local Baptist minister. Regular army forces present at the scene refused to 'participate. Chivington escaped court-martial by leaving Federal service prior to the preparation of military charges against him.

99. See Charles Royster, *The Destructive War: William Tecumseh Sherman, Stonewall Jackson, and the Americans* (New York: Vintage Books, 1991), 358.

100. General F. C. Ainsworth, Chief of the Records and Pension Office, to James Ford Rhodes, June 29, 1903, cited in James M. McPherson, *Battle Cry of Freedom: The Civil War Era* (New York: Oxford University Press, 1988), 802.

101. Davis's articles in *Belford's Magazine* in January and February of 1890 were cited and summarized by Col. Norton Parker Chipman in *The Tragedy of Andersonville: Trial of Captain Henry Wirz, The Prison Keeper* (Sacramento: N. P. Chipman, 1911), 19–26. Chipman, the judge advocate who prosecuted Wirz, wrote this work, at the behest of the membership of the Grand Army of the Republic, to respond to the Davis articles. Subsequent pro-Confederate claims of moral relativity between U.S. and C.S.A. prison policies and conditions can be found in Mildred Lewis Rutherford, *Facts and Figures vs. Myths and Misrepresentations: Henry Wirz and the Andersonville Prison* (Athens, Ga.: United Daughters of the Confederacy, 1921), 29. Subsequently, the Georgia chapter of the UDC proclaimed Wirz a martyr and erected a monument that is still standing, although the Georgia legislature refused—even at the height of southern anti-desegregation agitation in 1958-to use state funds to repair it.

102. McPherson, *Battle Cry of Freedom*, 706, 802.

103. Chipman, *The Tragedy of Andersonville*, 22.

104. House Executive Document (The Andersonville Trial), 706.

105. Captain Henry Wirz, C.S.A., Andersonville, Georgia, May 7, 1865, to General J. H. Wilson, U.S. Army, reprinted in Friedman, *The Law of War*, 784–785.

106. Text of Article 8 of the 1945 London Charter: "The fact that the Defendant acted pursuant to order of his Government or of a superior shall not free him from responsibility, but may be considered in mitigation of punishment if the Tribunal determines that justice so requires." This article was applied by the International Military Tribunal and in the subsequent Nuremberg trials, including the Hostage Case, the Einsatzgruppen Case, and the Command Case. See Howard S. Levie, *Terrorism in War: The Law of War Crimes* (Dobbs Ferry, N.Y.: Oceana Publications, 1993), 518.

107. House Executive Document (The Andersonville Trial), 773.

108. Chipman, *The Tragedy of Andersonville*, 28.

109. The other co-conspirators named in the final indictment, John H. Winder (deceased), Richard B. Winder, Joseph Isaiah H. White, W. S. Winder, and R. R. Stevenson, were not tried. A similar situation occurred during the prosecution of the perpetrators of the My Lai Massacre in Vietnam after the death of Col. Frank Barker and the difficulties his death created for the prosecution of Barker's subordinates (Capt. Ernest Medina) and superiors (Col. Oren K. Henderson, Gen. Samuel Koster, and Gen. George H. Young).

110. Although the United States attempted to distribute *General Order No. 100* to Confederate forces, the idea of applying its obligations to Confederate officers following its explicit rejection by the Confederacy (see note 13) is open to criticism by those who claim that such a process creates law ex post facto.

111. As recently as 2000, Peter Maguire in his seminal *Laws and War: An American Story* (New York: Columbia University Press, 2000), 40, called the Andersonville trial a "dramatic spectacle of vengeance."

2. The Doctrinal Development of the American Military Profession

1. Two recent biographies of Carl von Clausewitz are Raymond Aron, *Clausewitz, the Philosopher of War* (Englewood Cliffs, N.J.: Prentice-Hall, 1985), and Michael Howard, *Clausewitz* (Oxford: Oxford University Press, 1983).

2. All references to On War *(Vom Kriege,* 1832) are based on the edition and translation by Michael Howard and Peter Paret (Princeton: Princeton University Press, 1976; reprint Everyman's Library, 1993).

3. Major works of Clausewitz criticism published after World War I include B. H. Liddel Hart, *The Ghost of Napoleon* (London: Faber & Faber, 1933), J. F. C. Fuller, *The Reformation of War* (London: Hutchinson, 1932), and Hans von Seeckt, *Gedanken eines Soldaten* (Leipzig: Hase & Koehler, 1935).

4. The most substantial treatment of the influences of German idealist philosophy on Clausewitz is found in Aron's *Clausewitz, the Philosopher of War*, 223–232. Clausewitz's conception of "absolute war" has been described as a "Platonic ideal" outside any reference to German idealist philosophy. See Howard's *Clausewitz*, 49. While contemporary critics of Clausewitz stress his idealism in his characterization of "ideal" or "absolute" war, his contemporary apologists minimize it. See John Keegan, *A History of Warfare* (New York: Knopf, 1993), 16–21, for an example of the

former and Bernard Brodie's introductory essay ("The Continuing Relevance of *On War"*) to *On War*, 1976 *(Vom Kriege*, 1832), 52–53, for an example of the latter. Clausewitz is not alone among those considered to be political realists who have predilections toward German idealist philosophy. For the influence of Hegelian idealism on Hans Morgenthau, see Michael W. Doyle, *Ways of War and Peace* (New York: W. W. Norton, 1997), 106n.

5. Clausewitz, *On War*, 84.

6. Doyle, *Ways of War and Peace*, 19–28.

7. See Samuel P. Huntington, *The Soldier and the State: The Theory and Politics of Civil-Military Relations* (Cambridge: Belknap Press, 1957), Henry A. Kissinger, *Nuclear Weapons and Foreign Policy* (New York: Harper and Brothers, 1957), and Harry G. Summers Jr., *On Strategy: A Critical Analysis of the Vietnam War* (Novato, Calif.: Presidio Press, 1982).

8. For a discussion of how Clausewitz's direct influence on the American military profession intensified after the American defeat in Vietnam, see the editor's introduction to *Clausewitz and Modern Strategy*, ed. Michael Howard (London: Frank Cass, 1986), 9.

9. Clausewitz, *On War*, 99.

10. *General Order No. 100*, art. 30.

11. Edward M. Coffman, in his authoritative article on the subject, disputes the contention that the Constitution played a significant role in officers' decisions to fight for or against the United States and argues that the postwar allegiance oaths required by Congress were a significant development in both military professionalism and the American civil-military relationship. See Edward M. Coffman, "The Army Officer and the Constitution" *Parameters*, September 1987, 2–12. Even Samuel P. Huntington, who held that southern culture was more facilitating of military professionalism, noted: "On the one hand, the Southern officer's political allegiances drew him to the Confederacy; on the other, his professional responsibility drew him to the Union." See Huntington, *The Soldier and the State*, 211–212.

12. Cited in Coffman, "The Army Officer and the Constitution," 5.

13. Most officers have taken this oath as an enlisted soldier or a cadet prior to their commissioning.

14. Russell F. Weigley noted in *The American Way of War* that Clausewitz's writings were, compared to Jomini's, "difficult, circumlocutory, often apparently self-contradictory." See *The American Way of War: A History of United States Military and Policy* (Bloomington: Indiana University Press, 1973), 82, 211.

15. Huntington, *The Soldier and the State*, 143–62, 172–77.

16. Major Wallace E. Walker, USA, "Emory Upton and the Army Officer's Creed" *Military Review*, April 1981, 65–68, and Russell F. Weigley, *History of the United States Army* (New York: Macmillan, 1967), 279, 281.

17. Weigley, *History of the United States Army*, 277.

18. Bvt. Maj. Gen. Emory Upton, *The Military Policy of the United States*, 4th impression (Washington D.C.: GPO, 1917), viii, xi.

19. For a discussion of foundational or "keystone" doctrine, see Introduction, note 4.

20. For a discussion of Wagner's criticism of the Prussian military tradition, see

Kretchik, "Peering through the Mist: Doctrine as a Guide for U.S. Army Operations, 1775–2000," Ph.D. diss., University of Kansas (2001), 88–92.

21. Wagner, *Organization and Tactics*, 2d ed. (Kansas City, Mo.: Hudson-Kimberly Publishing, 1897), 3, 43.

22. Upton, in his criticism that Americans "have no military policy" and that "laws whose operation have been the same in all our wars," can be utilized systemically to achieve the wisest policy possible. See Upton, *The Military Policy of the United States*, xii. Contrarily, Wagner noted that because "many diverse sentiments can influence the same army," "knowledge of human nature is half of the science of war." See Wagner, *Organization and Tactics*, 46, 49.

23. Wagner, *Organization and Tactics*, 43–44.

24. Weigley, *The American Way of War*, 174, 177.

25. Janowitz, in the conclusion of *The Professional Soldier*, insisted "the worth of the military profession has been deeply rooted in the importance of its non-military functions." See *The Professional Soldier: A Social and Political Portrait* (Glencoe, Ill.: Free Press, 1960), 438.

26. Marine major Littleton Waller reported that Smith ordered him to kill "everyone over ten years old." See Peter Maguire, *Law and War: An American Story* (New York: Columbia University Press, 2000), 60.

27. Root's address is included in his preface to Upton's *Military Policy of the United States*, iii.

28. Ibid., iv.

29. While McClellan called President Lincoln a "gorilla," he called Scott a "perfect incubus" who is either a "dotard or a traitor" and demanded that both Halleck and Secretary of War Stanton be removed after they criticized his conduct toward the enemy. Quoted in James M. McPherson, *Battle Cry of Freedom: The Civil War Era* (New York: Ballantine Books, 1989), 360, 569. Author McPherson also emphasizes the policy differences over emancipation as being key to the motives of Stanton, Halleck, and Lincoln in removing McClellan; see ibid, 502–506.

30. Upton, *Military Policy*, 384–387. For Huntington's sympathetic approach to MacArthur's dismissal, see *Soldier and the State*, 367–389.

31. Upton wrote: "Since the Rebellion, with a fatuity pregnant with future disaster, we settled down to the conviction that out total neglect of military preparation, our defeats, our sacrifices in blood and treasure, were the predestined features of a war protracted through four long years, in order that the minds of the people might be prepared for the extinction of slavery. These views, so comforting now, were not held during the war." See Upton, *Military Policy of the United States*, 385. Article 24 of *General Order No. 100* addresses slavery and the war.

32. See citations of Root as found in Maguire, *Law and War*, 62, 66, 69.

33. Letter to General Genville Dodge, July 21, 1902, cited in ibid., 308, n. 88.

34. Elihu Root, "Francis Lieber: Presidential Address at the seventh annual meeting of the American Society of International law, Washington, D.C., April 24, 1913," in *Addresses on International Subjects*, ed. Robert Bacon and James Brown Scott (1916; reprint, Freeport, N.Y.: Books for Libraries, 1969), 103.

35. Ibid., 96. Four years prior, in a letter to Andrew Carnegie, Root called Germany "the obstacle to the establishment of arbitration agreements, to the prevention of war, to disarmament, to the limitation of armaments, to all attempts to

lesson the suspicions and alarm of nations toward each other . . . Germany . . . stands, and as persistently stood since I have been familiar with foreign affairs, against that kind of progress." Cited in Maguire, *Law and War*, 69.

36. Root, "Francis Lieber," 103.

37. Root wrote of the rising professional bureaucracies, "we shall expand them, whether we approve theoretically or not; because such agencies furnish protection . . . [which] cannot be practically accomplished by the old and simple procedure of legislatures and courts." See Robert H. Wiebe, *The Search for Order, 1877–1920* (New York: Hill & Wang, 1967), vii, viii, 228; Root cited on 295–296.

38. Department of War, *Field Service Regulations* (Washington, D.C.: General Staff, 1905). Capstone doctrine is the highest category in the "hierarchy of publications" that link doctrine to national strategy and the guidelines of other government agencies, including members of international alliances and coalitions. Keystone doctrinal publications provide the foundation for a series of doctrinal publications in the same hierarchy. See JP 1-02, *Department of Defense Dictionary of Military and Associated Terms* (Washington, D.C.: GPO, 2002), 62, 82.

39. This DOD assumption was accomplished under the incomplete and belated implementation of the Goldwater-Nichols Department of Defense Reorganization Act of 1986. In 2001, Field Manual 3-0 formally superseded the FM 100-5 series, in conformity with the joint (service) numbering system. Department of the Army, Field Manual 3-0, *Operations* (Washington, D.C.: GPO, 2001); available online at http://www.adtdl.army.mil/cgi-bin/atdl.dll/fm/3-0/toc.htm.

40. Kretchik, "Peering through the Mist," 99.

41. Department of War, *Field Service Regulations* (Washington, D.C.: General Staff, 1905), 190–204.

42. Chief of Staff of the Army, *Field Service Regulations, United States Army, 1923* (Washington, D.C.: GPO, 1924), iii.

43. Donald A. Wells, *The Laws of Land Warfare: A Guide to the Army Manuals* (Westport, Conn.: Greenwood Press, 1992), 6.

44. War Department, *Rules of Land Warfare* (Washington, D.C.: GPO, 1914), 7.

45. Ibid., 13. In its appendixes, the conventions considered binding based on ratification included: (1) Convention III of The Hague, October 18, 1907, relative to openings of hostilities; (2) Convention IV of The Hague, October 18, 1907, respecting the laws and customs of war; (3) Convention V of The Hague, October 18, 1907, respecting the rights and duties of neutral powers and persons in war on land; (4) Convention VIII of The Hague, October 18, 1907, relative to the laying of automatic submarine contact mines; (5) Convention IX of The Hague, October 18, 1907, respecting bombardment by naval forces in time of war; (6) Convention XI of The Hague, October 18, 1907, relative to the right capture in naval warfare (6) Convention XIV of The Hague, October 18, 1907, prohibiting the discharge of projectiles and explosives from balloons; (7) Table of ratifications and adhesions of the second peace conference at The Hague in 1907; and (8) the International Convention for the amelioration of the condition of the wounded and sick in armies in the field at Geneva, July 6, 1906.

46. War Department, *Rules of Land Warfare* (Washington, D.C.: GPO, 1940), iii–vi.

47. Verbatim quotations from *General Order No. 100* found in *Rules of Land War-*

fare (1914) include but are not limited to: military necessity (Articles 11–13), reprisals (Articles 380–381), and protections of prisoners of war (Article 47). In the case of *Rules of Land Warfare* (1940), see military necessity (Articles 23–25) and protections of prisoners of war (Article 77d).

48. Relevant articles expanding the prohibitions of *General Order No. 100* found in *Rules of Land Warfare* (1914) are: denying quarter (Articles 182–183), collateral damage (Articles 172, 184, 212, 217, 218), care of prisoners (Articles 49–64), and care for sick and wounded (Articles 105, 108). In the *Rules of Land Warfare* (1940), see: denying quarter (Article 33), collateral damage (Articles 26, 34, 45, 50, 51), care of prisoners (Articles 74–76, 81–90), and care for sick and wounded (Articles 173–201).

49. Maguire, *Law and War*, 77.

50. Henry Stimson to Warren G. Harding, January 28, 1921, Henry Stimson Papers at Yale University, cited in Jack C. Lane, *Armed Progressive: General Leonard Wood* (San Rafael: Presidio, 1978), 154, 148–149.

51. John K. Mahon, *History of the Militia and the National Guard* (New York: Macmillan, 1983), 152–153.

52. Lane, *Armed Progressive*, 148.

53. Milton M. McPherson, *The Ninety-Day Wonders: OCS and the Modern American Army* (Fort Benning, Ga.: U.S. Army Officer Candidate Alumni Association, 2001), 24–51.

54. John McAuley Palmer, *America in Arms: The Experience of the United States with Military Organization* (New Haven: Yale University Press, 1941), 136–137, and *Statesmanship or War* (Garden City, N.Y.: Doubleday, 1927), 29, cited in Weigley, *History of the United States Army*, 398.

55. War Department, Tentative Field Manual 100-5, *Operations*, 1939 (Washington, D.C.: GPO, 1939), 29–30. Kretchik, "Peering through the Mist," 126.

56. See *Infantry in Battle* (Washington, D.C.: Infantry Journal, 1939), 1, 14, cited in Weigley, *American Way of War*, 215.

57. Weigley, *History of the United States Army*, 426.

58. Interview between George Marshall and his official biographer, Forrest C. Pogue, on January 22, 1957. Cited in Pogue, *George C. Marshal: Ordeal and Hope* (New York: Viking Press, 1966), 461, n. 33. See also McPherson, *The Ninety-Day Wonders*, 63.

59. Gen. Marshall's address to the first Officer Candidate School (OCS) class in October 1941 as read by its commandant, Gen. Omar Bradley, and witnessed by the author's late father standing in formation with the other graduates. Reprinted in *Selected Speeches and Statements of General of the Army George C. Marshall*, ed. Major H. A. DaWeed (Washington, D.C.: Infantry Journal, 1945), 175–177.

3. Command Responsibility and the Meaning of Nuremberg

1. Department of Defense, Joint Publication 1-02, *Dictionary of Military and Associated Terms* (Washington, D.C.: GPO 2001), s.v. "command."

2. *Webster's Seventh New Collegiate Dictionary* (Springfield, Mass.: G. & C. Merriam, 1965), s.v. "responsibility."

3. See Leslie Greene, "Command Responsibility in International Humanitarian Law," *Transnational Law and Contemporary Problems* 5 (1995): 319–320.

4. During this conflict, U.S. Army troops acting in the self-interested, self-regulated mode of irregular forces carried out two notorious acts of atrocity. Over one million Philippine citizens died as a consequence of the army's retaliatory counterinsurgency operations.

5. From the reminiscences of Gen. Walter Krueger, U.S. Military Institute Archives at the Army War College, Carlisle Barracks, Pa., cited in Leonard Mosely, *Marshall: Hero for Our Times* (New York: Hearst Books, 1982), 22.

6. Change 1 of November 15, 1944, to War Department Field Manual 27-10, *The Rules of Land Warfare* (Washington, D.C.: GPO, 1940).

7. For a detailed description of U.S. reservations regarding the "Commission on the Responsibilities of the Authors of War and the Enforcement of Penalties," see Peter Maguire, *Law and War: An American Story* (New York: Columbia University Press, 2000), 76–78.

8. Memorandum of Reservations Presented by the Representatives of the United States to the Report of the Commission on the Responsibilities . . . ," April 1, 1919. See "Commission on the Responsibilities of the Authors of War and the Enforcement of Penalties, by Secretary of State Robert Lansing and Legal Advisor James Brown Scott," *American Journal of International Law* 14 (1920): 127–149.

9. "Annex to the Convention Regulations Respecting the Laws and Customs of War on Land, 1907 Hague Convention IV and Regulations," in *Documents on the Laws of War*, 2d ed., ed. Adam Roberts and Richard Guelff (Oxford: Oxford University Press, 1989), 48.

10. See Bradley F. Smith, "The Great German War on the Potomac," in *The Road to Nuremberg: How the Allies Finally Agreed to Try Nazi Leaders—Rather than Shoot Them* (New York: Basic Books, 1981), 12–47.

11. Quotation from Morgenthau diaries, reel 2, box 6, August 19, 1944, cited in Arieh J. Kochavi, *Prelude to Nuremberg: Allied War Crimes Policy and the Question of Punishment* (Chapel Hill: University of North Carolina Press, 1998), 81.

12. Melvyn P. Leffler, *A Preponderance of Power: National Security, the Truman Administration, and the Cold War* (Stanford: Stanford University Press, 1992), 100.

13. Reinhold Niebuhr, "Victors' Justice," *Common Sense* 15 (January 1946), 6–9.

14. George F. Kennan, *Memoirs 1925–1950* (New York: Bantam Books, 1969), 274.

15. Diary of Henry L. Stimson, vol. 48, 4, 7, 14, Yale University, quoted in Kochavi, *Prelude to Nuremberg*, 85.

16. 11 November Memorandum in Papers of Samuel L. Rothman, War Crimes, Harry S. Truman Library, Independence, Mo., cited in Bradley F. Smith, *The Road to Nuremberg* (New York: Basic Books, 1981), 72–74. For FM 27-10, see note 6.

17. "The Bernays Additions" and "the Nuremberg Ideas" are phrases utilized by Gen. Telford Taylor, the chief American prosecutor following Justice Jackson's return to the Supreme Court. The phrases indicate an association with those proposals initiated by the "Stimson group" of planners in the War Department. See Telford Taylor, *The Anatomy of the Nuremberg Trials: A Personal Memoir* (Boston: Back Bay Books, 1992), 35, 39, 639.

18. Kochavi, *Prelude to Nuremberg*, 118, 161.

19. Smith, *The Road to Nuremberg*, 148–151, 190, 195–196.

20. Taylor, *Anatomy of the Nuremberg Trials*, 639.

21. See Robert H. Jackson, *International Conference of Military Trials* (Washington, D.C.: GPO, 1947), 104–105.

22. Charter of the International Military Tribunal, reprinted as Appendix A in Taylor, *Anatomy of the Nuremberg Trials*, 645–653.

23. Hermann Goering and Ernst Kaltenbrunner, while holding military rank, are not included in this list of major military defendants because of the former's extensive nonmilitary role as the secondary head of state for the Third Reich and the latter's role as a penal administrator and executioner of the Final Solution, a role that was primarily non military in function.

24. Final Statement of Admiral Raeder on 31 August 1946, *Trial of the Major War Criminals Before the International Military Tribunal, Nuremberg, 14 November 1945–1 October 1946*, Blue Series, vol. 22 (1947; reprint, Buffalo: William S. Hein, 1995), 391.

25. Testimony of General Jodl on 6 June 1946, ibid., vol. 15, 507–508.

26. Ibid., 5 June 1946, 383.

27. Final Statement of Field Marshall Keitel on 31 August 1946, ibid., vol. 22, 377.

28. One of the better arguments for considering Allied bombing campaigns as war crimes is found in John W. Powers, *War without Mercy: Race and Power in the Pacific War* (New York: Pantheon, 1986), 37–41.

29. Maguire, *Law and War*, 124–125. The best source on the attitudes of contemporary American military professionals toward the trial, based on press articles of the period, is William J. Bosch, *Judgment on Nuremberg: American Attitudes toward the Major German War-Crimes Trials* (Chapel Hill: University of North Carolina Press, 1970), 166–202.

30. Taylor, *Anatomy of the Nuremberg Trials*, 559–570.

31. Principles of International Law Recognized in the Charter of the Nuremberg Tribunal and in the Judgment of the Tribunal. Adopted by the International Law Commission of the United Nations, *Report of the International Law Commission Covering Its Second Session, 5 June–24 July 1950*, Document A/1316 (New York: United Nations, 1950), 11–14.

32. Military Commission Convened by the Commanding General United States Army Forces, Western Pacific, reprinted in A. Frank Reel, *The Case of General Yamashita* (Chicago: University of Chicago Press, 1949), 80, n. 16.

33. Declaration of the President of the Military Commission in the Trial of General Tomoyuki Yamashita, United Nations War Crimes Commission, *Law Reports of Crimes of War Criminals* 1 (U.S. Military Command, 1946): 34–35.

34. Quoted from the position articulated by Secretary of State Lansing at the Paris Peace Conference in 1919 in "Memorandum of Reservations Presented by the Representatives of the United States to the Report of the Commission on the Responsibility," April 1, 1919; see "Commission on the Responsibilities of the Authors of the War . . . ," 127–149.

35. *Yamashita v. Styler*, 327 U.S. (1946), Majority Opinion, reprinted in *The Law of War: A Documentary History*, ed. Leon Friedman, 2 vols. (New York: Random House, 1972), 1605.

36. Murphy Minority Opinion, ibid., 1613.

37. Rutledge Minority Opinion, ibid., 1613–1623.

38. Action of the Confirming Authority, General Headquarters, U.S. Army Forces, Pacific, in the case of General Tomoyuki Yamashita, Imperial Japanese Army, February 7, 1946.

39. Opinion and Judgment of the United States Military Tribunal at Nuremberg in *United States v. Wilhelm von Leeb et al.* (hereinafter the German High Command case), reprinted in Friedman, *The Law of War,* 1456.

40. Ibid., 1449–1451.

41. Ibid., 1303.

42. Ibid., 1324.

43. Ibid., 1323.

44. Ibid., 1325, 1318–1319.

45. Green, "Command Responsibility in International Law, 333.

46. T. Taylor, "The Course of Military Justice," *New York Times,* February 2, 1972, A-39; Taylor, *Nuremberg and Vietnam: An American Tragedy* (Chicago: Quadrangle Books, 1970), 180–181; Reel, *Case of General Yamashita,* 80; Antonio Cassese, *Violence and Law in the Modern Age* (Princeton: Princeton University Press, 1988), 84–85.

47. Major Bruce D. Landrum, "The Yamashita War Crimes Trials: Command Responsibility Then and Now," *Military Law Review* 149 (1995): 289–301. Quotation from Robin Moore Campbell, "Military Liability For Grave Breaches of National and International Law: Absolute or Limited," Ph.D. diss., Duke University (1974), iv.

48. See note 43 and Cassese, *Violence and Law,* 84–85.

49. Parks wrote his graduate thesis on command responsibility and the Yamashita trial. Major William Hays Parks, "Command Responsibility for War Crimes, *Military Law Review* 62 (1973): 1–104; see esp. 22, 32, 63, 64.

50. That double standard posits that there is a difference between "us" and "them." The wall that separates "us" from "them" is built on racism, jingoism, religious prejudice, gender discrimination, and, above all, indifference toward others. Ann Marie Prevost, "Race and War Crimes: The 1945 War Crimes Trial of General Tomoyuki Yamashita," *Human Rights Quarterly* 14 (1992): 303–338.

51. Parks, "Command Responsibility for War Crimes," 82.

52. Convention for the Amelioration of the Condition of the Wounded and Sick in the Armed Forces in the Field (Geneva I), August 12, 1949, Articles 1–3, in International Committee of the Red Cross, *The Geneva Conventions of August 12, 1949* (Geneva: ICRC Publications, n.d.), 23–24; Convention for the Amelioration of the Condition of the Wounded and Sick in the Armed Forces at Sea (Geneva II), August 12, 1949, Articles 1–3, ibid., 51–53; Convention Relative to the Treatment of Prisoners of War (Geneva III), August 12, 1949, Articles 1–3, ibid., 75–76; Convention Relative to the Protection of Civilian Persons in Times of War (Geneva IV), August 12, 1949, Articles 1–3, ibid., 153–154.

53. Ibid., 283.

54. Jean S. Pictet, ed., *Commentary on the IV Geneva Convention Relative to the Protection of Civilian Persons in Times of War* (Geneva: International Committee

of the Red Cross, 1960), 10; and Judith Gail Gardam, *Non-Combatant Immunity as a Norm of International Humanitarian Law* (Dordrecht: Martinus Nijhoff, 1993), 25.

55. 1948 United Nations Convention on the Prevention and Punishment of the Crime of Genocide, Resolution 260 (III) A of the General Assembly on 9 December 1948, reprinted in *The Human Rights Reader*, ed. Micheline R. Ishay (New York: Routledge, 1997), 421–422.

56. 1948 United Nations Universal Declaration of Human Rights, Article 11, reprinted in Ishay, *The Human Rights Reader*, 409.

57. Maguire, *Law and War*, 224, 270, 285.

58. Robert H. Jackson, introduction in Whitney R. Harris, *Tyranny on Trial: The Evidence at Nuremberg* (Dallas: Southern Methodist University Press, 1954), xx–vii.

59. A generalized call for "effective collective measures for the prevention and removal of threats to the peace, and for the suppression of acts of aggression or other breaches of the peace" is found in Article I of the Charter of the United Nations, T.S. No. 993, signed on June 26, 1945. The General Assembly on December 4, 1977, adopted the following definition of aggression: "Aggression is the use of armed force by a State against the sovereignty, territorial integrity or political independence of another State, or in any other manner inconsistent with the Charter of the United Nations as set out in this Definition." See General Assembly Resolution 3314, GAOR, 20th sess., supp. 31, UN Doc. A/9631 (1974).

60. Henry L. Stimson, "The Nuremberg Trial: Landmark in Law," *Foreign Affairs* 25 (January 1947): 179–181, 183–189.

61. Taylor, "Nuremberg Trials: War Crimes and International Law," reprinted as Appendix B of *Final Report to the Secretary of the Army on the Nuremberg War Crimes Trials Under Control Council No.10* (Washington D.C.: Department of the Army, 1949).

62. Ibid., 221, and Taylor, *Anatomy of the Nuremberg Trials*, 629. In the former work, Taylor noted that the Internal Military Tribunal for the Far East, unlike the trials under Control Council Law No. 10, convicted twenty-five Japanese defendants for crimes against peace.

63. Article Five of the Rome Statute for the International Criminal Court, UN Doc. A/CONF.183/9. Even in the case of the Rome Treaty establishing an International Criminal Court (ICC), aggression is to be defined at a review conference seven years after ratification. See Donna K. Axel, "Toward a Permanent International Criminal Court," in *War Crimes: The Legacy of Nuremberg*, ed. Belinda Cooper (New York: TV Books, 1999), 324.

64. Eugene Davidson, *The Nuremberg Fallacy* (New York: Macmillan, 1973), 6, 15.

65. Otto Kranzbuhler, "Nuremberg Eighteen Years Later," *De Paul Law Review* 14 (1964–1965): 335–347.

66. Quincy Wright, "Positivism and the Nuremberg Judgment," *American Journal of International Law* 42 (1948): 405–414.

67. During the trial, Professor Hermann Jahrreiss, a defense council, argued form the positions associated with legal positivism, while Sir Hartley Shawcross, the chief British prosecutor, and Justice Jackson argued for positions associated with natural law theory (Shawcross) and legal realism (Jackson). See Stanley L. Paulson,

"Classical Legal Positivism at Nuremberg," *Philosophy and Public Affairs* 4 (1975): 132–158.

68. For an example of the former, see Richard A. Falk, "Nuremberg: Past, Present, and Future," *Yale Law Journal* 80 (1971): 1505–1528. Two contemporary critiques of the IMT from the conservative perspectives of legal positivism and the "English-speaking concept of law" are "The Nuremberg Novelty," by the editors of *Fortune Magazine* (December 1945), and Senator Robert A. Taft, "Equal Justice under Law: The Heritage of the English-Speaking Peoples and Their Responsibility," speech delivered at Kenyon College, Gambier, Ohio, October 5, 1946; both are reprinted in *From Nuremberg to My Lai*, ed. Jay W. Baird (Lexington, Mass.: D. Heath, 1972), 101–113. For a recent example of a conservative describing Nuremberg as an "anomaly," see George F. Will, "Lessons from Nuremberg," *Washington Post*, December 15, 2003, A31. See also "Positivism, Pragmatism, Natural Law, and Nuremberg," in Bosch, *Judgment on Nuremberg*, 41–52.

69. Mark S. Martins, " 'War Crimes' during Operations Other than War: Military Doctrine and Law Fifty Years after Nuremberg—and Beyond," *Military Law Review* 149 (1995): 145–187.

70. Justice Robert Jackson, "The Significance of the Nuremberg Trials to the Armed Forces," *Military Affairs* 10 (1946): 2–15.

71. See Martins, " 'War Crimes' during Operations Other than War," 182.

72. After the Second World War, American policy, as in the earlier case of the Lieber Code, emphasized command and control issues that were more reflective of the worldview of military commanders than they were of that of international lawyers. After World War I, American policy was drawn up by the Department of State; after World War II, as in the case of the Andersonville trial after the Civil War, it was planned and executed by the Department of War.

73. Department of the Army, Field Manual 27–10, *The Law of Land Warfare* (Washington, D.C.: GPO, 1956), 178–179.

74. Ibid., 3, 178–179.

75. Maj. Mark S. Martins, while deputy director of the Center for Law and Military Operations at the Judge Advocate General's Corps School, Charlottesville, Va., noted the direct reference in a draft copy of FM 27-10: "the language of the command responsibility standard proposed and ultimately adopted for the Army's field manual was based on the court's judgment against List [Hostage case] as well as on *In Re Yamashita*." See Martins, " 'War Crimes' during Operations Other than War," 154, n. 42. Maj. Richard Baxter's draft of FM 27-10, para. 8.8A (1 March 1954); copy was on file with the library of The Judge Advocate General's Corps School. A Freedom of Information Act request for this document produced the information, from the chief librarian, that this document was lost as a result of flooding in 1999 and believed destroyed.

76. FM 27-10 (1956), 178–179.

4. The American Military Ethic in the Early Cold War

1. Inspector General of the Army, "No Gun Ri Review" (Washington, D.C.: Department of the Army, 2001).

2. Under General Assembly Resolution 177 (II), paragraph (a) [English text], as

published in *Report of the International Law Commission Covering its Second Session, 5 June–29 July 1950* (UN Document A/1316), 11–14.

3. Like the War Department's 1940 edition of FM 27-10 along with its 1941 and 1944 editions, the first Department on the Army editions maintained the distinction between capstone doctrine—publications offering the highest authoritative doctrinal guidance and reflecting the military component of national-international alliance strategy—and keystone doctrine—statements of a subject-specific nature to which other subject-area publications defer—by issuing two separate publication series.

4. Walter Edward Kretchik, "Peering through the Mist: Doctrine as a Guide for U.S. Army Operations, 1775–2000," Ph.D. diss., University of Kansas (2001), 154–162.

5. For the first postwar naval and air force manuals on law-of-war matters, see *Tentative Instructions for the Navy of the United States Governing Maritime and Aerial Warfare* (Washington, D.C.: GPO, 1941; reprinted, with changes, 1944) and U.S. Department of the Air Force, Air Force Pamphlet AFP 110-31, *International Law: The Conduct of Armed Conflict and Air Operations* (Washington, D.C.: Headquarters of the Air Force, 1976).

6. Lt. Col. P. F. Gualt, a military lawyer writing in a civilian law review, questioned the ability of civilian judges serving on military tribunals to deal with issues of military professionalism. See P. F. Gault, "Prosecution of War Criminals," *Journal of Criminal Law and Criminology* 36 (1945): 180–183.

7. *Army and Navy Journal*, December 1, 1945, 325, commenting on the IMT; and ibid., February 9, 1946, 744, commenting on the Yamashita trial. Cited in William J. Bosch, *Judgment on Nuremberg: American Attitudes toward the Major War-Crimes Trials* (Chapel Hill: University of North Carolina Press, 1970), 168.

8. During a tour of liberated Europe with newsmen, Eisenhower clarified that earlier statements attributed to him may have indicated a lukewarm position on his part toward the trials. See Bosch, *Judgment on Nuremberg*, 172.

9. Robert H. Jackson, "The Significance of Nuremberg to the Armed Forces," *Military Affairs* 10 (1946): 2–15.

10. George F. Kennan, *Memoirs 1925–1950* (New York: Bantam Books, 1969), 274.

11. William H. Whyte, Jr., "Groupthink" (1952), reprinted in *Interpretations of American History*, eds. Gerald N. Grob and George Athan Billas (New York: Free Press, 1982), 2:448–459.

12. Douglas MacArthur, *Revitalizing a Nation: A Statement of Beliefs, Opinions, and Policies Embodied in the Public Pronouncements of General of the Army Douglas MacArthur*, ed. John Pratt (Chicago: Heritage Foundation, 1952), 61.

13. T. Harry Williams, "The Macs and the Ikes: America's Two Military Traditions," *American Mercury* 75 (1952): 32–29.

14. Russell F. Weigley, *History of the United States Army* (New York: Macmillan, 1967), 517–519.

15. For Huntington's critique of the Williams thesis, see Samuel P. Huntington, *The Soldier and the State: The Theory and Politics of Civil-Military Relations* (Cambridge: Belknap Press), 367–373.

16. Eliot A. Cohen, "The Unequal Dialogue," in *Soldiers and Civilians: The Civil-Military Gap and American National Security,* eds. Peter D. Feaver and Richard H. Kohn (Cambridge: MIT Press, 2001), 433.

17. Officer candidates are usually issued *Soldier and the State* in an edited form such as found in Malham M. Wakin, ed., *War, Morality, and the Military Profession,* 2d ed. (Boulder: Westview Press, 1985), 23–56.

18. Williams, "The Macs and the Ikes."

19. See Huntington, *The Soldier and the State,* 7–18.

20. Samuel P. Huntington, *The Clash of Civilizations and the Remaking of the World Order* (New York: Simon and Schuster, 1996), and *Who Are We? The Challenges of American Identity* (New York: Simon and Schuster, 2004). For a brief comparative analysis of Huntington's major works, see Daniel Lazare, "Diversity and Its Discontents," *The Nation* 278 (June 14, 2004): 18–24.

21. Huntington, *The Soldier and the State,* 79.

22. Whyte, "Groupthink," 448–459.

23. Huntington, *The Soldier and the State,* 79.

24. Huntington frankly admits that his concept of "objective civilian control" of the military is extra-constitutional. He is critical of constitutional allegiance because it represents "cutting loose from the safe grounds of objective civilian control" as achieved by establishing "a distinct class of specialists in the management of violence" and "rendering them politically sterile and neutral." See ibid., 80–85.

25. Huntington also classed those not involved in the direct application of violence, such as quartermasters and intelligence officers, as persons lacking the expertise of the line or of combat arms officers. See *The Soldier and the State,* 7–18.

26. Forest C. Pogue, Marshall's official biographer, wrote that Marshall considered the "enlisted soldier's voice [as] the voice of a democratic army." See Pogue, *George C. Marshall: Organizer of Victory* (New York: Viking Press, 1973), 93.

27. Ibid., 55–58.

28. Huntington, *The Soldier and the State,* 77–78

29. Ibid., 98.

30. For Eisenhower's position, see Bosch, *Judgment on Nuremberg,* 174; and for Jackson's, see his "The Significance of Nuremberg," 14.

31. Telford Taylor, *Sword and Swastika: Generals and Nazis in the Third Reich* (New York: Simon and Schuster, 1952), 364, 366.

32. Ibid., 370, 373.

33. Memorandum, Captain A. C. Wedemeyer for the Adjutant General, 3 August 1938, Subj: German General Staff School, NARA RG 165, G-2 Regional Files—Germany (6740), Washington National Record Center, Suitland, Md.

34. Albert C. Wedemeyer, *Wedemeyer Reports!* (New York: Henry Holt, 1958), 417–418; and Forrest C. Pogue, in *George C. Marshall: Ordeal and Hope. 1932–1942* (New York: Viking Press, 1966), 141.

35. Edward A. Shils and Morris Janowitz, "Cohesion and Disintegration in the German Wehrmacht in World War II," *Public Opinion Quarterly* 12 (1948): 280–315.

36. T. N. Dupuy, *A Genius for War: The German Army and General Staff, 1807–1945* (New York: Prentice-Hall, 1977), 2, 5, 309.

37. Mantecue J. Lowrey, *The Forge of West German Rearmament: Theodor Blank and the Amt Blank* (New York: Peter Lang, 1990), 3–4.

38. Ibid., 98–99, 122, 123. Theodor Blank as cited in Huntington, *The Soldier and the State*, 123.

39. Remer was convicted in October 1992 for publicly denying the Holocaust, a crime in Germany; he died in exile in Spain on October 4, 1997.

40. Count Wolf Baudissin, "The New German Army," *Foreign Affairs* 34 (1955): 1–13; and Donald Abenheim, *Reforging the Iron Cross: The Search for Tradition in the West German Armed Forces* (Princeton: Princeton University Press, 1988), 258–296.

41. For a general discussion of the place of the Wehrmacht in the *Historikerstreit*, see Charles S. Maier, *The Unmasterable Past: History, Holocaust, and German National Identity* (Cambridge: Harvard University Press, 1997), 19–22. A more extended discussion by a number of scholars writing in German can be found in Rolf-Deiter Muller and Hans-Erich Volkman, eds., *Die Wehrmacht: Mythos und Realität* (Munich: R. Oldenbourg Verlag, 1999).

42. Omer Bartov, *Hitler's Army: Soldiers, Nazis, and War in the Third Reich* (New York: Oxford University Press, 1991), 3–11, 59–105.

43. "More to the Holocaust than SS and Special Police," *Deutsche Press Agenteur,* in English translation in *Indian Express,* July 12, 1999, 1; and Donald G. Schilling, "Review of *Die Wehrmacht: Mythos und Realität,*" *Journal of Modern History* 73 (2001): 208–211.

44. Ten thousand of seventy thousand French soldiers who served in the First Indochina War were veterans of the Wehrmacht or Waffen SS. Included were ethnically German French citizens who were drafted into the Wehrmacht after the fall of France, and German-speaking volunteers to the French Foreign Legion. See Sebastian Fellmeth, "Frankreichs Stalingrad," *Die Zeit,* April 3, 2003, 11.

45. Andrew F. Krepinevich, *The Army in Vietnam* (Baltimore: Johns Hopkins University Press, 1986), 27–55.

46. General Maxwell Taylor, *The Uncertain Trumpet* (New York: Harper and Bros., 1959), 39–40.

47. By Taylor's definition, "a just war may be one waged for a just cause that can be achieved no other way; one capable of producing a better peace than the one existing before the war; one waged in self-defense or for legal rights; one to protect the nation's natural right; one with a high probability of producing more good consequences than bad for the human race; or one conducted non-aggressively in accordance with the United Nations Charter." See General Maxwell Taylor, "A Do-It-Yourself Professional Code for the Military," *Parameters: Journal of the U.S. Army War College* 10 (1980): 12–13. See also "A Professional Ethic," *Army* (May 1978): 18–21.

48. Cecil B. Currey, *Edward Lansdale: The Unquiet American* (Boston: Houghton Mifflin, 1988), 196–199. Graham Greene, *The Quiet American* (New York: Viking, 1955), William E. Lederer and Eugene Burdick, *The Ugly American* (New York: W.W. Norton, 1985).

49. S. L. A. Marshall, "Arms in Wonderland," *Army* (November 1959), 131–132.

50. Krepinevich, *The Army in Vietnam,* 27–55.

51. Robert J. McMahan, *The Limits of Empire: The United States and Southeast Asia Since World War II* (New York: Columbia University Press, 1999), 110.

52. Paul L. Savage and Richard A. Gabriel, "Cohesion and Disintegration in the American Army, An Alternative Perspective," *Armed Forces and Society* 2 (1976): 340–376.

53. Officer Debrief: Interview with Gen. William E. DePuy by Lt. Cols. Bill Mullen and Les Brownlee, 26 March, 1979, reprinted as *Changing an Army: An Oral History of General William E. Depuy, U.S. Army Retired* (Carlisle Barracks, Pa.: U.S. Army Military History Institute, 1986), 194.

54. Examples include Lt. Col. Thomas B. Cameron, "The German General Staff System Revisited," USAWC Military Studies Paper, U.S. Army War College (1989), and Col. William H. Groening, "The Influence of the German General Staff and the American General Staff," USAWC Military Studies Paper, U.S. Army War College (1993).

5. Command Responsibility and the My Lai Massacre

1. Phạm Thành Công, director of Khu Chứng Tích Són Mỹ, interviewed by the author at My Lai Memorial on March 16, 1996.

2. Christian G. Appy, *Working-Class War: American Combat Soldiers and Vietnam* (Chapel Hill: University of North Carolina Press, 1993), 267. In a number of articles in 2004–2005, Nicholas Turse credited Appy with coining the phrase "doctrine of atrocity" to describe the institutionalization and bureaucratization of brutality exercised by American forces during the Vietnam War. See "The Doctrine of Atrocity: U.S. against 'Them'—A Tradition of Institutionalized Brutality," *Village Voice*, May 11, 2004, 1; and "The Tip of the Iceberg: Report on Vietnam 'Tiger Force' Atrocity," posted on www.Antiwar.com, accessed February 18, 2006. See Turse's " 'Kill Anything That Moves': U.S. War Crimes and Atrocities in Vietnam, 1965–1973," Ph.D. diss., Columbia University (2006). To use the term "doctrine of atrocity" is to overlook the fact that official U.S. military doctrine on the laws of armed conflict, as embodied in FM 27-10, did not change during the war; nor was it modified during the institutional reactions following the war.

3. Officer Debrief: Interview with Gen. William E. DePuy by Lt. Cols. Bill Mullen and Les Brownlee, 26 March, 1979, reprinted as *Changing an Army: An Oral History of General William E. DePuy, U.S. Army Retired* (Carlisle Barracks, Pa.: U.S. Army Military History Institute, 1986), 40.

4. Andrew F. Krepinevich Jr., *The Army and Vietnam* (Baltimore: Johns Hopkins University Press, 1986), 85 and 271.

5. Report of the Department of the Army Review of the Preliminary Investigations into the My Lai Incident: Volume I, The Report of the Investigation (Washington, D.C.: Department of the Army, 1970), henceforth referred to as Peers Report. Reprinted in The My Lai Massacre and Its Cover Up: Beyond the Reach of Law?, ed. Joseph Goldstein, Burke Marshall, and Jack Schwartz (New York: Free Press, 1976), 314.

6. In addition to training received during basic training, Charlie Company personnel received at least one MACV supplemental briefing following their arrival in country. Ibid., 320, 316, 320, 334, 337.

7. Letter of Specialist Tom Glen, U.S. Army to MACV Commander, General Creighton Abrams, 1968, reprinted in Michael Bilton and Kevin Sim, *Four Hours in*

My Lai (New York: Viking, 1992), 207–213. In his response to his brigade's adjutant general, Powell dismisses Glen for not coming forward earlier and not providing specifics, although Powell did not directly ask Glen for further information. See Charles Lane, "The Legend of Colin Powell," *New Republic*, April 17, 1995, 20–32.

8. U.S. Army War College (USAWC) Senior Leader Oral History Program. Gen. William C. Westmoreland interviewed by Lt. Col. Martin L. Ganderson, 1982, vol. 2 (box 15), 238–239. Part of USAWC Military History Research Collection, William C. Westmoreland Papers, Carlisle Barracks, Pa.

9. U.S. Army War College (USAWC) Senior Leader Oral History Program. Lt. Gen. William R. Peers interviewed by Col. James H. Breen and Col. Charlie B. Moore. Reel 4, April 14, 1977, 33–36. USAWC Military History Research Collection, William R. Peers Papers, Carlisle Barracks, Pa.

10. Peers Report, 314–345.

11. Bilton and Sim, *Four Hours in My Lai*, 320, 329, 381–384.

12. U.S. House of Representatives, *Committee on Armed Services, Investigation of the My Lai Incident: Hearing of the Armed Services Investigating Subcommittee*, 91st Congress., H.A.S.C. no. 94-47, April 15–June 22, 1970, 202–248.

13. Ibid., 53–84. Later, on hearing of Lt. Calley's conviction, Congressman Hebert would remark that "it is terrible to let Cassius Clay walk the streets of America, while William Calley, who was trying to do his duty, is incarcerated." Quoted in Mark D. Carson, "F. Edward Hebert and the Congressional Investigation of the My Lai Massacre," *Louisiana History* 37 (1976), 73.

14. Bilton and Sim, *Four Hours in My Lai*, 340–344.

15. Ibid., 329.

16. Instructions from the Military Judge to the Court Members in the *United States vs. First Lieutenant Calley, Jr.*, reprinted in *The Law of War: A Documentary History*, ed. Leon Friedman (New York: Random House, 1972), 1722.

17. Wayne Greenhaw, *The Making of a Hero: A Behind-the-Scenes View of the Lt. William Calley Affair* (Louisville: Touchstone Publishing, 1971), 193.

18. Herbert C. Kelman and Lee H. Lawrence, "American Response to the Trial of Lt. William L. Calley," in *The Military in America*, ed. Peter Karston (New York: Free Press, 1980), 41–45.

19. The popular films of Stephen Spielberg offer a contemporary view of this duplicity in human affairs. After making his epic Holocaust commemorative, *Schindler's List* (1993), he followed with two films, *Saving Private Ryan* (1998) and *Band of Brothers* (2001), that depict American soldiers handling prisoners of war in a clearly criminal manner.

20. Captain Hugh Thompson, U.S. Army Ret, interviewed by author during Human Rights Week at the U.S. Army School of the Americas on January 23, 1999; Colonel William C. Wilson, "I Had Prayed to God That This Was Fiction," *American Heritage*, Spring 1983, 63; General Peers, USAWC Oral History, 41. For Capt. Daniel's public denunciation, see "The Captain Who Told The President Off," *Newsweek*, April 19, 1971, 19.

21. U.S. House of Representatives, *Investigation of the My Lai Incident*, 56–58.

22. Peers Report, 439–441.

23. Mary McCarthy, *Medina* (New York: Harcourt Brace, 1972), 59.

24. Col. Will G. Eckhardt later described his theory of the case as follows:
During these particular three hours, Captain Medina remained on the outskirts of the village. No evidence placed Captain Medina at the scene of any of these killings. The incident occurred in dense jungle growth. However, since the area involved was approximately ten thousand square yards, the size of five footballs fields, the prosecution's position was that Captain Medina knew precisely what was transpiring and that he had the ability to issue orders stopping the slaughter and to seek help in controlling his men. In short, the prosecution felt that he had *actual knowledge* [italics mine] that unarmed, unresisting, noncombatants were being killed by men under his command. The evidence was clear that he had the communications ability to stop this carnage. He had two basic choices. He could have taken affirmative action, for example, issuing orders or seeking help to control his men. Seeking assistance would, of course, have reflected poorly on his military leadership ability. The other course of action would be to remain silent and hope that the incident would be relatively insignificant and would not be discovered. Apparently, he chose his military career over the lives of unarmed, unresisting, noncombatants who were being slaughtered by his troops within earshot. His crime, in the prosecution's eyes, was abandoning his command responsibility on the battlefield.
"Command Criminal Responsibility," *Military Law Review* 97 (1982): 1–34.

25. The military judge, Col. Kenneth Howard, summarizing the evidence for the defense in *United States v. Captain Medina*, cited in ibid., 34.

26. Prosecution Brief on the Law Principles in *United States v. Captain Medina* titled "A Company Commander Is Responsible for Controlling and Supervising Subordinates During Combat Operations," reprinted in ibid., 31. FM 27-10 (1956), 178–179.
Military commanders may also be responsible for war crimes committed by their subordinates. When troops commit massacres and atrocities against the civilian population of occupied territory or against prisoners of war, the responsibility may rest not only with the actual perpetrators but also with the commander. Such a responsibility arises directly when the acts in question have been committed in pursuance of an order of the commander concerned. The commander is also responsible *if he has actual knowledge, or should have had knowledge* [italics mine] from reports received by him or through other means, that troops or other persons subject to his control are about to commit or have committed a war crime and he fails to take the necessary and reasonable steps to insure compliance with the law of war or to punish violators thereof.

27. Instructions from the Military Judge to the Court Members in the *United States v. Captain Ernest L. Medina*, reprinted in Friedman, *War Crimes: A Documentary History*, 1732:
In relation to the question pertaining to the supervisory responsibility of a Company Commander, I advise you that as a general principle of military law and custom a military superior in command is responsible for and required, in the performance of his command duties, to make certain the proper performance by his subordinates of their duties as assigned by him. In other words, a commander must remain alert and make timely adjustments as required by a changing situa-

tion. Furthermore, a commander is also responsible if he has actual knowledge that troops or other persons subject to his control are in the process of committing or about to commit a war crime and he wrongfully fails to take the necessary and reasonable steps to ensure compliance with the law of war. You will observe that these legal requirements placed on a commander require *actual knowledge* [italics added] plus a wrongful failure to act. Thus mere presence at the scene without knowledge will not suffice. That is, the commander-subordinate relationship alone will not allow an inference of knowledge. While it is not necessary that a commander actually see an atrocity being committed, it is essential that he know that his subordinates are in the process of committing atrocities or about to commit atrocities.

28. Eckhardt, "Command Criminal Responsibility," 12–13.

29. Opinion and Judgment of the United States Military Tribunal at Nuremberg in *United States v. Wilhelm List et al.*, reprinted in Friedman, *The Law of War*, 1323.

30. William Clark, "Medina: An Essay on the Principles of Criminal Responsibility for Homicide," *Rutgers School of Law-Camden Law Review* 5 (1973): 59–78.

31. Telford Taylor, "The Course of Military Justice, *New York Times*, February 2, 1972, 37.

32. Douglas Robinson, "Henderson Trial: More Is Involved than a Colonel," *New York Times*, November 29, 1971, as cited in Bilton and Sim, *Four Hours in My Lai*, 408.

33. Taylor, "The Course of Military Justice," 37.

34. Peers felt that even in the assignments of active duty officers, the case was stacked against the prosecution. In his USAWC debrief, Peers used the example of the Henderson trial where "you have a Major, a fine officer, but a young officer not near as experienced as Rothblatt and the lieutenant colonel from JAG that were defending Henderson. So I do not think the Army put its best foot forward. I think they could have assigned much stronger individuals on teams and I am not exactly pleased with the composition of some of the court-martials. I think they could have put on a more representative kind of people there—people that could have understood what went on in warfare and not necessarily service support kind of individuals." USAWC Senior Leader Oral History, Lt. Gen. Peers, 33–36.

35. Cited in Prevost, "Race and War Crimes," 329.

36. General Taylor's remarks during a January 8, 1971, appearance on the *Dick Cavett Show*. A condensed version of the interview, edited by Neil Sheehan, appeared in the *New York Times*, January 9, 1971, p. 3, col. 1.

37. Taylor, "Judgment on My Lai," *New York Times*, January 10, 1970, 29; "Nuremberg in Son My," *New York Times*, November 21, 1970, 30; and "The Course of Military Justice," *New York Times*, February 2, 1972, 39. Taylor's books of the period include *Nuremberg and Vietnam: An American Tragedy* (Chicago: Quadrangle Books, 1970).

38. Sheehan, *New York Times*, January 9, 1971.

39. Taylor, *New York Times*, January 10, 1970, and November 21, 1970.

40. Taylor, *Vietnam and Nuremberg*, 180–181, 191.

41. In Sheehan's *A Bright Shining Lie*, his 1988 blockbuster epic on the war, West-

moreland is depicted in an uncomplimentary manner. For Sheehan, while it was Lt. Gen. William DePuy who was the "main architect of the building and deployment" of the American military machine in Vietnam and the mastermind of America's destructive tactics—"prodigious firepower" and "attrition"—Westmoreland was its the unimaginative and self-deluded executioner. See Sheehan, *A Bright Shining Lie: John Paul Vann and America in Vietnam* (New York: Random House, 1988), 10–11, 16, 558.

42. Taylor, *New York Times*, February 2, 1972.

43. Taylor, *Nuremberg and Vietnam*, 13–15, 119–121.

44. See Richard A. Falk's review of Taylor's *Nuremberg and Vietnam*, "The Problem With War Crimes," *New York Times*, December 27, 1970, 165.

45. Waldemar A. Solf, "A Response to Telford Taylor's *Nuremberg and Vietnam: An American Tragedy*," *Akron Law Review* 5 (1972): 43–68.

46. Under Article 102 of the 1949 Prisoner of War Convention, which stipulated that prisoners of war "can be validly sentenced only if the sentence and been pronounced by the same courts and according to the same procedure as in the case of members of the armed forces of the detaining powers." See Solf, ibid., 61–64. Arguments that find in the Medina trial a refinement or liberalization of jurisprudence are available in Robyn Campbell, "Military Liability For Grave Breaches of National and International Law: Absolute or Limited?," Ph.D. diss., Duke University (1974), 180–214; and Major Bruce D. Landrum, "The Yamashita War Crimes Trial: Command Responsibility Then and Now," *Military Law Review* 149 (1995): 289–301.

47. W. Hays Parks, "Command Responsibility for War Crimes," *Military Law Review* 62 (1973): 1–104.

48. Taylor, *New York Times*, February 2, 1972. For background on Gen. Yamashita's command, see Prevost, "Race and War Crimes," 304–338; for the same on Capt. Medina's, see Bilton and Sim, *Four Hours at My Lai*, 47–141.

49. Parks, "Command Responsibility," 1. F. Lee Bailey cited in Luther West, *They Call it Justice : Command Influence and the Court-Martial System* (New York: Viking Press, 1977), 186.

50. For the three-day turnaround between Westmoreland's receipt of the Peers Report and his order for the Army War College study, see Cincinnatus, *Self-Destruction: The Disintegration and Decay of the United States Army during the Vietnam Era* (New York: W. W. Norton, 1981), 130.

51. U. S. Department of the Army, *Study on Military Professionalism* (Carlisle Barracks, Pa.: U.S. Army War College, 1970), 55.

52. Ibid., iii, 23–29. The description of Westmoreland's meeting is based on the observations of Lt. Col. Walt Ulmer and Lt. Col. Mike Malone as cited in James Kitfield *Prodigal Soldiers: How a Generation of Officers Born of Vietnam Revolutionized the American Style of War* (New York: Simon & Schuster, 1995), 107–112.

53. File on Lt. Col. Anthony B. Herbert, May 20, 1969, Final Action, HQ 1st Field Force, Vietnam, Approved Barnes Relief of Herbert. USAWC Military History Research Collection, John W. Barnes Papers, Carlisle Barracks, Pa.

54. Memorandum for Lt. Gen. Kerwin from Westmoreland, November 29, 1971, and MACV Directive 20-4, May 18, 1968, MACJA *Inspections and Investigations for War Crimes*, For the Cdr. by Chief of Staff Walter T. Kerwin, Jr. USAWC

Military History Research Collection, William C. Westmoreland Papers, Carlisle Barracks, Pa.

55. Besides Paul L. Savage and Richard A. Gabriel, "Cohesion and Disintegration in the American Army, An Alternative Perspective," *Armed Forces and Society* 2 (1976): 340–176 (as discussed in Chapter 4 of the present book), included among these texts are: Hayes Johnson and George Wilson, *Army in Anguish* (New York: Pocket Books, 1972); Lt. Col. Edward L. King, *The Death of an Army: A Pre-Mortem* (New York: Saturday Review Press, 1972); Lt. Col. William L. Hauser, *America's Army in Crisis: A Study in Civil-Military Affairs* (Baltimore: Johns Hopkins University Press, 1973); and Stuart H. Loory, *Defeated: Inside America's Military Machine* (New York: Random House, 1973).

56. Sir John Winthrop Hackett's Harmon Memorial Lecture at the United States Air Force Academy in October 1970, included in *War, Morality, and the Military Profession*, ed. Malham M. Wakin (Boulder: Westview Press, 1979), 107–126.

57. Ibid.

58. Gen. Edward C. Meyer, *Who Will Lead? Senior Leadership in the United States Army* (Westport, Conn.: Praeger, 1995), 132.

59. Gen. Bruce Palmer Jr., *The 25-Year War: America's Military Role in Vietnam.* (Lexington: University Press of Kentucky, 1984), 86.

60. David L. Anderson, ed., *Facing My Lai: Moving beyond the Massacre* (Lawrence: University Press of Kansas, 1998), 126.

61. Col. David H. Hackworth and Julie Sherman, *About Face: The Odyssey of an American Warrior* (New York: Touchstone, 1989), 818.

62. Anderson, *Facing My Lai,* 126.

63. Transcript of "States and Law of War Panel," Tulane University My Lai Conference, December 1–3, 1994, 9, 16.

64. Participants included Robert Komer, Maj. Gen. Edward Lansdale, Ambassador Henry Cabot Lodge, Brig. Gen. S. L. A. Marshall, Sir Robert Thompson, and Gen. William Westmoreland.

65. W. Scott Thompson and Donaldson D. Frizzell, eds., *The Lessons of Vietnam* (New York: Crane, Russak, 1977), 40–46, 52–53.

66. Edward N. Luttwak, a well-known critic of Vietnam War revisionism, argues that interference from civilian officials was of "only a most superficial scope." He also asserts that not only did the army fight the war it wanted to fight, it fought the way it did more for the purposes of organizational convenience than for military success. Luttwak, *The Pentagon and the Art of War* (New York: Touchstone, 1985), 23–27, 41–42).

67. Palmer, *The 25-Year War,* 200–201, 170–171.

68. Andrew F. Krepinevich Jr., one of the major critics of the revisionist "no more Vietnams" school of thought, documents the great lengths to which army leaders went to resist what they considered President Kennedy's counterinsurgency "fad." The army preferred "to fight the kind of conventional war that it was trained, organized, and prepared (and wanted) to fight instead of the counterinsurgency war it was sent to fight." Krepinevich, *The Army and Vietnam* (Baltimore: Johns Hopkins University Press, 1986), 271. Krepinevich, a retired major, was assigned to the Executive Secretariat of the Office of the Secretary of Defense in the mid-1980s. His argu-

ment is somewhat undermined by the fact that those chosen to lead the army's counterinsurgency effort, like Generals Edward Meyer and William DePuy, lacked background in the discipline of counterinsurgency operations. Officers with that training and experience, such as Edward Lansdale, Roger Hilsman, and others, played less substantial roles in the so-called counterinsurgency "kick" (see ibid., 5–7, 70–74, 270–275).

69. Hackworth, *About Face,* 817.

70. FM 100-5. *Operations,* July 1, 1976, with Change 1, April 29, 1977 (Washington, D.C.: GPO, 1977). Walter E. Kretchik, "Peering through the Mist: Doctrine as a Guide for U.S. Army Operations, 1775–2000," Ph.D. diss., University of Kansas (2001), 188.

71. Michael Walzer, *Just and Unjust Wars: A Moral Argument with Historical Illustrations* (New York: Basic Books, 1977), 304, 309–316.

6. The 1977 Geneva Protocol I and Post-Vietnam Military Doctrine

1. Department of Defense Directive 5100.17, *The Department of Defense Law of War Program,* Part V (November 5, 1974), 1–8.

2. General Assembly Resolution 2444, *Respect for Human Rights in Armed Conflicts,* December 16, 1968, 23 GAOR Supp. No, 18, at 50, U.N. Doc. A/7218 (1969), and General Assembly Resolution 2597, December 16, 1968, 24 GAOR Supp. No, 30, at 62, U.N. Doc. A/7630 (1970).

3. International Committee of the Red Cross, *Commentary of the Additional Protocols of 8 June 1977 to the Geneva Conventions of 12 August 1949* (Dordrecht: Martinus Nijhoff, 1985), xxx–xxxv.

4. Maj. Gen. George S. Prugh, *Law at War: Vietnam 1964–1973,* Vietnam Studies series (Washington, D.C.: GPO, 1975).

5. George S. Prugh, "Judges in Command: The Judicialized Uniform Code of Military Justice in Combat," *Harvard Journal of Law and Public Policy* 3 (1980): 57–63. For a discussion of Prugh's role in leading the effort to normalize the treatment of enemy POWs, see Col. Fred L. Bunch, "Review of Stuart Rochester and Fred Kiely, *Honor Bound," Military History Review* 163 (2000): 151–152.

6. Michael Bothe, Karl Partsch, and Waldemar Solf, *New Rules for Victims of Armed Conflict: Commentary on the Two 1977 Protocols Additional to the Geneva Conventions of 1949* (The Hague: Martinus Nijhoff, 1982), 4.

7. *Report of the United States Delegation to the Diplomatic Conference on the Reaffirmation and Development of International Humanitarian Law,* Fourth Session (Submitted to the Secretary of State by George Aldrich, Chairman of Delegation, September 8, 1977) (Washington, D.C. Department of State, September 8, 1977), 28–29; hereinafter cited as U.S. Delegation Report.

8. *Official Records of the Diplomatic Conference on the Reaffirmation as Development of International Humanitarian Law Applicable in Armed Conflicts 1974–1977* (Bern: Federal Political Department, 1978), 10–11. The official records of the diplomatic conference were published in 17 volumes and followed the sessions chronologically regardless of content. In 1981, Howard Levie converted the official record into a four-volume thematic arrangement with cross-referenced citation iden-

tifiers from the "Official Record"; see *Protection of War Victims: Protocol I to the 1949 Geneva Convention* (Dobbs Ferry, N.Y.: Oceana Publication, 1981).

9. *Basic Principles of the Legal Status of the Combatants Struggling against Colonial and Alien Dominated and Racist Regimes* (U.N Gen. Ass. Res. 3103, Dec. 12, 1973).

10. Gen. Walter Reed, "Laws of War: The Developing Law of Armed Conflict—Some Current Problems," *Case Western Reserve Journal of International Law* 9 (1977): 20–21.

11. George H. Aldrich, "Establishing Legal Norms through Multilateral Negotiation—The Laws of War," *Case Western Reserve Journal of International Law* 9 (1977): 9–15.

12. This trigger is drawn from the de Martens Clause that appeared in the preamble to the 1899 Hague Convention (II) whose purpose was to extend protections to civilians in cases not addressed by current humanitarian law. It was later associated with Protocol I's "principles of humanity" that prohibits any unnecessary violence against soldiers and, especially, civilians. See J. Pictet, *Development and Principles of International Humanitarian Law* (Dordrecht: Martinus Nijhoff, 1985), 62. For a discussion of de Martens Clause in context of the American negotiation of the Protocols, see remarks of Waldemar Solf at the American Red Cross-Washington College of Law Workshop on Customary Law and the 1977 Protocols Additional to the 1949 Geneva Conventions, summarized in the *American University Journal of International Law and Policy* 2 (1987), 481–484.

13. Richard Baxter, "Humanitarian Law or Humanitarian Politics? The 1974 Diplomatic Conference on Humanitarian Law," *Harvard International Law Journal* 16 (1975): 11–18.

14. Army Pamphlet 27-1-1, *Protocols to the Geneva Conventions of 12 August 1949* (Washington, D.C.: Headquarters, Dept. of the Army, 1979), 1.

15. Statement for General Debate by George H. Aldrich, U.S. Representative, March 5, 1974, USIS Press Release, U.S. Mission, Geneva; see Diplomatic Conference on the Reaffirmation and Development of International Humanitarian Law Applicable in Armed Conflicts (CDDH/SR) 11 at 71.

16. Aldrich, "Establishing Legal Norms"; Baxter, "Humanitarian Law"; and Reed, "Laws of War."

17. Baxter, "Humanitarian Law," 13–18; and Georges Abi-Saab, "Wars of National Liberation and the Laws of War," *Annals of International Studies* 3 (1972), 93–117.

18. Baxter, "Humanitarian Law," 13–18.

19. Ibid.; Reed, "Laws of War," 21.

20. Baxter's cited source for his use of the term "just war" is the late Col. G.I.A.C. Draper, the UK delegate to the conference. Draper lamented the interdependence of the *jus ad bellum* and the *jus in bello* because he believed stress on the former undermined compliance and rationalized noncompliance with the latter. See Draper, "The Development of International Humanitarian Law," *International Dimensions of Humanitarian Law* (Geneva: Henry Dunant Institute, 1988), 65–67; and "The Christian and War," *International Affairs* 2 (1962): 13–19. Regarding the use of just war terminology to describe U.S. negotiating positions, Aldrich listed "humanity" and "military necessity" as two of three major precepts that were widely shared be-

tween the U.S. and other delegations—the third precept being "sovereignty," which is not usually associated with just war doctrine. Gen. Reed listed "Principle of Distinction" and "Rule of Proportionality" as central rules addressing the content of the negotiations. Aldrich, "Establishing Legal Norms," 13; Reed, "Laws of War," 23–25.

21. Charter of the United Nations (1945) reprinted in *The Human Rights Reader*, ed. Micheline Ishay (New York: Routledge, 1997), 407–412. For a discussion of the UN Charter as modern codification of just war doctrine, see Hans Kelsen, *General Theory of Law and State* (Cambridge: Harvard University Press, 1946), 50–57, and Judith Gail Gardam, *Non-Combatant Immunity as a Norm of International Humanitarian Law* (Dordrecht: Martinus Nijhoff, 1993), 38–39.

22. U.S. Delegation Report, 7.

23. Bothe et al., *New Rules for Victims of Armed Conflicts*, 8–9, and CDDH/SR 36, 33–64.

24. See Waldemar A. Solf, "A Response to Douglas J. Feith's *Law in the Service of Terror—The Strange Case of the Additional Protocol*," *Akron Law Review* 20 (1986): 261–289.

25. The American delegation's concern over the introduction of subjective *jus ad bellum* criteria was shared by other western delegates and even Jean Pictet, the leading ICRC authority on the Geneva Conventions and Protocols. See Gardam, *Non-Combatant Immunity as a Norm*, 83, and remarks of the United Kingdom delegate to the conference, Col. Draper, at CDDH/I/SR. While the opposition to the ratification of Protocol I would outlive the official pariah status American officials and policy held out to the Democratic Republic of Vietnam, the PRDSV, the Palestine Liberation Organization, and the National African Congress, the political impact of contemporary American foreign policy officials' attitudes should not be underestimated.

26. Solf, "A Response to Douglas J. Feith," 268, 287.

27. As traditional just war doctrine predates modern international law, Graham's argument derogatively places these "newly evolved states" on an evolutionary scale on par with the West's dark ages. While one can find in Baxter writings traces of the American cold war establishment antirevolutionary worldview, one does not find any social devolutionary anti–Third World chauvinism. Rather, Baxter's central point is that the application of *jus ad bellum* principles to internal conflicts is considered novel by many authoritative sources. This concern over the creation of legal innovations was, in fact, shared by the supporters of amended Article 1, who wanted Protocol I to be applied to wars of liberation instead of the completely novel Protocol II. For the claim that Protocol I represented a return to the eleventh century, see David E. Graham, "The 1974 Diplomatic Conference on the Law of War: A Victory for Political Causes and a Return to the 'Just War' Concept of the Eleventh Century," *Washington and Lee Law Review* 32 (1975): 25–63. In another contemporaneous article, Baxter discusses the novelty of specifically *jus ad bellum* provisions to internal conflict outside the direct context of Protocol I. See Baxter in John Norton More, ed. *Law and Civil War in the Modern World* (Baltimore: Johns Hopkins University Press, 1974), 518–536.

28. Quote from Gardam, *Non-Combatant Immunity*, 97. Gardam, like the pres-

ent author (see Chapter 1), recognized the principle of noncombatant immunity and finds that it can be traced to Augustine. See ibid., 5.

29. The principle of granting humanitarian treatment with recognition of combatant status, evocative of Article 157 of the Lieber Code (see Chapter 1), was interjected into the Final Act. Quoted from Appendix D, U.S. Delegation Report, 2.

30. The two largest and most comprehensive tomes on the issue of the noncombatant protections of Protocol I are William Hays Parks, "Air War and the Law of War," *Air Force Law Review* 1 (1990): 135–145, and Gardam, *Non-Combatant Immunity,* in favor of ratification.

31. CDDH/1; I, Three, 24; and Levie, *Protection of War Victims,* 4:302.

32. CDDH/I/74; and Levie, *Protection of War Victims,* 4:306.

33. Bothe et al., *New Rules for Victims of Armed Conflicts,* 525; and CDDH/I/SR.61, 53–54.

34. U.S. Delegation Report, 3–4.

35. Ibid.

36. Solf, "Response to Douglas Fieth," 265.

37. Aldrich, "Progressive Developments of the Laws of War: A Reply to the Criticisms of the 1977 Protocol I," *Virginia Journal of International Law* 26 (1986): 693–720.

38. William Hays Parks, Solf's successor, credits the intervention of Gen. Alexander Haig, then the Supreme Allied Commander Europe (SACEUR), with pushing through the JCS approval with the misleading claim that "signing doesn't mean anything and has no binding effect." Parks claimed that Haig's action was a result of his friendship with Ambassador Aldrich. According to Parks, the "U.S. delegation unilaterally made the decision to sign and ratify" and then went on to prepare documents supporting its decision. The quote of Haig by Parks is not cited. See Parks, "Air War," 88–89. Parks, who participated in this working group as head of the Law of War branch in the International Law division of the Navy Judge Advocate General, argued that there were military concerns related to the protocols that were raised in the meetings of the working group but not addressed to the satisfaction of some members of the group. The author requested the records of the working group, DAJA-1A 1980/6084, the Ad Hoc Law of War Working Group. Parks, now serving as head of the U.S. Army Operational Law Division (as functional successor to Solf), reported that his office had destroyed the records of this group as part of an office move. He claims that these destroyed files were significant because they documented that there was significant military dissent regarding the signing of the protocols by the United States. Source: Parks, letter to the author, August 2, 2001. I must accept Parks's characterization. On the face of it, Parks's position appears inconsistent with his statement in a 1978 article that the protocols, however, "were the subject of *detailed review* [italics mine] by the Department of Defense and Joint Chiefs of Staff prior to their signature." See "The 1977 Protocols to the Geneva Convention of 1949," *Naval War College Review* 31 (1978), 17–27.

39. U.S. Declaration made upon signature included the understanding that provisions of the protocol were "not intended to have any effect on and do not regulate or prohibit the use of nuclear weapons" and that, in reference to Article 44, Combatants and Prisoners of War, paragraph 3, The Protocols and the Law of War that the

phrase 'military deployment preceding the launching of an attack' means any movement toward a place from which an attack is to be launched." International Committee of the Red Cross, *State Parties and Signatures*. Available online at http://
www.icrc.org/ihl.hil, accessed October 15, 2004. See discussion of NATO evaluation of the protocols in U.S. Army War College, Strategic Studies Institute, *Protocols
I and II—International Humanitarian Law Applicable to Armed Conflict*, Final
Report, CAN 78027 (20 March 1979), 11; hereinafter cited as Army War College
Study.

40. Parks, "The 1977 Protocols," 20.

41. DCSOP Letter to Commandant, U.S. Army War College Study, "Study Directive: Protocols I and II—International Humanitarian Law Applicable to Armed Conflict," August 5, 1978. Included as Appendix A in U.S. Army War College Study,
A-1–A-3.

42. U.S. Army War College Study, 15, 25–32 (quote on 26).

43. Ibid., vii, 5–8 (quote on 10).

44. Parks, "Air War and the Law of War," 89–90, n. 283.

45. Ibid., 90–93. See also supra, note 38.

46. Department of Defense, Department of Defense Working Group Review and
Analysis of Protocol I Adopted by the Diplomatic Conference on International Law,
I-51-99, (1987) [hereinafter Law of War Working Group], 5–89. It was in connection
with an American position regarding the nonapplicability of the articles to the
apartheid policies of South Africa that a reservation was recommended for Articles
85–87. See pp., 83–85.

47. Parks, "Air War and the Law of War," 91.

48. Cover letter to Secretary of Defense U.S. Department of Defense, May 3, 1985,
Law of War Working Group.

49. Law of War Working Group, 1–4.

50. Sofaer was at that time architect of the Reagan administration's nonrecogni-
tion of the International Court of Justice's (ICJ) judgment that the United States pay
Nicaragua more than $1 billion in reparations for the illegal mining of that country's
harbors in 1984.

51. See Feith, "Law in the Service of Terror: The Strange Case of the Additional
Protocol," *National Interest* 1 (1985): 36–47; Feith, "International Responses," in
*Hydra of Carnage: The International Linkages of Terrorism and Other Low-
Intensity Operations*, ed. Uri Ra'Anan et al. (Lexington, Mass.: Lexington Books,
1986), 265–285; Feith, "Protocol I: Moving Humanitarian Law Backwards," *Akron
Law Review* 19 (1986): 531–535.

52. Letter of Transmittal from President Ronald Reagan, Protocol II Additional to
the 1949 Geneva Convention, and Relating to the Protections of Victims of Non-
international Armed Conflict, S Treaty Doc. No.2, 100th Congress, 1st Session
(1987) at 111; reprinted in the *American Journal of International Law* 81 (1987): 910–
912.

53. Hans-Peter Gasser, "The U.S. Decision Not to Ratify Protocol I to the Geneva
Conventions on the Protection of War Victims: An Appeal for Ratification by the
United States," *American Journal of International Law* 81 (1987): 912–925; Aldrich,
"Prospects for United States Ratification of Additional Protocol I to the 1949 Ge-

neva Conventions," ibid. 85 (1991): 1–20; and Sofaer, "Agora: the U.S. Decision Not to Ratify Protocol I to the Geneva Conventions on the Protection of War Victims: The Rationale for the United States Decision," ibid. 82 (1988): 784–787; and Sofaer, "Terrorism and the Law," *Foreign Affairs* 64–65 (Summer 1986): 901–922.

54. The level of this official effort to dissuade the United States' allies is a matter of dispute. For a discussion of the effort in regard to Australia, see Gardam, *Non-Combatant Immunity,"* 160, n. 185; Parks, "Book Review," *George Washington Journal of International Law and Economics* 28 (1994), 207–223, and "Air War and the Law of War," 222.

55. According to Parks, "The Middle East peace process continues, albeit slowly, and the dialogue between the ANC and the South African government increases, the negative value of Articles 1(4), 43, and 44 may diminish, if not all together disappear. See "Book Review," 677.

56. Aldrich, "Comments on the Geneva Protocols," *International Review of the Red Cross* 320 (October 31, 1997): 508–510. Parks, in "Air War and the Law of War," portrayed the negotiations conducted by Baxter, Solf, Prugh, and Reed as compromised by the negotiators' lack of experience with technology and the strategy of aerial bombardment. See "Air Power," 79, n. 261.

57. For a hagiographic narrative, see James Kitfield, *Prodigal Soldiers: How a Generation of Officers Born in Vietnam Revolutionized the American Style of War* (New York: Simon and Schuster, 1995).

58. The author first made the acquaintance of Parks at the author's court-martial in 1995 for various charges related to the attempt by the author, as the counterintelligence general staff officer for the multi-national forces during Operation Restore Democracy in Haiti, in September 1994, to conduct an unauthorized census of political prisoners held by the de facto government of Haiti. Col. Parks was called as an expert witness for the government to refute the author's expert witness testifying in support of a justification defense for an affirmative duty under international humanitarian law. Park's description of his position and his doctrinal decision-making history, offered in the course of qualifying as an expert witness, led the author to the idea of the present book. During his testimony, Parks admitted to holding the unofficial rank of "the old fox" in the area of the law of war. His official duties up to that time included the review of weapons systems for compliance with international provisions for the Judge Advocate General of the Army and for U.S. Special Operations Command; the legal review of the law-of-war treaties and other international agreements that have included the review of the Hague Convention of 1954 for the protection of cultural property in war time, the 1981 Conventional Weapons Convention, and most important, the "new" review of 1977 Additional Protocol I; serving as army representative on U.S. delegations to law-of-war negotiations in Geneva, The Hague, Vienna, and the United Nations; and serving as a lecturer of international law at the Judge Advocate General School, all four of the war colleges, the Industrial College of the Armed Forces, the Armed Forces Staff College, and as an adjunct professor at the George Washington National Law Center. See testimony of Colonel William Hays Parks, U.S. Marines (Retired), 12 May 1995, *United States v. Rockwood*, 1998, WL 47532, 2. Official trial transcript included in the Lawrence Rockwood Papers, 1981–2000, Hoover Institution Archives, call no. XX(5688985.1), Stanford University, Stanford, Calif.

59. For Parks unofficial elucidation of his Clausewitzian concerns in regard to the protocol, international humanitarian law, and the ICRC, see "Air War and the Law of War."

60. Comment attributed to J. Pictet by Solf and quoted by Parks in "Air War and the Law of War," 75.

61. Ibid., 64, 72 at n . 245, 81, 182.

62. *United States v. Rockwood*, 12 May 1995.

63. JCS Publication No. 1, *Dictionary of Military Terms* (Washington, D.C.: GPO, 2000), s.v. "operational art."

64. FM 100-5, *Operations* [1982] (Washington, D.C.: GPO, 1982), and FM 100-5, *Operations* [1986] (Washington, D.C.: GPO, 1986). For a discussion of the Clausewitzian content of Air-Land Battle doctrine, see Walter Edward Kretchik, "Peering through the Mist: Doctrine as a Guide for U.S. Army Operations, 1775–2000," Ph.D. diss., University of Kansas (2001), 210–211.

65. North Atlantic Treaty Organization, Allied Tactical Publication 35 (A), *Land Forces Tactical Doctrine*, December 5, 1990 (Ft. Leavenworth: U.S. Army Command and General Staff College).

66. See John F. Otis, "Clausewitz: On Weinberger," *Marine Corps Gazette* 72 (February 1988): 16–17; and John L. Byron, "A Response to 'Clausewitz: On Weinberger,' " *Marine Corps Gazette* 73 (January 1989): 17–18.

67. The author served as a strategic intelligence offer in support of Operation Restore Hope and a counterintelligence staff officer in support of Operation Restore Democracy.

68. John Hirsh and Robert Oakley, *Somalia and Operation Restore Hope: Reflections on Peacemaking and Peacekeeping* (Washington, D.C.: United States Institute of Peace, 1995), vi–xvi.

69. Statement by Colonel Harry S. Summers Jr., U.S. Army (retired) before the Committee on Armed Services, United States House of Representatives, 170th Congress, Federal Document Clearing House Congressional Testimony, October 7, 1994.

70. Richard Holbrooke, *To End a War* (New York: Random House, 1998), 336.

71. *The News Hour with Jim Lehrer*, From a conversation with Richard Holbrooke and Elizabeth Farnsworth in San Francisco, May 19, 1998, Transcript #6130 (MacNeil/Lehrer Productions, 1998).

72. Robert F. Baumann, "Operation Uphold Democracy, Power Under Control," *Military Review* (July–August 1997), 13–16; and Donald E. Schultz, *Whither Haiti* (Carlisle Barracks, Pa.: Strategic Studies Institute, 1996), viii, 20.

73. Morris Janowitz, *The Professional Soldier: A Social and Political Portrait* (New York: Free Press, 1964), 438.

74. Kretchik, "Peering through the Mist," 201–208.

75. FM 100-5, *Operations* [1993]; FM 100-20, *Military Operations in Low Intensity Conflict* (Washington, D.C.: GPO, 1990); and FM 100-23, *Peace Operations* (Washington, D.C.: GPO, 1994).

76. *United States v. Rockwood*, 12 May 1995.

77. Department of Defense Directive 5100.17, (1974) 1–8. This phrase was repeated verbatim in the 1979 edition of the directive. See Department of Defense Directive 5100.17 (Washington, D.C.: Headquarters, Department of Defense, July 10, 1979), 2–3.

78. Department of Defense Directive 5100.17 (Washington, D.C.: Headquarters, Department of Defense, December 9, 1998), 5.

79. *United States v. Rockwood*, 12 May 1995, and *United States v. Noriega*, 808 F. Supp. 791 (S.D. FL. 1992). In the former, the military judge gave instructions to the jury in reference to Parks's claim. In the latter, the court ruled against Parks's claim, concluding that Noriega had a legitimate claim as a POW in that certain provisions of the Geneva Conventions were enforceable in Panama.

Conclusion: Drinking from the Poisoned Chalice

1. Richard R. Baxter, "Humanitarian Law or Humanitarian Politics? The 1974 Diplomatic Conference on Humanitarian Law," *Harvard International Law Journal* 16 (1975): 11–18; and Antonio Cassese, *Violence and Law in the Modern Age* (Princeton: Princeton University Press, 1988), 6.

2. *International Review of the Red Cross* 306 (June 30, 1995): 316–322.

3. UN Secretary-General Kofi Annan, "Statement on Receiving the Report of the Independent Inquiry into the Actions of the United Nations during the 1994 Genocide in Rwanda," S/1999/1257 (December 16, 1999), available online at http://www.un.org/News/ossg/sgsm_rwanda.htm, accessed November 3, 2004, and "Report of the Secretary-General pursuant to General Assembly resolution 53/35: The Fall of Srebrenica," A/54/549 (November 15, 1999) at http://www.un.org/News/dh/latest/rwanda.htm, accessed November 3, 2004.

4. James Bennet, "Clinton Declares U.S. and the World Failed Rwandans," *New York Times*, March 26, 1998, A-1.

5. Mark John, "NATO Ready to Help in Darfur, but Not with Troops, *Washington Post*, February 14, 2006, A-1.

6. Samantha Powers, *A Problem from Hell: America and the Age of Genocide* (New York: Basic Books, 2002); Hannah Arendt, *Eichmann in Jerusalem: A Report on the Banality of Evil* (New York: Viking Press, 1964).

7. Preamble, *The Rome Statute of the International Criminal Court* (ICC), U.N. Doc. A/CONF.183/9 (July 17, 1998), available online at http://www.un.org/law/icc/statute/romefra.htm.

8. Article 7, Statute of the International Criminal Tribunal for the former Yugoslavia (ICTY), Security Council Resolution 827, U.N. SCOR, 3217th mtg. (May 25, 1993), online at http://www.un.org/icty/basic/statut/stat2000.htm#7, accessed November 4, 2005; and Article 6, the Statute of the International Criminal Tribunal for Rwanda (ICTR), Security Council Resolution 955, U.N. SCOR, 3453rd mtg. (November 8, 1994), at http://www.un.org/ictr/statute.html, accessed November 4, 2005.

9. Celebici Judgment: *Prosecutor v. Delacic, Mucic, Delic, and Landzo*, case no. IT-96-21-T, at http://www.un.org/icty/celebici, accessed November 4, 2004.

10. Blaskic Judgment: *Prosecutor v. Blaskic*, case no. IT-95-14-AR-108, at http://www.un.org/icty/blaskic/trialc1/judgement/, accessed November 4, 2004.

11. Kambanda Judgement: *Proseutor v. Jean Kambanda*, case no. ICTR 97-23-S, at http://www.ictr.org/ENGLISH/cases/Kambanda/judgement/kambanda.html, accessed November 4, 2004.

12. Letter from Ramsey Clark to UN Secretary-General Kofi Annan in reference to "The Trial of Slobodan Milosevic, Former President of the Federal Republic of Yugoslavia before the International Criminal Tribunal for the Former Yugoslavia," February 12, 2004, posted online by the International Committee to Defend Slobodan Milosevic (ICDSM) at http://www.icdsm.org/more/rclarkUN1.htm, accessed on November 4, 2004.

13. Article 33 made an exception to the prohibition of the defense of superior orders in cases that concurrently met all three of the following tests: (1) the accused was "under a legal obligation to obey orders"; (2) the accused "did not know that the order was unlawful"; and (3) "the order was not manifestly unlawful." *Rome Statute of the International Criminal Court,* U.N. Doc. A/CONF.183/9 (July 17, 1998), at http://www.un.org/law/icc/statute/romefra.htm, accessed November 4, 2004.

14. *Hearing before the Subcommittee on International Operations of the Committee on Foreign Relations of the United States Senate,* 105th Cong. 2nd. Sess. S. Hrg. 105-724 (1998) (statement of David Scheffer, Ambassador at Large for War Crimes Issues). See also Michael Scharf, "The Politics behind the U.S. Opposition to the International Criminal Court," *New England International and Comparative Law Annual* 5 (1999), posted online by the New England School of Law at http://www.nesl.edu/intljournal/vol5indx.cfm, accessed November 8, 2004.

15. *Hearing before the Subcommittee on International Operations of the Committee on Foreign Relations of the United States Senate.*

16. Dana Milbank, "Who's Pulling the Foreign Policy Strings?," *Washington Post,* May 14, 2002, A-19.

17. *Report of the International Committee of the Red Cross (ICRC) on the Treatment by the Coalition Forces of Prisoners of War and Other Protected Persons by the Geneva Conventions in Iraq during Arrest, Internment, and Interrogation* (February 2004), 3; posted by GlobalSecurity.org at http://www.globalsecurity.org/military/library/report/2004/icrc_report_iraq_feb2004.htm, accessed November 5, 2004.

18. Report of Maj. Gen. Anthony Taguba into allegations of prisoner abuse at Abu Ghraib titled *Article 15-6 Investigation of the 800th Military Police Brigade* (March 9, 2004), 16–17, posted online by the Center for Public Integrity at http://www.publicintegrity.org/docs/AbuGhraib/Taguba_Report.pdf.

19. Final Report of the Independent Panel to Review DoD Detention Operations, August 2004, 43; hereinafter cited as the Independent Panel Review.

20. For on overview of these studies, see Lt. Col. Dave Grossmen, *On Killing: The Psychological Cost of Learning to Kill in War and Society* (Boston: Little, Brown, 1995), 299–323.

21. In the 1944 movie *Passage to Marseilles,* Humphrey Bogart plays a hardened, cynical escaped convict from Devil's Island turned patriot who shoots down an attacking German bomber and then machine-guns the helpless pilots seeking quarter (Warner Bros., Hal Wallis, dir., 1944).

22. Steven Spielberg, *Band of Brothers* (New York : HBO Video, 2002), and *Saving Private Ryan* (Universal City, Calif.: Dreamworks Home Entertainment, 1998).

23. The campaign to pay William West's fine was organized by Geoff Metcalf. See campaign letter of December 15, 2003: "Let's Pick Up the Tab: Please Make a Christ-

mas Gift Donation to Lt. Col. West," posted at http://www.newsmax.com/archives/
articles/2003/12/14/183703.shtml, accessed November 6, 2004.

24. Presidential Memorandum, "Humane Treatment of al Qaeda and Taliban Detainees" (February 7, 2002), included as Appendix C in Independent Panel Review.

25. Independent Panel Review, 2–17.

26. In the months after 9/11, an interagency task force, which included the thirty-
four-year-old John C. Yoo, White House staff, met under the leadership of Alberto F.
Gonzales, White House council, and Vice President Dick Cheney to overhaul domestic and international law for the war. According to a serialized *New York Times*
report, they received little or no input from military lawyers. See Tim Golden, "After Terror: The Secret Rewriting of Military Law," *New York Times,* October 24,
2004, A-1.

27. Quoted in Telford Taylor, *The Anatomy of the Nuremberg Trial* (Boston: Back
Bay, 1992), 168.

28. Matthew 7:1 (King James Version). For an outline of St. Augustine's writings
on just war doctrine, see Chapter 1 of the present book.

INDEX

Captain Lawrence P. Rockwood is a former U.S. Army counter-intelligence officer. He was born in Trenton, N. J. After his separation from active military service, he served as a Fellow for the Center for International Policy, a consultant for the Institute for Policy Studies and for Amnesty International's Military, Police, and Security Working Group, and has been contracted as a human rights instructor for the Department of the Army and Department of Defense. He received his Ph.D. in American diplomatic history in 2005 from the University of Florida. Captain Rockwood has recently served as an investigating commissioner for the International Tribunal on Haiti and a member of the Intelligence Ethics Section Organizing Committee of the Joint Services Committee on Professional Ethics. He presently resides with his wife, Amelia Simpson, Ph.D., in San Diego and teaches at the University of Maryland University College.